To the memory of those with whom I served, Vietnam, 1966-67

Also By the Author

Corporate Governance (1993)

Problems in Corporate Governance (1997)

Understanding Corporate Law (with A. Pinto) (1999)
(2d ed. 2004)(3rd ed. 2009)

Forensic Social Work (with R. Barker) (2d ed. 2000)

Boardroom Chronicles (2002)

Questions and Answers: Business Associations (2004)(2d ed. 2012)

No Seat at the Table—How Corporate Governance and Law Keep
Women Out of the Boardroom (2007)

Business Enterprises: Legal Structures, Governance, and Policy
(with J. Hemingway, et al)(2009)

The Last Male Bastion—Gender and the CEO Suite at
America's Public Companies (2010)

The Sage Handbook of Corporate Governance (with T. Clarke)(2012)

TABLE OF CONTENTS

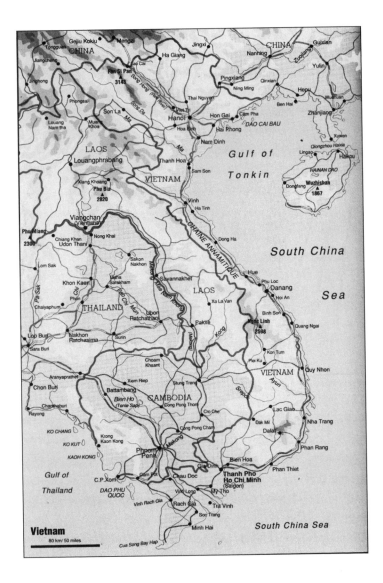

Preface

NUOC MAM IS THE SALTY, "FERMENTED" FISH SAUCE Vietnamese put on their food. I was stationed in Phan Thiet, 200 kilometers east and slightly north of Saigon, a fishing town where workers manufacture great quantities of the stuff. Phan Thiet is known as Vietnam's "Nuoc Mam Capital."

I spent a year there from 1966-67. Twice more (1995 and 2011) I returned to see how the small city had evolved, leading to the title of this book, *Three Tastes of* Nuoc Mam. In it, I describe my role as an officer in the "Brown Water Navy" as well as my subsequent visits.

The Brown Water Navy consisted of a hodgepodge of wooden junks, coast guard vessels, inshore minesweepers and, later, swift boats and riverine craft. The U.S. Navy and the Republic of Vietnam (South Vietnam) assembled this hodgepodge to patrol Vietnam's extraordinarily long coast and its many rivers and canals.

Forty-four years intervened between the time I came home from my tour in Vietnam (April 1967) and the time I began this book (early 2011). The reason I delayed writing for so long was not revulsion at recalling the horrors of war, as many U.S. military experienced and of which James Lee Burke so eloquently wrote in his book, *Swan Peak*:

Sometimes in his dreams Clete saw a straw hooch with a mamasan in the doorway engulfed in an arc of liquid flame ... He saw a seventeen-year-old door gunner go apeshit on a wedding party...the brass cartridges jacking from an M60 suspended from a bungee cord. He saw a Navy corpsman with rubber spiders on his steel pot try to stuff the entrails of a Marine back inside his abdomen...He saw himself inside a battalion aid station, his neck beaded with dirt rings, dehydrated...his flak jacket glued to the wound in his chest.

I didn't see anything like that, or only a bit or two of it. Most of us who were in Vietnam didn't.

The delay in writing about my Vietnam experience also was not due to the overwhelming anti-war sentiment I encountered when I came home. I did encounter that and it did play a part in the reversal of my views about the War. I was never a John Kerry, a future U.S. Senator who in 1971 dressed in his Navy fatigues, leading "Vets for Peace" (some, perhaps many of whom were not vets at all). In turn, those "vets" led a 100,000 war protesters' march upon the U.S. Capitol. By contrast, with little fanfare at all, I slowly and quietly turned against the War.

The real reason I delayed in writing about my combat experiences was that I thought for the longest time that I had very little, or nothing, to say. I was not a war hero. I was seldom in nose-to-nose combat. I got shot at three or four times but I am not absolutely certain of one of those incidents.

Our country, though, has a long tradition of seeing the human and the funnier side of things military. Sometimes the tradition manifests itself in black humor about war and the Army or Navy. World War II had G.I. Joe, the cartoon figure drawn by Bill Mauldin, and *Mr. Roberts*, a 1946 novel by Thomas Heggen made into a movie in 1955 starring Henry Fonda, James Cagney, and Jack Lemmon. Not much of that lighter side came out of the Vietnam War, the "American War" as the Vietnamese call it. All the history books, biographies and chronicles were grim, recalling the terror and the horror of the War, the high costs in civilian and military lives, and the geopolitical implications. In no particular order, we had historical works such as *Platoon* (Dale Dye), *Bright Shining Lie* (Neil Sheehan), *Fire in the Lake* (Frances Fitzgerald), and *The Things They Carried* (Tim O'Brien). More in the hard combat genre are *The Killing Zone* (Frederick Downs), *Blood Trails: The Diary of a Combat Foot Soldier* (Christopher Ronnau), *Hamburger Hill* (Samuel Zaffiri), *The Bloodbath at Hamburger Hill* (John DiConsiglio), *Days of Valor* (Robert Tonsetic), and *A Rumor of War* (Philip Caputo). One fiction novel, Nelson Demille's *Up Country* (2002), devotes itself to Vietnam after the War, examining the humorous side of things as well.

Overall, however, it was as though the vociferous, near universal and loud anti-war movement, which went on for years, heard all around the world, silenced even the prospect of laughter. The Vietnam War "movement" drowned out, masking from view, any report of the humorous events that happened or the lighter side to things that occurred.

Well, time has passed. The Mercedes emblem has replaced the peace symbol as the icon of the times. Although some individuals still harbor strong anti-war views, they are fewer and fewer, and perhaps now someone like me, who actually was there, may attempt a snapshot of the lighter side of things, a Mr. Roberts of the Vietnam War.

So, presentation of the lighter side (not necessarily hold-your-sides humor) is a first goal for this book.

A second goal, or byproduct, is to show how loose and unrestricted (or with very few restrictions) things were. This was particularly true in the War's early years. Many U.S. military wore pearl-gripped six shooter revolvers, handle bar mustaches, and an "out there" Wild West mien. It seemed as though every U.S. serviceman left the past and, to some extent, the present, behind, going off in search of fortune or adventure. Army Special Forces troops were notorious for wearing necklaces of Viet Cong ears or of dried human tongues.

The average citizen does not realize how often in a military establishment, known for its regimentation, there may be room for a large amount of "play in the joints," even extreme outlandish behaviors, some of which may lead to barbaric acts while others result in extreme incongruity.

At times, soldiers, Marines, and others needed the flexibility and room for creativity a certain amount of looseness permitted. Chapter 5 recounts some of the red tape and regulation military had to go through to obtain air support. A twelve-to-fifteen-minute delay in procuring an air strike could mean life or death in certain situations but such a delay there had to be in order to obtain approvals from rung after rung of higher-ups. The contrast between Korean troops, several battalions of whom operated in the northern reaches of our area, virtually without restriction, and U.S. troops, who had numerous restrictions and complex rules of engagement, are striking. Excessive political correctness sometimes entered into the equation, probably as a byproduct of the growing anti-war sentiment back home.

As troops in the field, we were fighting a war with one arm tied behind our backs. At times, though, U.S. troops were able to be flexible and creative. They would get the job done, eventually, in nonconventional ways.

This volume also recounts the differences and similarities between then and now, with a lengthy visit in 1995 sandwiched in-between (then, then, and now—hence *Tastes of Nuoc Mam*). I returned to Vietnam in 1995, just after the country had emerged from nineteen years literally in the Dark Ages, with no foreign contact; prison and re-education camps for Vietnamese with the remotest connection to the South Vietnamese government; sky high unemployment; an out-of control birth rate; and an absence of any foreign currency or foreign goods that could be purchased with "hard" foreign exchange (francs, marks or dollars).

In 1995, excruciating poverty was everywhere. I traveled from Saigon to Hanoi, seeing no Americans and very few foreigners at all, from anywhere. The country was then in worse shape, far worse shape, economically and otherwise, than it had been in the War years of 1966-67.

More than what I saw in 1966-67, what I saw on later trips proves how unwinnable the Vietnam War was, how unwise or even foolish was the U.S. presence there. Vietnam was engaged in a civil war in which we had no business intervening. The U.S.'s prolonged support for a worthless South Vietnamese regime did nothing more than harden resolve and embolden hardcore Marxists, who took control and plunged the country into a near twenty-year nightmare. Even if a political justification existed for American involvement, geography militated against any lasting success.

Vietnam is a string bean (wet noodle) of a country, more than 1,700 kilometers (1,100 miles) long, and very narrow. It has only one principal thoroughfare, Highway One, which runs from Hanoi to Ho Chi Minh City (Saigon). The U.S. built state-of-the-art airbases every seventy five to eighty kilometers the length of the country, the best and most comprehensive aviation infrastructure in the world. The U.S. had the best technology, weaponry, and equipment in existence.

Yet we (U.S. and South Vietnamese forces) were never able to keep Highway One open, even for a few weeks. In my patrol area, 200 kilometers from Saigon, the Viet Cong (VC) blockaded the road at least once a month, sometimes more often. Seemingly, they (the VC) could disrupt Highway One at will.

It was said that the U.S. and South Vietnamese forces owned the cities and towns while the Viet Cong owned the countryside. That was only partially true. The Viet Cong owned many of the towns as well, as the early 1968 Tet offensive vividly demonstrated. Even in so-called secure towns, as U.S. forces we did not wander about or go down side streets. The Viet Cong were everywhere and also nowhere. They raided or ambushed, melting back into their civilian occupations, or into the countryside, or into neighboring Cambodia or Laos.

The Vietnam War was one then that could not, and probably should not, have been won.

Earlier I said that I never wrote of my Vietnam experiences because I believed that I had little or nothing to say. Actually that was not always true. From time to time I did write about them.

As a professor, I may be the only, or one of two legal academics who fought in Vietnam (law dean Rudy Hasl is the other). Later in my career I became a finalist for the position of dean at several law schools. The script for the decanal selection process requires candidates to list their most significant achievements. I always listed my year in Vietnam when, at age twenty-two, I led sixteen enlisted men through a year of combat.

Almost invariably, when it came time for my campus visit as a dean candidate, I found that my biography had been sanitized. Someone had removed any reference to Vietnam. So not only was it that I thought that no one cared, in certain quarters, twenty-five to thirty years after the War, it remained taboo as a subject. For many years after they came home, Vietnam veterans were vilified as killers, or derided as losers, or both. For a veteran, the better course of action was to call no attention to Vietnam service at all.

Mark Twain termed fiction as a "superior form of lying." This book is not fiction but it is what some term "creative non-fiction." Not all of the events recounted in this book happened to me, or happened precisely in the way I describe. Rather the portrayals in this book many times represent amalgams, or capture the spirit more than the exact letter of what went on.

I was not a war hero and I hope that nothing in this book makes me out to have been, in the slightest way. If it does, I now expressly disclaim that I was in any way a hero. It was not my intent to portray myself as heroic.

Some of the names have been changed so that no one may be held up to scorn or ridicule. If I misreported some matter, or put anyone in a false light, I apologize. I researched this book as best as I was able.

That said and done, everything recounted in this book did happen, in one form or the other.

The spelling of Vietnamese place names follows the conventions adopted by the U.S. and international press corps. In newspapers, on road signs, and elsewhere, the Vietnamese themselves write all place names and other terms as discrete syllables (Viet Nam, Ha Noi, Sai Gon). The War era press corps compounded any of the names they used frequently (Vietnam, Hanoi, Danang) but not those which appeared less often in their reports (Nha Trang, Bien Hoa, Nha Be, An Loc). I have utilized the press corps usage, although my 2011 trip revealed that nearly all the old two word (non-compounded) spellings have re-emerged, seemingly used exclusively.

TASTE ONE

THE BROWN WATER NAVY
IN VIETNAM—1966-1967

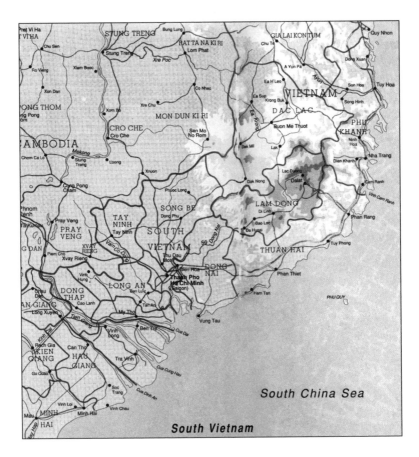

South Vietnam

1

III Corps in the Morning

*With God's help, we will lift [Vietnam] up and up,
ever up, until it is just like Kansas City.*

—Senator Kenneth Wherry, Nebraska, 1940 (speaking of Singapore)

The only thing that I am afraid of is fear.

—Arthur Wellesley, Duke of Wellington, 1831

*Vietnam is a mostly cloudy place. The ragged mountains suck
the clouds down, and most people remember the fogs and
the mists, like the ground itself is always steaming.*

—Lee Child, *Tripwire* (1999)

FEAR MANIFESTS ITSELF IN DIFFERENT WAYS IN different individuals.
For some, their knees knock, their hands shake. Others stutter or
speak more quickly. A few actually do pee their pants (usually just a
bit). With me, when first I arrived in my patrol area in Viet Nam,
where I would spend the next twelve months, my mouth went all
dry. I'm a cotton mouth kind of guy, I discovered.

I was cotton mouthed but not by the sight of some barren land,
devastated by war. Viet Nam is absolutely beautiful. Binh Thuan
Province, toward the southern end of III Corp (the U.S. had sliced
South Vietnam north to south, into I, II, III and IV Corps), resembled
Italy or Greece, semi arid, filled with cacti and Poinciana trees.

1

So why was I cotton mouthed? I had hitched a ride on a U.S. Coast Guard cutter (an eighty-two foot WPB) from *Nha Trang,* 200 kilometers north of Binh Thuan, where III Corps coastal patrol forces were headquartered and where I received my indoctrination training. We motored along at thirteen to fourteen knots, half a kilometer off the coast, through patches of early morning fog.

Gradually the morning mists lifted, giving way to a stainless steel gray sky, as we motored on down toward Phan Thiet. It was early May 1966.

In this enchanted setting, with wreaths of fog still encircling the hilltops, the Coast Guard Officer in Charge (OIC) was trying to scare the bejesus out of me. He was succeeding. I was this twenty-two-year-old Lieutenant Junior Grade—Lt.(jg)—eleven months out of college, sent to Viet Nam at a time supposedly when the Department of Defense still sent only volunteers. I never volunteered for anything.

The "coastie" told me about Duckett, the Navy guy whose place I was taking. I don't remember Duckett's first name, if I ever did know it. Duckett had been shot up, badly, by the Viet Cong (*viet* = people, *cong* = man) as he, his Vietnamese crew, and his fellow U.S. advisers were on patrol in the small inlet just north of Phan Thiet Bay, a grand sweeping bay with thirty or more kilometers of sand beach, at the south end of Binh Thuan Province. Phan Thiet Bay was centered on the outfall of the Phan Thiet River into the sea, where Phan Thiet, the provincial capital, was located and where I would be stationed.

Patrolling close in, Duckett's two Yabudda junks (wooden, ten meters, or thirty-nine feet, long, with a General Motors diesel engine in each, painted haze gray with eyes and a fierce red mouth painted on the bow) had been hit by shore fire. Although it was difficult to get straight information, Duckett had been hit in the lower back and shoulder. He was seriously wounded, airlifted out by helicopter to Cam Ranh Bay, the huge U.S. installation and natural harbor 130 kilometers to the north. I never did hear whether Duckett survived, but

I am pretty sure he did. I never heard anything to the contrary.

But "Jesus Christ," as they say, and as I thought to myself. I was an economics major who got into Navy ROTC because he liked the uniforms. The Navy was supposed to be safe, erudite, certainly gentlemanly: steaks and bone china in the ward room every night; waited on by stewards; tailored blue officers' uniforms in winter, crisp whites in summer; and high-minded conversation with fellow officers following dinner. See the world: Barcelona, Naples, Antibes, Cape Town, Sydney, Honolulu, Tokyo, Hong Kong, and Singapore.

The small Coast Guard coastal patrol boat (WPB) upon which I rode, was commissioned, as I recall, the *Point Comfort*. So far it and its skipper were offering the opposite—extreme discomfort.

I wound up in Phan Thiet, a sad-sack collection of two-table restaurants and used electronics stores, all with corrugated tin roofs, and movie tents, spread out along Vietnam's Highway One, on both sides of the Phan Thiet River. The most noteworthy landmark was a water tower painted to resemble a pagoda. To boot, Phan Thiet stunk, worse than raw sewage.

The Coast Guard WPB navigated around the sand bar protecting Phan Thiet harbor's entrance, letting me off at the small public dock midst the 1000 or more fishing vessels filling the harbor. Another adviser, Jim Ewers, from Cincinnati, met me (at that time all U.S. personnel were still labeled "advisers"; the fiction persisted for another six to eight months, even though by mid- 1966 more than 150,000 U.S. troops were engaged in actual combat). Ewers walked me past the much smaller inner harbor boat basin where our patrol craft were moored.

Many of the Vietnamese walking and bicycling the dirt streets wore black cotton loose-fitting tops and bottoms, resembling pajamas, with homemade sandals. All the women and many of the men wore straw conical hats to protect them from the sun. A few men wore pith helmets. Westerners were still new to them. They stopped in the street, staring at Ewers and myself as though we were circus animals.

The U.S. Coast Guard *Point Comfort.*

Our billet, to be my home for the next year, was located two to three city blocks inland from the harbor, and a few dozen meters north of the Phan Thiet River. A ten foot stone wall, plastered and white washed, topped with barbed wire, surrounded a compound half the size of a city block. In that area lived forty-five or so U.S. military, roughly half U.S. Army personnel who acted as advisers to the Vietnamese ranger battalion which garrisoned the town and bivouacked out near the airport. The other half consisted of Navy guys, assigned to coastal patrol duty.

Within the wall was a two-story building, once a convent I think, maybe a hospital, useful for our purposes as it contained numerous small bedrooms which we shared, two to a room. In the courtyard stood several recently constructed plywood huts which served as lounge areas and a mess. The armory, where weapons and ammunition were stored, was in a more secure stone and concrete building off to one side.

4

I was busy meeting my new mates, junior officers like myself and enlisted guys with whom I would spend many hours on patrol. The trepidation and fear I had felt hearing about Duckett and other battles or skirmishes fought with the VC was fast dissipating, swirling away like bathwater down a drain. Then I heard a "whoosh" and a "thump," followed by an explosion in the street outside or, possibly, in the vacant area next to the river. My body tensed up once again. I dived for cover. No one needed to tell me what was happening: we were under mortar attack.

The guys with whom I had been standing jogged toward several vacant doorways facing onto the courtyard. They didn't sprint, didn't fling themselves under a jeep—just more of a hurried but orderly exit from the open area. Along came another "whoosh," "thump," and explosion, again outside. I can't remember if there was a third.

My fear was back. I didn't care whether I had exhibited the requisite amount of courage. I knew right then that I did not want to be here for a whole year, especially if the year would be like that. I wanted to be in the real Navy, on board a cruiser or a destroyer ("greyhounds of the fleet"), maybe even an aircraft carrier.

"Happens once a while," Ewers apologized.

"What happens?" I had thought that Phan Thiet was "secure," that is, free of VC presence.

"Charlies bicycle into town, or ride up the back streets on a motorbike. They set up a mortar tube in the back streets, fire two to three rounds at us and run like hell. They're probably gone before the last round hits the ground."

"How many of our guys have been killed?" I asked what I thought to be a logical follow up question.

Ewers and the others laughed. "They haven't hit the compound yet. They never even come close. They're lousy shots."

Big consolation, I thought. The odds are stacking up in favor of them hitting something one of these days. And I now had two slivers under my skin—Duckett's unfortunate incident and a mortar attack on my new residence—which caused me great consternation.

The next day, early in the morning, two Yabudda junks, one with me aboard, sailed out on my first patrol. A breeze blew, making a light chop on Phan Thiet Bay. White sand beaches, and above them, brown hills surrounded all sides of the huge bay. Nearer us we could see the fish traps of bamboo and nets set by local fisherman. Closer still we could see down into depths of the clear ocean water. Outward from the sides of our bow wake we saw schools of small fish swimming away, appearing as though someone had scattered fistfuls of silver dollars into the water, suspended less than a meter from the surface and glinting in the sunlight.

From Phan Thiet, our (my) patrol area reached northward from Point Ke Ga to the south, across Phan Thiet Bay and then northward for sixty-five to seventy kilometers to Con Na Beach and Point Mui Dinh (*Mui* means cape or point). If you look at a map of Vietnam, at Phan Rang (where a large U.S. airbase used to be), just below Cam Ranh Bay, the coast turns southwesterly. That first seventy kilometers or so of the long southwesterly chord is Binh Thuan Province, its rocky coast and inland waters, our patrol area.

I was in the "Brown Water Navy," to be distinguished from the decidedly more upscale "Blue Water Navy" my parents had told me about and about which I had dreamt in college days. Instead of spotless white uniforms or Navy dress blues, *Officer and a Gentleman* uniforms, it was to be baseball hats, t-shirts, shorts, and body armor, riding tiny wooden patrol craft.

We were issued part leather, part khaki colored canvas combat boots but we never wore them. For traction, jumping from vessel to vessel, we wore tennis shoes. We were also issued olive drab fatigues with spacious cargo pockets on the pant legs. We soon abandoned those in favor of Bermuda shorts and T-shirts, sometimes olive drab ones. That's the closest we got to military garb. We had nothing close

Brown Water Navy patrol (Vietnamese Junk Forces).

to the camouflaged battle dress uniforms (BDUs) or tan combat desert uniforms (CDUs) the modern military favors.

I had heard of Southeast Asia or, indeed, all of Asia, as teeming with people. Long stretches of Viet Nam bore little evidence of human habitation. There were no roads into many areas, especially in Binh Thuan. Brown and green hills rose up 800 or 900 feet right beyond the water's edge. The beaches were circles of white sand ringed with stands of tall palm trees. Big rolling sand dunes. No people, at least that could be seen.

The Binh Thuan coast was a variegated one, with bay after bay interspersed with hour glass shaped coves and inlets. The whole province lay in the rain shadow of the Truong Son mountains, visible and brooding ten to twelve miles inland, where we were told Charlies (Viet Cong or National Liberation Front [NLF]) were based. U.S. forces called this "Indian Country" (all land from the foothills up to and including the mountains and anything above the coastal plain). Both the latitude (11° N) and the protection of the mountains moderated what weather extremes did exist.

Earlier, in 1954, the Geneva Convention on Viet Nam had laid out the Demilitarized Zone (DMZ) (in black humor referred to as the "Dead Marine Zone"), a ten-kilometer wide area bracketing seventeenth latitude north. The Ben Hia River bisects the zone. The DMZ cut the country in two, separating North Viet Nam from the Republic of South Viet Nam.

We were in III Corps, the third "fourth" of South Vietnam, about 200 kilometers (klicks) east and a bit north of Saigon. Below us was Vung Tau (Cape St. Jacques on French charts, still in use in the War's early years) at the mouth of the Long Tau ship channel to Saigon.

Below the ship channel, stretching to the tip of the country was the Delta (meaning the delta of the Mekong River), which cuts west across Viet Nam and turns northwards at Phnom Penh, the Cambodian capital. The great river, a mile wide, 4200 kilometers long, known as the "Amazon of Asia," stretches north to Vientiane in Laos and from there to northern Thailand, Myanmar (Burma), and China. On U.S. forces' maps, the Delta was IV Corps but everyone called it the Delta, a 200 kilometer long, flat, densely populated area of several thousand square miles, with a countless number of estuaries, lakes, and swamps, as the Mekong splits into nine channels and approaches the South China Sea.

The Delta was the "rice bowl" of Vietnam, a seemingly idyllic landscape carpeted in a dizzying variety of greens. The Delta also was a water world, where boats, houses, and markets float upon the endless number of streams, canals, and rivers that flow through the area. Bucolic though the Delta may have seemed in the shimmering light of day, it was a hot bed of Viet Cong activity, unsafe day or night for any American not heavily armed and traveling in numbers. I was pleased not to be there.

Binh Thuan and Phan Thiet, where I wound up, have several distinguishing features, aside from beautiful beaches and enchanting landscapes.

First, Phan Thiet was the fifth largest city in South Viet Nam, after

(I guess) Saigon, Danang, Nha Trang, and Hue, although nobody ever heard of Phan Thiet, including U.S. military who had served in-country. That Phan Thiet was the fifth largest was not saying a whole heck of a lot because Phan Thiet had only 80,000 residents, out of thirty-five to forty million in total population (North and South) back then (said to be ninety-two million today). But 80,000 was more, much more, than just a village. On the other hand, that Phan Thiet was the fifth largest city signaled what a rural country Vietnam was.

Second, Phan Thiet was the fishing capital of Viet Nam. As you crossed the river on the Highway One bridge through town (practically everything in Viet Nam abuts Highway One), and looked out to seaward, where the Phan Thiet river approached the bay, there was a basin filled, as I said, with hundreds (a thousand or more) of fishing vessels. Sea life in the waters off Phan Thiet was so abundant that during several times each year eighty and one hundred foot, steel hulled fishing trawlers, big ones, sailed down from Taiwan and Korea, a thousand or more kilometers to the north, to fish a few klicks off the Binh Thuan coast.

Third, Phan Thiet was (is) the *nuoc mam* capital. In *nuoc mam* factories, workers line wooden vats, much like large wine vats (ten to twelve feet across) with fish. On the fish, the workers layer salt. On top of the salt they load on another tier of fish, and so on and so on, until the whole shebang is three meters high. Then the *nuoc mam* producers let the whole thing rot. Workers mix the juice that comes off with peppers and spices. *Nuoc mam* is on every home and restaurant table in Viet Nam, as well as on many Vietnamese tables in America. Many refer to *nuoc mam* as the "Vietnamese ketchup." Vietnamese put it on everything. Phan Thiet is chock-a-block with *nuoc mam* and *nuoc moi* (made with shrimp) factories—down every street and every lane.

Now Phan Thiet is in Asia. Then, in 1966-67 especially, the city was undeveloped. Sanitation was not the best. There were open sewers. Here, there, and practically everywhere, you got a strong smell of human waste, overpowering at times. Now combine that smell with the pervasive smell of rotting fish. In other cities and towns of Vietnam, the odor of burning charcoal wafted in on the breezes, as Vietnamese used charcoal fires both for cooking and for heat. But Phan Thiet had an odor like no place any of us had ever been, ten times stronger than the foulest barnyard. But they say the human olfactory sense is the quickest to adapt. That proved true, although when we came back off patrol we always had a period in which we had to re-adapt. We joked about it—"fish and shit," a rhyme of sorts with "fish and chips."

Fourth, Vietnamese's forebears came from Mongolia via central China. They began a descent into the upper reaches of the Indochina Peninsula in the Twelfth or Thirteenth Centuries. The early Vietnamese's predecessors were the Chams, a warlike Hindu people. Phan Thiet approximates the southernmost point this Cham civilization reached and was one of its principal centers. The Vietnamese destroyed the Champa capital city of Indrapura in 1471; thereafter, except for a few outliers such as Cham Island, after the sixteenth century the Chams ceased to exist as a distinct people.

Just north of Phan Thiet, and a mile or so out to the east, in or slightly inland from the sand dunes, are Cham towers. Built of red brick, these towers are three to four stories and thirty to thirty-five feet (nine to ten meters) high. Their limestone decorations resemble the Khmer decorations on the temples of Angkor Wat in Cambodia. Undoubtedly the towers (sanctuaries) had religious significance. They are 1,000 or more years old (the historical marker says built in the ninth century), well preserved, their beauty enhanced by the sand dunes, seashore, and landscape that surround them. We saw them nestled up above the sand dunes as we motored out from Phan Thiet to begin our patrols.

There are Cham towers elsewhere in Viet Nam (Phan Rang and

above Nha Trang, to the north, for instance) but Phan Thiet is a good place to see them.

Fifth, Phan Thiet was, as I said, a city of 80,000 or so, termed "secure" (but not necessarily safe). But the remainder of Binh Thuan Province was sparsely populated with few roads, hilly and mountainous terrain, bays, inlets, and other places to hide, allegedly filled with Viet Cong (lots of them). The VC, however, did not populate the outer reaches of the province to bring power to the people. Binh Thuan was supposedly a Viet Cong R & R (rest and relaxation) center to which VC soldiers repaired after a hard month of fighting. The Charlies (Chuck, Sir Charles) undoubtedly appreciated beautiful beaches and warm ocean waters as much as the next guy. Binh Thuan was the VC's Hawaii.

Charlie's presence while on R & R had two consequences. Whenever anyone shot at U.S. or South Vietnamese forces, the shooters were usually (not always) backing up. Few on either side, save for the men and women who shot at Duckett (in what came to be known as Duckett' Cove), wanted a fire fight. That's not what they (the VC) were there for.

The other consequence, however, cut in precisely the opposite direction. While Phan Thiet proper was deemed "secure," the entire remainder of the province was not, most decidedly so. North of Duckett's Cove a range of large sand dunes began. This area, and another farther to the north, were deemed beyond merely "unsecure." They were "free fire zones." These areas had been the scene of hostile VC activities in the past. The mapmakers marked them out, including several hundred meters to seaward, with bold red borders. Ordinary rules of engagement (when armed and deadly force may be used, which is much more circumscribed than many non-military believe) did not apply. Within a free fire zone, U.S. or Vietnamese troops could shoot at anything that moved, or did not move, for that matter. They could shoot automatic weapons, machine guns, mortars, what-have-you, with no provocation necessary and no questions asked.

I was ordered to go to a war, I did my job, took care of my guys, and my guys took care of me. After a year, we all came home. In retrospect, boarding and searching junks and sampans (a junk large enough to hold a standing water buffalo, according to one popular test) put us at an extremely high level of risk, but we saw little gunfire, death and destruction. I got shot at maybe three, perhaps four times.

One of the few destructive things I did see was in the free fire zone I just described. Again, Viet Nam is a long string bean of a country, especially the former South Vietnam (below the DMZ), fifty kilometers across at its narrowest and not more than 130-140 kilometers at the widest, at least north of the Mekong Delta. The most expeditious way in which to move people, supplies, foodstuffs, animals, or what have you (guerilla fighters, war materiel, etc.) is by sea. Up and down the Vietnamese coast, then, besides the thousands of fishing vessels, moved thousands of passenger and cargo junks and sampans. Many of them had steel rather than wooden hulls. They could be up to seventy-five feet in length. Like bugs, they crept up and down the coast, night and day, in an endless parade.

Most sampan skippers knew where the free fire zones were. They navigated their sampans out to sea a bit and around the free fire zone. A few kilometers onward, after passing well clear of the free fire zone, the skipper turned his vessel back close to shore and to calmer waters.

One night at dusk, I was aboard a Yabudda junk tied to another junk, just on the boundary of a free fire zone. We saw a faint movement in the darkness several hundred meters away. The other Yabudda untied and headed toward the movement. The ARVN (Army of the Republic of Viet Nam) lieutenant aboard suddenly picked up an armed M-79 grenade launcher. Without having spoken with or conferred with anyone, he took aim quickly and fired. He vaporized the junk. God knows how many were aboard. Most surely they were not Viet Cong. They may have been smugglers or black marketers but not Viet Cong.

They could have been a wholly innocent family. In any case, they did not deserve the fate which befell them.

There was nothing left but flaming debris. The Yabudda junk and the ARVN lieutenant moved off into the night. I never saw them again.

One of the lasting impressions of that era comes from the incidents or episodes of violence I saw in my year in Viet Nam. I saw several incidents similar to the indiscriminate destruction of that junk and intervened to prevent several others from occurring. What struck me was how little regard Vietnamese seemed to have for each other and for human life.

Based upon those experiences, I tended to spread my opinion, or judgment, across all Asian peoples and particularly all Vietnamese. But I know now that is not true. We all cry at funerals and find great joy in marriage ceremonies and births of children. People are people. I think that the cruelty and low regard for fellow human beings that I saw comes from poverty, certainly as a byproduct of war, and from subservience. The subservience of colonialism, which Vietnam endured for 1000 years under China, and for nearly 100 years under France, accentuates or emboldens men and women to demonstrate their superiority and control over others of their kind. Often they do so through evident and extreme disregard of others, morphing into violence and extreme brutality. Witnessing those episodes of violence and brutality slipped a third sliver of discomfort and consternation under my skin.

Vietnamese fisherman aboard their junk.

2

The Mission

We have a problem making our power felt. Vietnam is the place.

—President John F. Kennedy, 1961

Let no one doubt that we have the resources and the will to follow this cause as long as it may take. No one should think for a moment that we will be worn down, nor will we be driven out, and we will not be provoked into rashness.

—President Lyndon B. Johnson, 1966

We are swatting flies and we should be going after the manure pile.

—General Curtis LeMay, U.S. Air Force, 1965

BUT YOU WOULD HAVE THOUGHT WE WERE there for a wild west show. In May, 1966 there were 150,000 or so men in-country. Regimentation was wanting (it came thereafter, as the number of U.S. in country soared to above 460,000, peaking at 505,000). Many military did their own thing while off duty. In the early years, many also did their own thing, or some of their own things, while on duty. Being a cowboy was one of them.

I saw several Army and Navy senior enlisted men and officers wear chrome plated, pearl handled six shooters. Some wore matched pistols, backwards (butts facing out). Large engraved western belt buckles (a buffalo, an antelope, the American flag) were popular. Handlebar mustaches were in. I never did see a cowboy hat, at least worn while on duty, but nearly everyone wore a baseball cap of some kind rather than official military headgear, at least while not on patrol. In *A Rumor of War*, Philip Caputo describes how he saw helicopter pilots who, in 1965, wore "Terry and the Pirates costumes," with bush hats and low slung holsters containing pearl handled revolvers. It wasn't only helicopter pilots.

New vocabulary took over. Instead of "carry," or "place," or "set down," or "hike," or "patrol," "hump" became the universal solvent. Instead of walking from point A to point B, or patrolling, ground forces "humped." Were I to direct another to pick up a box, carry it across the room, and place it on the window sill, I might simply say, "Hump it to the window."

"Saddle up" first undoubtedly meant for grunts, or ground pounders, to put on their packs, pick up their weapons, and move out. We saddled up as well. We put on our body armor (eight-pound vests), our ammunition, and side arms, picked up our other weapons, radios, first aid supplies, and combat rations (Cee-rats), and "humped" the two city blocks from our compound to our patrol craft. After stowing what needed to be stowed, we backed out into the stream and "humped" off on coastal patrol.

The swift boats, which found new notoriety in the 2004 presidential campaign, as Democratic nominee John Kerry's alleged heroism as a swift boat Officer in Charge (OIC) came under scrutiny, were put in service about halfway through my year in Vietnam. Swift boats and their crews were especially known for cowboy antics.

Swift boats (PCFs—Patrol Craft Fast) could reach speeds of thirty-six to thirty-seven knots, with a crew of six (fewer witnesses to their antics) and a lot of firepower (twin 50-caliber machine gun turrets over the pilot house, over-and-under machine gun, 81-millimeter mortar on the main deck). A swift boat had a junior officer, lieutenant junior grade, as OIC. The scuttlebutt was that swift boat crews, instead of going to their patrol areas, after leaving their home base

U.S. Navy Swift Boat on coastal patrol, 1967.

would pull the boat into a secluded cove to enjoy a day of water sports, water skiing behind the craft.

My favorite Wild West show story: Two swift boats had a firefight with one another. The prosecutor questioning one of the OICs asked, "Joe, you knew it was a friendly. Why did you open fire?" Joe didn't blink an eye: "Ya, but he shot at me first."

Such were the early days of the Vietnam War—a lot of cowboy stuff. We did it, too. Early on in our year there, the OIC of our little detachment was off on an errand somewhere. So, during a slow Sunday afternoon, a couple of officers, including me, and a handful of enlisted men put on Australian slouch hats and body armor. We took the most menacing automatic weapons we could find. Off we went, in a couple of small boats, venturing a hundred meters out on Phan Thiet Bay. There, while our boss was away, we struck various manly Wild West poses, taking pictures for the folks and our friends back

The author playing cowboy.

home. We were "starring in our own war movie," as Philip Caputo notes troops did everywhere, at least in those early years.

But we had a more serious purpose in being there.

Highway One, which reaches from Hanoi in the north to Saigon, was really the only long distance highway in the country. It was much watched and heavily travelled, at least for Vietnam back then. Local farmers, men and women, often blocked long stretches of the highway to dry their rice or their manioc root. To attempt to keep the highway open, the military (ARVN) had checkpoints all along the highway. American Special Forces camps overlooked chokepoints and junctions that the VC would be likely to attack or disrupt. Movement by either motorized vehicle or ox cart (just as likely) was slow going.

As I described, Vietnam has a long, variegated coast. The quickest method then for the VC to move men, ammunition, weapons, or foodstuffs was by water, sometimes only at night and often more brazenly, in full light of day. So Commander Military Assistance Command Vietnam (COMMACV) ordered Commander Naval Forces Vietnam (COMNAVFORV) (the military is fond of jaw breaking acronyms) to blockade the entire South China Sea coast (called the "East Sea Coast" by Vietnamese). Navy and Vietnamese patrols were to board and search vessels they encountered, apprehending suspected VC, and turning suspected VC, draft dodgers, and smugglers over to the Vietnamese National Police.

A secondary purpose was blocking. As Army or Marine detachments conducted "search and destroy" missions ("offensive sweeps" in official jargon) in coastal areas they would sweep toward the coast. Inshore waterborne forces (Brown Water Navy forces) had to patrol off the coast to prevent ex-filtration by sea. I remember doing this duty as the First Air Calvary (the Big Red One) conducted operations in our province. We constantly had difficulty obtaining the Army radio frequencies so that we could communicate and hopefully coordinate our efforts. By and large, coastal patrol forces retained the same radio frequencies while the ground based Army forces changed frequencies monthly.

First a formation of Cobra or Huey helicopter gunships, six or eight of them, would sweep in low over the jungle in a nose down attitude. They would begin firing Gatling guns and rockets into the area where the VC were suspected of being ("thump, thump, thump," the noise of rockets being fired was a distinctive sound). Two minutes later another fleet, this one of Huey helicopters, eight or ten of them, would sweep in low, landing sixty to seventy troops. Each Huey carried seven infantry and four crew members. These ground forces would do a sweep, wheeling toward the coast. Offshore we would hear gunfire. Forty minutes later the helicopters would return, taking the Army ground forces away. To this day, when I hear helicopter sounds close overhead, I get chills; the hair on the back of my neck stands up.

We did blocking operations a score or more times, as Big Red One troops did sweeps toward the beach, in a variant on the classic "hammer and anvil" tactic. We saw Vietnamese emerge running from the bush, and then running along the sand. We fired at them but we never were never able to capture anyone or effectively seal off the coast. We were too slow. Our Yabudda junks could barely go as fast as a man could run.

The difficulty in all of these coastal patrol operations was that the U.S. Navy did not have the equipment with which to do the job. To be sure, the Navy had handsome, haze gray destroyers, long frigates, even longer cruisers ("the big guns"), and gargantuan aircraft carriers—but it had nothing small or capable of inshore patrol. So the Navy pulled together a motley collection of water craft, including the aforementioned Yabudda junks, Coast Guard WPBs (twenty-five plus meters, or eighty-two feet, in length with eleven crew and names such as *Point White, Point Welcome, Point Comfort, Point Gresham, Point Hudson, Point Partridge, Point Lomas, Point Kennedy*), and inshore minesweepers (wooden, named after birds such as the *Bluebird* and the *Oriole*). Old World War II destroyer escorts, which had outlived their useful lives as radar picket ships, ready for the scrap yard, were pressed into service for offshore patrols. We were a garage band navy, not the U.S. Navy seen in the movies and on recruiting posters.

Meanwhile, the Navy instituted a crash program to develop proper vessels. They designed two: the swift boat and the smaller riverine craft known as PBRs (Rover Patrol Craft) for the Delta. The swift boat's fast track design and construction were evident. At fifty feet (fifteen meters), the craft were too small to stay on station very long. If the transit time from their base to their patrol area was lengthy, a swift boat might only be on station for twelve hours. In fact, many swift boat crews would pull in the first secluded cove or bay, anchor, and sleep off crew members' hangovers. When it finally reached their station, a swift boat might only stay there for four to five hours.

The windshields on swift boats popped out all the time as well. Early on, until the Navy got the problem fixed, swift boats had to return to base right away if they had encountered rough seas. The vessels could not take weather at all.

There was a swift boat base at Cam Ranh Bay to the north of us. I visited there several times. I had served with a guy, Jim Columbo, from Detroit, in my first month in Vietnam. Jim had come back for a second tour in Vietnam, the second time as OIC of a swift boat. He was stationed at Cam Ranh.

At the Cam Ranh Navy base, you couldn't walk ten meters before someone stuck a can of beer in your hand (San Miguel, from the Philippines, was the favorite but the saying was that there was "a headache in every bottle"). There were volleyball and basketball courts. Elsewhere on the base they had a golf course, with sand putting greens, coated with motor oil, then rolled firm. Much of the aura and reports of heroics surrounding the swift boats in Vietnam were myths. Swift boat crews cultivated the Wild West appearance and mentality even after it had died out everywhere else. Swift boats were more famous for not doing the jobs assigned to them than they were for any heroics by their crews.

Navy riverine craft in Mekong Delta, 1967.

How John Kerry, the presidential candidate in 2004, did his much ballyhooed heroics, and got his medals, on a river I haven't figured out, as the Navy assigned swift boats exclusively to coastal patrol. Duty on the rivers was left to the smaller riverine craft, shorter hydrojets with four-person crews and open cockpits, which drew only eighteen inches of water. Nonetheless, as with many other Vietnam vets I know, we are reluctant to mention our Vietnam service around political conservatives or Tea Party advocates lest we get "swiftboated" (vilified for any claim we make), a word now in many dictionaries.

When we came home forty years ago we had to keep our mouths shut because the War was so unpopular, as many times were those of us who had fought in it. Forty years later, things haven't changed much: once again you feel as though you can't mention what you did, this time because there might be a swiftboater in your midst.

One more swift boat story: In Vietnam, we all purchased or had relatives back home send us Radio Shack or similar walkie-talkies, which you could stick in your back pocket. A principal reason was that to use Navy or Army frequencies we were required to encode everything. We then often had to relay messages through the Coastal Patrol Centers (Nha Trang for us) to communicate with someone we could see several hundred meters away, who would then have to take valuable time to de-code the message. Navy portable radios were PRC 10s, big and cumbersome. Encoding and decoding took time, a pain in the ass, so we got the little "illegal" handsets, communicated in plain English and broke the rules. We even made up funny call signs for our store bought walkie-talkies: "Snoopy," "Lucy," and Peanuts" for the goody two shoes; "Fuck You One," "Fuck You Two," and "Fuck You Three" for the more rough hewn.

Another swift boat captain I knew, who we called Horrible, and his crew had walkie talkies. When they left their base at Cam Ranh, they went straight to the bay next to the U.S. Air Force base at Phan Rang, about twenty klicks south of Cam Ranh. Horrible and his senior petty officer would man the swift boat while the other troops went into the enlisted men's club to have a few (more than a few) drinks. Then they would reverse it. Horrible and his friend would go ashore while the troops manned the patrol craft.

Now the officers' club at Phan Rang sat up in the sand dunes overlooking the bay. Horrible would take a seat at the bar. Inevitably, some Air Force guys (many were pilots) would come over and by way of introduction say, "Hey, we don't get many Navy guys in here. Whatcha doing?"

Horrible would put them on. "See that boat out there. It's remote controlled."

The pilots didn't believe him. "You're putting us on."

"No, I'm not. Watch this." Picking up his walkie talkie, Horrible would say, "Right full rudder" and the swift boat in the distance would move smartly to starboard, heading for the coast. He would speak into the handset again, "Left full rudder." The boat would turn to port, moving back to seaward.

The Air Force guys would clamor for the walkie talkie. "Gimme that. Gimme that. I want to try it." Horrible said he never had to buy a drink. After four or five pops, paid for with Air Force dollars (script actually, because U.S. personnel were not allowed greenbacks), Horrible would return to his swift boat. He and his crew would proceed to their patrol area, or at least to the first cove, where Horrible and his crew could sleep it off.

The massive effort to patrol an 1100 kilometer coast, and to interdict VC, black marketers, and smugglers, boarding and searching a hundred thousand or more vessels, was known as Operation Market Time. In 1966, just after I arrived off the coast, Market Time took on a further sense of urgency. The higher ups' biggest fear was that a steel hulled trawler, eighty or ninety feet long, and capable of carrying great quantities of weapons and ammunition, rather than a little dinky wooden one, would sneak down from the north, offloading its cargo in a secluded cove, under cover of darkness.

Well, sure enough it happened, near Ba Dong, in the Delta, at the mouth of the Co Chien River, 200 kilometers to the south of us. Patrol aircraft uncovered a 100-foot trawler as she was approaching the coast. The Coast Guard WPB *Point Comfort* shouldered the trawler aground.

With rockets and strafing machine gun fire, after a fire fight, assisted by other Coast Guard WPBs, the *Point Comfort* caused the now burning North Vietnamese Army (NVA), VC, and trawler crew to run the vessel aground toward the beach and abandon her. The 250 tons of weapons and supplies did not reach the enemy forces. The trawler was largely destroyed.

But the whole incident changed a lot for us, substantially increasing our risk. From on high, we were ordered to board and search

Offshore fishing trawler.

every steel hulled, offshore trawler we saw. As I said before, we saw quite a few, as periodically, foreign fishing vessels came from Taiwan and other countries to fish off the Vietnam coast. Whenever a larger fishing trawler was sighted, we had to drop whatever we were doing at the time. We would leave the shelter of bays and inlets, going out three to four klicks to sea where the weather was always much rougher, substantially so, with stronger winds and five to seven foot waves. With our little wooden patrol craft tossed by the waves, we would climb a rope Jacob's ladder up and over the side of a fishing boat that was itself bobbing up and down, many times five to six feet. We worried constantly about an ankle getting caught, or a leg crushed between the two vessels, especially if you slipped, as they bobbed up and down and banged violently together.

Now factor in that as we tried to board and search these offshore fishing vessels we were all armed. We wore bullet proof vests (body

armor) but they provided incomplete protection at best, and probably none at close range. The weaponry the Navy provided us was out-
dated, but heavy duty, World War II weaponry. We had .45 caliber
pistols and Thompson submachine guns, also .45 caliber, which we
needed because if anything arose we would be a in a relatively confined
space. Thompson's are short, snubbed nose weapons. We needed them
because we needed a broad field of fire.

We had shotguns, too, maybe illegal ones because the barrels had
been sawn off, or just cut down really. After World War II, the Geneva
Convention outlawed true sawed off shotguns, or so we were told.
The term "sawed off shotgun" conjures up the pistol-like weapon
liquor store owners keep under the counter, or gangsters hide under
their coats. The guns we had were still long guns, with shoulder
stocks rather than pistol grips, but with four to five inches taken off
the barrel to ease handling in confined spaces. They were Winches-
ters, I believe: single barrel, 12-gauge, pump action, holding six rounds.
The only safety was a half cock on the hammer.

By accident, those things went off all the time. Accidental misfir-
ing seemed to occur every time we boarded offshore trawlers, at least
in high seas. As the boarding officer, I usually went first. I can't count
the times a shotgun behind me misfired, buckshot whizzing by my
ear. One of my best enlisted guys, Sam Houston of San Angelo, Texas,
usually handled a shotgun, going up the ladder right behind me.
Under his handlebar mustache, he would lick his lips nervously, apol-
ogizing to me for his weapon's accidental discharge, but there was
nothing he could do. Sam Houston was one of our best weapons guys.
The fault was the way in which Winchester designed the shotgun,
not Sam's.

These operations put tens of thousands of men at risk for years,
year after year, but not the obvious ones of being killed by VC bombs
or bullets. The risks were less serious and less obvious: the risk of
getting a foot crushed, of being shot by an accidental misfire, or of

killing or wounding a crew member on a friendly vessel who would have been completely bewildered by all these big, heavily armed, seemingly bellicose Americans disturbing their space and rocking their world.*

And, turns out, the really big one got away. There was a serious risk offshore but quite a bit offshore, one which U.S. intelligence sources never picked up upon until the War was over. By 1968, as the United States bombed and otherwise interdicted traffic on the Ho Cho Minh Trail, the North Vietnamese searched for other means whereby they could supply NLF and NVA troops in South Vietnam. They expanded the trail so that in certain parts of Laos there were ten trails or even twelve, not one.

Tom Bissell in *The Father of All Things: A Marine, His Son and the Legacy of Vietnam* recounts that by July 1968 as many as 1100 trucks a day began the 600-800 mile journey down the trail. When U.S. bombing commenced the number was cut in half in a week, and cut in half again in another week.

The North Vietnamese then began transporting supplies by ship, not only offshore but far offshore. Ocean going freighters of 12-15,000 tons and 300-400 foot long (not seventy to seventy-five foot) coastal freighters or disguised fishing trawlers, laden with supplies, would make the 1600 kilometers plus journey from Haiphong in the North, rounding the horn in the south (the southern tip of Vietnam), sailing into the Gulf of Thailand. They would sail northward, offloading their cargos at Shinoukville, Cambodia, only 200 kilometers southwest of the Parrot's Beak and the Cambodian-Vietnamese border. That the U.S. forces crimped down (they never shut it altogether) the Ho Chi Minh Trail then resulted not in a reduction but in a redi-

---

* Stanley Karnow, in *Vietnam: A History* (Penguin, New York, 1983), the definitive account which won the Pulitzer Prize, recounts that from 1959 onward the North Vietnamese had a study committee, denominated "Group 759," which existed solely to devise means whereby men and supplies could be shipped into South Vietnam by sea.

rection of supplies. Bissell reports that by 1970 eighty percent of the NLF's and NVA's supplies and equipment came by sea, through the backdoor at Shinoukville in the west.

Market Time, the massive U.S. coastal patrol effort in which I and the Brown Water Navy engaged, involved scores of ships, patrol craft, airplanes, and thousands of men. The Navy and Coast Guard patrolled inshore, close-in off shore, and offshore. But never very far or far enough offshore. Neither the U.S. nor the South Vietnamese had any regularized means which could have discovered let alone intercepted traffic forty, fifty, sixty miles or farther offshore.

We had a job to do, a mission to undertake, to patrol and protect inshore, close to the coast. We undertook the mission and did the job, but not without misgivings, even at the time, and serious lapses, which have become evident but only after the War ended.

3

Men to Accomplish the Mission

I don't go to town often, but I like to have a good time when I do.

—Seaman Bones Caldwell, U.S. Navy, 1966

*They were to a man thoroughly American ... idealistic, insolent,
generous, direct, violent, and provincial in the sense that they
believed that the ground upon which they stood was now forever
a part of the United States simply because they stood on it.*

—Philip Caputo, *A Rumor of War* (1977)
(Describing enlisted marines he commanded in 1965)

*It wasn't like the San Francisco Forty Niners on one side of the field
and the Cincinnati Bengals on the other. The enemy was all around you.*

—Captain E.J. Banks, U.S. Marine Corps, 1965

"JOIN THE NAVY AND SEE THE WORLD"—the recruiting slogan proved
true. All of the men with whom I served in Vietnam had done exactly
that. They came from the heartland, none from either coast. They
came from small towns or cities, places like Liberal, Kansas, or Fairbanks, Iowa, or from farms in Nebraska, Minnesota, or Eastern Col-
orado. They liked to have a good time but they all had small town
values and country-bred dignity about them. They were extremely
loyal to one another and to me and the other officers (most of them,
anyway). They took quiet pride in being proficient at their jobs. They
also got into their share of scrapes and did some funny things.

A favorite was Leroy Lambert from Liberal, Kansas. Leroy was our electronics technician. He took care of gear but occasionally went out on patrol. Leroy was average height but seemed taller than he was, perhaps because he was lean and laconic. Quiet types always seem taller to me than they really are. He always had a cigarette, lit or unlit, dangling from his mouth. His flat, Midwestern drawl might mislead you into thinking he was a not-too-smart farm boy. He was, and presumably still is, quick acting and smart as a whip.

Another guy was Bones Caldwell from Red Star, Arkansas, the skinniest sailor in the Navy. Bones was 5' 11" but could not have weighed more than 115 pounds. He had tattoos running up and down both arms. He wore eye glasses, with cheap plastic frames and oversized lens, which always made him look even skinnier and frailer than he was. Out of nervous energy, Bones would push his glasses up onto the bridge of his nose every fifteen seconds, whether he needed to or not.

Bones was legendary as a short hitter; he could not hold his liquor. In a prior duty station, after he had been paid in cash (outside Vietnam the Navy always paid in cash), Bones would go ashore, say, in Subic Bay in the Philippines. After going to a bar, and drinking a few beers, Bones would take out his cash, throwing it in the air. In the ensuing mad scramble for the bills, Filipino and other customers nearly killed one another. Bones would join in the scramble, emerging with his uniform torn and dirty.

The Shore Patrol would half drag, half carry Bones back to ship. His liberty would have lasted forty-five minutes. Coming aboard, he would rouse himself long enough to say to whoever would wonder about his condition, in his piney woods accent, "I don't go to town often but I like to have a good time when I do." Then Bones would pass out. Lucky for us, or for Bones in particular, the Navy paid us in script (Military Payment Certificates) while we were in Vietnam. There were very few places to spend it anyway.

A certain coarseness crept into dealings. Now I was a Catholic schoolboy who up until that point in his life had gone to mass every Sunday of his life (after a year in Vietnam I did not step inside a church for ten years). Back then I was a bit of a "goody-two-shoes." One overweight, rather crude enlisted guy named Durante was lolling about a few days after I arrived. As I passed by him, I asked Durante what was for lunch. "Horse cock sandwiches," he replied. I was not certain that I heard him right but the term seemed incredibly crude to me. I later learned that Durante was no coarser than anyone else. Horse cock, or some similar phrase, is the name Navy personnel universally use for sliced lunchmeat (bologna, salami, etc.).

We ran our little station as if it were a ship at sea, a notion with which the Army advisers agreed. That was another source of coarseness which crept into the equation.

One of my collateral duties was to serve as station Welfare and Recreation Officer, a formal title and office aboard a Navy ship. My "duties" consisted of bringing some softballs back from Cam Ranh Bay and stocking the station's library, which consisted of two to three cartons of used paperback books. Periodically (twice, I think) I went to Cam Ranh to trade in our stock of books for a new batch, which had come in with a shipment of used books from the U.S. (maybe courtesy of the USO?). Word would get around that I was going and the enlisted troops would begin lobbying me.

Now one would think that the categories of books requested would run the gamut: biography, history, self-help, geography, maybe philosophy, as well as fiction. In truth, only two requests would be made: "Mr. B, we need more f*** books," meaning soft-core pornographic romance novels. Other enlisted guys would counter the first group's request by asking, "Mr. B, can you get us some more good shit kickers?" meaning western adventure novels with multiple shoot-ups, bank robberies, duals, fast draw artists, and so on. I tried as best I could to accommodate both groups.

In truth, after long patrols none of us was up to more serious reading. A fellow officer's mother was an English teacher in Concord, North Carolina. She was appalled at the low-brow reading material we requested but dutifully sent over Travis Magee novels by John Macdonald and similar fare.

A similar scenario played out over the content to be played over the station entertainment network. Lambert had rigged loudspeakers for the mess area and several other common areas. Here the fight was not for classical, jazz, martial, or any other type music: it was exclusively rock n' roll versus country and western, known also as "shit kickin' music." Here the latter won out. During daylight hours easy listening country and western endlessly played. I can still remember the lyrics: "Silver threads and golden needles will not mend this heart of mine," or "The race is on and here comes Heartache, and the winner loses all."

Tattoos, which I dislike, probably growing out of my experiences in the Navy, were widespread among enlisted guys. They were not the abstract, and occasionally artistic, tattoos you may see today, often passed off as "body art." These were old fashioned sailor tattoos. Flags, pinups, or girl friends' and wives' names were popular. Spider webs or hinges on each elbow were a bit more creative, as were "hot" and "cold" on the upper chest. Several men had a small devil tattooed on the bicep. The devil held a trident; script below read "Born to Raise Hell."

In my earlier incarnation, aboard a ship, one of my enlisted guys went out, got drunk, and visited a tattoo parlor. There he had a cross etched on his forearm with "RIP" (Rest in Peace) above it and "Mom" below it. The next day he came to see me about the tattoo. He was in tears. The problem was that his mother, back in Nebraska, was still alive, actually quite young.

For some reason, sailors coming back from liberty would always have me awakened, or wake me themselves, to show me their fresh tattoos. They would be proud of them in the evening, when drunk, usually filled with remorse in the morning, when sober. In my opinion, there are fewer things uglier than a new, fresh tattoo. The colors are runny, blood and pus oozing out around the tattoo. You can barely make out what it is or what it says. To each her own I guess, and I have always been just medium strength on the belief that your body is a temple, but I don't like tattoos and I cannot comprehend why so many young people get them. Luckily, Vietnam had no tattoo parlors for my troops to patronize.

Back to Vietnam and the troops. One particularly able guy was VD Donner. VD was a Boatswain's mate. He was very good at what he did. He moved smartly and swiftly. He was incredibly strong and durable. He was a very good weapons handler. When he was behind you as you went on patrol and boarded a junk or sampan, you always knew that, if he was with you, VD "had your back."

Off duty, VD was always in trouble. He had been busted (punished by demotion in rank) several times by summary courts martial (the second lowest level of disciplinary proceeding) or non-judicial punishment (Captain's Mast, the lowest form of proceeding). Each time VD picked himself up, did his job in exemplary fashion, and got promoted back to where he had been.

Once the California Highway Patrol stopped VD at 4:00 A.M.on the San Diego Freeway. He was in a Buick convertible, top down, going ninety miles per hour. When they ordered VD out of the car, the officers saw a burly African American guy, naked except for Argyle socks.

Evidently VD had a way with, or at least involvement with, less savory women. He had contracted gonorrhea, I think, four times. VD told me once that when he went to the doctor, the physician had said, "When they named you VD, they weren't kidding."

"Doc" Desjardins was the medical corpsman assigned our unit. He was, as I recall, from upper Michigan somewhere and had French

Canadian ancestry. Nonetheless, everyone pronounced his surname in a Midwestern way, sounding out every letter, "D-e-s-j-a-r-d-i-n-s," rather than in the French or French Canadian way, "DeHardin." Doc (all medical corpsmen are "Doc"; all electricians "Sparky"; all cooks "Stewburner") was famous for his "surprise package."

Recreational drugs, hallucinogenic ones, pills of all kinds (uppers and downers), and plain old marijuana, became widespread in Vietnam. By 1971 it had become worse. Estimates were that thirty percent of U.S. troops experimented—not only with recreational drugs such as marijuana, but with opium and heroin. Isolated as we were, we never saw any of that. Maybe we were too square, or maybe it all came after our time. We were in Vietnam in 1966 and early 1967.

The only drugs we regularly used were what Doc would give us before we went out on long twenty-four, thirty-six, or forty-eight hour patrols. He would give each of us a small paper cup in which he had mixed twelve to thirteen tablets. I am certain there were amphetamines and other forbidden substances in there, but I do not know that for a fact.

You could take Doc's "surprise package," stay awake for a thirty-six hour patrol, come back to quarters, have a beer or two, sleep twelve hours, and awake with no hangover or other ill effect. Doc should have patented his mix and sold the patent to one of the major pharmaceutical companies.

I said that the men all came from small towns or farms. Frank Gagne came from Las Vegas, Nevada, but I guess that Las Vegas was a small town, or city, back then. Gagne was a University of Nevada graduate. Under pressure of being drafted and sent to Vietnam, Gagne joined the Navy to avoid all that. Guess where he wound up? Vietnam. Moreover, he was the biggest risk taker in the group. I would say that he would have volunteered for the most dangerous missions, but we did not have any per se. Instead Gagne always volunteered for the toughest assignments—overnight patrols, boarding and searching in bad weather, going out on the darkest, moonless nights.

A big guy, almost 6' 5", and muscular, Gagne had a baby face with a slight blush to his cheeks offset by piercing coal black eyes. Everyone in our billet, as far as I know, came from middle class, or more humble, economic circumstances. Gagne was the exception. His father was the CEO of a mid-size bank back in Las Vegas. Gagne could move comfortably in any surrounding. He was at ease moving among admirals or generals, flirting with bar girls, or talking business, politics, or philosophy.

I saw him in some of those settings because periodically some of us would get to go to Vung Tau, seventy kilometers to the south, where there were bars and numerous occasions of sin. I went there with Gagne at least twice (in Vietnam, at least where I was, officers and enlisted men moved comfortably with and supported one another—none of that Hollywood-officers-versus-enlisted hype). Vung Tau was also near the home base (Nui Dat) for the 4,500 Australian troop contingent (later 6,000) which fought in Vietnam. The Aussies were outgoing, welcoming and wild, at least when off duty—fun people. The saying was that to imitate an Australian all you had to do was walk around with a beer in your hand.

The Aussies were the ground troops closest to our station, about fifty-five or sixty kilometers south of us. Nonetheless, we never operated with them. Instead, the Big Red One, stationed further away (in Bien Hoa?) always did the sweeps in our area.

Vung Tau was our in-country R & R destination, which some single guys referred to as I & I (Intoxication & Intercourse). Supposedly, at least early in the War, in a year's tour of duty, a soldier, sailor, or Marine, was to receive R & R four times, that is, once a quarter. Three of those were to be in-country, one farther afield (out-country). Everyone got the latter but most never came close to getting three in-country R & Rs.

For out of country, the married guys went to Hawaii where they could rendezvous with their wives. They could also get free beach front accommodations at Fort Derussey which takes up two to three city blocks of Waikiki Beach. Single guys went to Thailand, Australia, or Hong Kong. I went to Hong Kong, staying in the famous Peninsula Hotel, where big gangly Americans in flying suits and others in combat fatigues mixed with Englishmen in three piece suits and Hong Kong Chinese who spoke perfectly accented English English.

One enduring memory of my week's R & R, otherwise a blur, was a food fight which broke out in the dining room of the Hong Kong Hilton (since torn down). One group of Army troops were flipping raw oysters with the tines of forks at an Air Force group, who were firing back with bread rolls and pads of butter. They went well beyond the Ugly American, and not subtle at all.

Our two other most frequent in-country destinations were Cam Ranh Bay, 130 or so kilometers to the north, and Nha Trang, the beautiful coastal city fifty kilometers north of Cam Ranh. Cam Ranh is a huge natural harbor, the Pearl Harbor of Vietnam, ten to twelve kilometers deep and eight to nine wide, completely protected from the South China Sea by a long arm of land and sand dunes from the north.

In fact, after the final U.S. forces left Vietnam in 1975, taking advantage of the natural harbor, the Russians took over the installations at Cam Ranh. They stationed naval ships in a base there and used it as a port for cargo ships as well, until well after the Berlin Wall fell in 1989 and the Soviet Union disbanded.

During the war, the large U.S. base included an airbase to and from which would fly commercial jet charters from and to the United States. U.S. troops generally got to Vietnam on commercial charters from Travis Air Force Base east of San Francisco rather than on military planes. Continental Airlines was the leading carrier followed by World Air, a charter company.

We would go to Cam Ranh to use the PX there, buying toothpaste, soap, underwear, books, and snacks; to visit our friends at the swift boat base, drinking copious amounts of beer (San Miguel but also Pabst, Miller's, or Budweiser) with them; and ostensibly to liaison with our air support. Believe it or not, in 1966, coastal patrol forces were still supported by flying boats, Navy PBYs (sea planes). Anchored "out in the stream" (out in the bay) at Cam Ranh was the USS *Currituck Sound*, a sea plane tender. We would go aboard ship to talk with the pilots and the operations people. I say ostensibly, though, because our real purpose was to get a first class lunch in the *Currituck Sound's* ward room or enlisted mess.

About halfway through my year in Vietnam, the Navy recalled the seaplanes, shortly thereafter retiring them from duty. Our air support from then on became P3 Orion aircraft out of Tan Son Nhut in Saigon. Large, four engine turboprop P3s were, and are (still flying forty-four years later) anti-submarine (ASW) aircraft that can stay aloft for thirteen to fourteen hours. I still remember the call sign for the squadron that used to overfly our patrol area—Cape Cod, as in "Cape Cod 11," "Cape Cod 12," etc.

The Navy outfitted the P3s with rocket pods on the wings so that they were capable of airborne support, albeit limited. The patrol craft were invaluable to us. If we had something suspicious going on, P3 patrol craft would circle, seemingly for hours, ready and able if we needed their help.

But the P3s were even more valuable for a trivial reason. They relieved the boredom. We would be out on patrol, for hours on end, moving along at three to four knots. Much of the time the boredom was excruciating. When a patrol aircraft came up on the radio, then, which they would do upon entering our patrol area, we would give the pilot our coordinates (all maps had a grid superimposed on them —we would take the coordinates from those). If it was nighttime and dark, we then would "request illumination." The patrol craft would circle our location, launching a para-flare, a parachute rigged with an illumination device. The para-flare would light up the entire night sky; for several minutes it seemed as though it were daylight. We could see each other's faces and clearly make out the individual palm trees on the shore. It was like standing under a giant streetlight.

I don't think we ever called for a para-flare because saw anything remotely suspicious. Each one of those para-flare devices probably cost the taxpayers $2000-2500, even back then. What a waste, but God we were bored and the illumination gave us a moment's relief.

Nha Trang was our favorite destination. We got to go there fairly often because our operational command, Coastal Patrol Center III Corps ("Halo Shampoo"), was there, as I said. Nha Trang had a long six to seven kilometer swimming beach, shaded by palm trees, fronted on by white stucco guest houses and small hotels, with flowering bougainvillea climbing up the walls and power poles. Offshore a half a mile or so were sixty or seventy forested islands, including Hon Mieu (South Island), Hon Tam, Hon Mat, Hon Cu Loa (Monkey Island), and Hon Tre (Bamboo Island), some of which arise suddenly to several hundred meters in elevation. Travel writers—then and later—unanimously termed Nha Trang Vietnam's most beautiful swimming beach.

We (U.S. forces) would arrive by patrol craft in the commercial harbor at the south end of the beach. From the large rectangular loading dock built out over the water, the road would begin and quickly go up a rise. Off to the right was a forested peninsula where Bao Dai, the last emperor of Vietnam (deposed in 1955), had his villa (now a hotel, the Cau Da Villas, and a small museum). Beyond was an almost gothic French girl's school. The only difficulty was that the U.S. military had commandeered those places. Up went packing crate partitions. Parked in front, on the lawn, now churned into mud, would be a half dozen dirty jeeps. Passing the airfield on the left, the city and the long tourist beach would begin.

We liked Nha Trang because of the change of pace and because we could drink ourselves silly. The military played a role in the latter.

Like Phan Thiet, Nha Trang was designated a "secure" town, although the Viet Cong overran it in the Tet Offensive of 1968. Even so, we were actively discouraged, even forbidden, from walking about or exploring the town. If we had detoured, however slightly, upon entering a U.S. compound we would have to tell the sentries that our vehicle was "not secure," or "unsecure." The sentries would then wave us aside. When they had time, they would use mirrors to screen the underside, look under the hood, search the back seat, and so on.

So to avoid the rigamarole, and also because we seldom felt even somewhat safe, when we went to Nha Trang we would go from U.S. compound to U.S. compound. In these compounds, the U.S. personnel would begin their nightly happy hours at 3:30 or 4:00 PM. So we drank—beer and "college party cocktails" (potent mixed drinks in tall highball glasses, also called "silver bullets")—often for seven or eight hours straight, every night we were in Nha Trang.

We, my troops along with myself and fellow officers, were in Nha Trang on the occasion when the first Korean troops (ROKs, Republic of Korea) came to Viet Nam. The VC were nearly, but not completely, fearless. They were deathly afraid of the Koreans, who were notoriously rugged and, some said, mean. Taking two prisoners up in an aircraft, pushing one out and saying to the other, "Now talk," was a tactic first ascribed to the Koreans.

The Koreans, the White Horse Division, came to Vietnam and to Nha Trang by ship. Their landing craft (LSTs) put their ramps down on the beach and the Koreans marched ashore, presumably to their new quarters in Nha Trang, where they would be based. Instead, as my enlisted guys and I watched, with flags flying, and vehicles laden with supplies, the Koreans marched on right through town and out into the field for their first operation. The ROKs didn't screw around. The Viet Cong quickly learned that.

Bouncing around in the back of a jeep (the roads were filled with huge potholes) I first experienced severe back pain. I got a jolt so hard that I thought I heard a snap in my vertebrae. I also got to know a bit more about one of my favorites from that year, Charlie Miller from Fairbanks, Iowa, with whom I spent some time in Nha Trang.

Charlie was a baby faced, slightly pudgy kid who had worked for a year in the John Deere factory in Waterloo, Iowa before he joined the Navy. He was a small town boy of small town boys. He would always ponder a second before answering you or responding to a comment, not in an argumentative but in a thoughtful way. Seemingly somewhat slow moving, Charlie was another who always "had your back." If you had some scary assignment, or were boarding a junk in the dark, you could count on Charlie Miller, with his cherub face, being right behind you, with a shotgun or an automatic weapon. He might not always have liked it but he did it.

I remember talking with Charlie for hours while we were on patrol. We had to talk not only to relieve the boredom but to preserve our sanity. What Tim O'Brien wrote in *The Things They Carried* about sentry duty applied equally to our long patrols:

The hours go by and you begin to lose your gyroscope. Your mind starts to roam. You think about dark closets, madmen, murderers under the bed, all those childhood fears. Gremlins, trolls, and giants. You try to block it out but you can't. You see ghosts. You blink and shake your head.

And you talk, even though you're not supposed to. Charlie Miller loved cars but not just any cars. He loved racing cars. His good friend back home, Lee Kunzman, had already made a name for himself as a race car driver. Charlie couldn't wait to get back to Iowa to be part of Lee's racing team. We used to talk about racing and autos.

Charlie was a great teammate. He knew what you wanted done before you asked for it. As I said, we encountered physical dangers only from time to time but when we did Charlie could be counted upon as one who would not have backed down from it.

But for some reason or other Charlie suffered from severe stress and anxiety attacks. He would become extremely restless, incapable of sleep, and then lapse into depression. I think twice during my year there Charlie had to spend time in the hospital at Cam Ranh Bay. He would come back good as new but these episodes were not the kind of thing you would ever think happening in a war zone or to a standup guy such as Charlie. When in the movie *Patton*, General Patton slaps an enlisted soldier supposedly suffering from shell shock, I always used to sympathize with Patton. Charlie Miller's episodes reminded me then, and remind me now, that the psychological stresses and strains of combat duty, much less nose-to-nose combat, are real and their manifestations difficult to predict.

North Vietnamese gun runner.

4

Captain Munster
(Creases Across the Ass)

THE SENIOR OFFICER IN CHARGE OF OUR LITTLE contingent was
Lawrence Leonard, a Navy lieutenant commander who thought himself the John Wayne or Audie Murphy of the decade, in the vanguard
of those who stood for freedom. He preferred to be called by the
name he had devised for himself: "Rocky." We preferred to call him
(never to his face) "Munster," after Herman Munster on the popular
television show "The Munsters."

Leonard was a tall, lanky guy with dark black hair that he combed
into a pompadour. I suppose he was not bad looking (he thought he
was exceedingly handsome) but he had a square head. He looked a
bit like Jeff Goldblum, the television actor. The square head and the
way Leonard loped along as he walked led to the Munster, or Captain
Munster, appellation.

On the surface, or on initial impression, he could be quite pleasant. After we had been around him only for a short while, we quickly found that he could be, and was, as judgmental as an older sibling, or a traffic cop. He was always right; we were always wrong. In public, at least when others were present, he smiled, frequently making little jokes. We quickly learned that it was an Eddie Haskell smile—practiced, phony, and as wicked as a rattle snake. As soon as the two of you, Munster and yourself, were outside the presence of others, the snake came slithering from its hole.

He fell short, far short, of being the John Kennedy or George Patton he fancied himself as being.

Alone among us, Captain Munster planned to make the Navy a career. Perhaps because of it, or maybe because it just came naturally, Munster was a supreme butt kisser, as I found many career military to be. He never failed to cozy up to a senior officer, or to anyone he thought could do him good. He could be the most pleasant, understanding, and smiley commander when he was in the presence of those he perceived as having some power. His only insistence was that they got his name right.

After a session with a superior was over, Munster could spin on a dime. If a subordinate (like me) had failed to kow-tow to him, or provide the correct documentary or logistical support at precisely the right moment, Munster would call you a "dumb son-of-a-bitch," "stupid," or an "idiot," as soon as you were out the senior officer's hearing range. He would tell you "never to do it again," or else "he would see to it that you got your ass kicked." He was as two faced a son-of-a-gun as ever I had encountered in my short life.

If Munster felt that you had done something to make him look bad, he would call you to his room to question you and give you a long lecture about "second guessing" him. I never did come to an understanding about what he meant about "second guessing."

Munster would also give you "the glare," as in cementing in your

44

memory the criticisms he has just leveled at you. His question marks turned to exclamation points, a whole series of them. The long piercing stare followed "the glare," as in "I told you so." The cartoon bubble floating over his head seemed to read, "Do I have to tell you everything to do? You're incompetent."

Now Munster's room had single bed where you would sit as he sat at a small table that served him as a desk. Sitting there, Munster lectured and swore at you. Surrounding the bed was a metal rail raised about three inches above the surface of the bed. If Munster's tirades lasted more than a minute or two, and they always did, this rail would begin to bite into the back of your thighs or into your butt. So it became part of the milieu that when you saw a colleague heading towards Munster's room, or a colleague saw you heading for a chewing out, the joke was "Gonna get your ass creased again?"

Munster was also fond of laying traps, playing mind games with us. He would have daytime crew place a large wooden box, or simulate a wrecked junk, in a secluded cove. When our patrol failed to detect the object on the beach, or to radio in a finding, Munster would read me, or whoever had been the officer in charge, the riot act after we returned. He would place me, or other officers, on restriction, confined to quarters. We thought we were there with a job to do. Munster evidently thought we were there to do things precisely his way (play games?), and no other.

Toward the end of my time in the service, there came into office as Chief of Naval Operations (CNO), Admiral Elmo Zumwalt, who before that had commanded the naval forces in Vietnam (COMNAVFORV). CNO is the highest military position in the Navy, second only to the Secretary of the Navy, a political appointee and a civilian.

CNO Zumwalt attempted to put an end to some of the endless butt-kissing games that occurred in the military. He regularly sent messages and commentaries directly to the unit level and thus to the troops in the form of "Z-grams," rather than downward through the

chain of command where senior officers could shortstop pronounce-
ments they did not like.

For example, one practice Zumwalt wanted to stop was the practice of washing or "painting sides." When Navy ships came back from
long six and eight month deployments, during which they had been
at sea for weeks at a time, a common practice was that the captains
would cause the ships to race ahead toward home (wasting great
quantities of fuel in the process). The ships would then hove-to a day
or two offshore, putting sailors over the side to apply fresh paint to
the hull. The process would take up the day or two they had gained
by racing ahead.

In a variant, the captains would cause the crew to use up most of
the fresh water, which always is in short supply on a Navy ship, to
scrub the ship's sides and superstructure. The crew would not be able
to shower or otherwise clean up but the ship could then return to its
home port looking spotless.

Why did Navy ship captains almost universally order these things
done, wasteful and irritating to crew as they were? To impress the admiral, that's why. So while the ship would look spotless, with flags flying, pennants fluttering, and officers decked out in spotless dress
white uniforms as the ship came into its home port, the crew would
have to greet their families, whom they had not seen in eight to nine
months, all smelly and unwashed. Career Navy officers preserved this
and other traditions of butt kissing as near sacred.

CNO Zumwalt tried to put a stop to such practices. He sent Z-
gram after Z-gram on the subject. And he caused a near revolt. Career
Navy officers liked the system just the way it was, and still is (I guess)
today. They rebelled. Admiral Zumwalt made little or no headway
against the practice of painting sides.

In another Z-gram, Zumwalt tried to get commanders to allow
enlisted men to wear their hair a bit longer. In those days, the late
'60s, in the civilian world many young men wore hair down to or over

their shirt collars. Commanders in the field almost universally, I think, ignored Zumwalt's entreaties. Because of their obscenely short hair, often with "whitewalls" around the ears, Navy personnel continued not only to stick out but embarrassingly so anytime they went into the civilian world.

Lest I did not adequately convey my message, let me repeat: Munster was an ass kisser par excellence, in the very mold Admiral Zumwalt tried to re-mold. There were none better than Munster. Z-grams, or the Vietnam version of which of which were promulgated at that time, were not only totally lost on but studiously ignored by the Munster.

Role two (Role one was Munster the butt kisser) was Munster the prima donna, aka the paranoid, I don't know which fits better. One lazy Sunday afternoon we were on what is known as holiday routine during which troops could read books, play catch, take a nap, or do whatever they wished. Usually, no patrols or a single patrol would be scheduled. The cook would often make up a big lunch.

Now where we were, the forty or so of us (which included the Army advisors) would eat in one mess. The custom was, as it is in the field or in most military installations, that the enlisted men ate first and the officers ate last, only after all the men had been fed.

Now Munster loved chocolate. He loved chocolate sauce on chocolate ice cream served over chocolate cake with chocolate frosting. He carried chocoholic to new heights. When he saw the troops coming through the chow line, ahead of us, Munster saw chocolate ice cream on their trays. Munster rubbed his hands with glee. He could not wait. It was the biggest event of the month for him. Once served, Munster might have eaten the ice cream before the roast beef.

But when we officers went through the chow line, lo and behold, the cook ("Stewburner") plopped strawberry ice cream on our trays. Now Munster could have been disappointed, crestfallen even. Instead he went ballistic.

He ordered everyone to stop eating. He ordered the cook out from behind the counter. He made the cook stand at attention. Munster then ordered the officer whose collateral duty it was to oversee meals and supply also to stand at rigid attention, next to the cook. He proceeded to question the two of them— interrogate really—as to where in our compound there might be additional chocolate ice cream. Muster was convinced that the cook and the supply officer deliberately were hiding chocolate treats from him.

In college, I had read Herman Wouk's *The Caine Mutiny* in which the skipper of an old destroyer (played by Humphrey Bogart in the movie) tears the ship apart, convinced that there were fresh strawberries aboard that crew members were conspiring to hide from him. Now, the nearly identical incident was unfolding, right before my eyes, except it involved chocolate, not fresh strawberries. I never thought such paranoia actually could run rampant anywhere, let alone on a military post in a combat zone.

After making the two poor souls stand at rigid attention for twenty minutes, Munster decided he would conduct a search of the freezer facility we had in quarters. He made the cook and the supply officer lead him to the walk-in freezer used for cold storage. Sure enough, no chocolate ice cream was found. This finding might have calmed him, or brought home to ordinary mortals how stupid or greedy they had acted. Instead, it enraged him.

He called off holiday routine. He announced that in two hours he would conduct a material inspection of the installation. Enlisted had to turn out of their bunks, put down their books, or lay aside the baseball they had been throwing in order to pick up broom and mop, cleaner and wax. This probably was the only material inspection ever ordered in Vietnam, at least in the war zone. Nobody could believe this was happening. At the appointed hour, Munster did his inspection, finding little about which to complain. But the day had been ruined. His antics cast a pall over the entire week that followed, and even beyond that.

Rob, the officer for whom supply was a collateral and not primary duty, had had enough. He put himself into the hospital at Cam Ranh. While there he requested a transfer. His request was granted. We never saw him again.

Only one slightly mitigating factor in Munster's favor was that ice cream—strawberry, chocolate, or any other flavor—was a somewhat rare commodity in Vietnam, at least for us. Larger ships out at sea received ice cream all the time, as well as movies, fresh vegetables, lettuce, and mail from home. Every day, or every other day, a large supply ship (400 feet long, 18,000-25,000 tons) called a "reefer"— as in refrigerator ship— would leave the Philippines for the Vietnamese coast. No matter what their main cargo all of these supply ships also carried ice cream, movies, and mail.

These ships would send a radio message to all U.S. ships called a PIM (Position of Intended Movement). We did not have the equipment to have access to those messages but the larger ships did have the radios and teletypes needed. The PIM would set out the day and times along with coordinates of the positions the supply ships would cross in the next five to seven days. The supply ships would replenish first the aircraft carriers and escort vessels to the far north, at Yankee Station in the Tonkin Gulf, from which the carriers launched air strikes against North Vietnam.

Next, supply ships would steam south, bringing alongside the gunfire support ships (destroyers and frigates) that would be close in to the shore in I Corps, firing five inch shells ten to twelve miles inland in support of Marine Corps operations there. One by one, the gunfire support ships would cease firing, one at a time, going four to five miles seaward. Once there, the combat ships would go alongside supply ships for underway replenishment.

Steaming south the replenishment (supply) ships would service the DDR's (old destroyer escorts) doing offshore patrols. They would finish their supply runs by servicing the LSTs, which served as mother ships for the riverine craft that patrolled the rivers and canals that thread up into the Delta.

Now even if we could have gotten a copy of a PIM message we could never have gotten the four to five miles out to sea to get ice cream, movies, or fresh vegetables. Often it was too rough out there for a thirty-nine-foot wooden sampan. Even if seas were glassy smooth, our Yabudda junks were just too slow. It might take us as long as two hours to get out there along the line of intended movement for the supply ships, an hour or so to wait, and two hours back again. So we did without, contenting ourselves with the supplies the Air Force C-123s brought into Phan Thiet's dirt airstrip.

Except for the USS *Vesuvius*—an older but still big (20,000 tons) ammunition ship. The *Vesuvius* and her captain were the only supply ship that would abandon the PIM, coming often in as far as a half mile offshore to mete out to us little guys some of the perks the big boys had.

The first time it happened I was aghast. Here was this huge, haze-gray military ship, with running lights ablaze and signal lights flashing, coming in dangerously close toward us and the shore. The sailors on board her lowered a forty-foot utility boat, which would then motor over toward us. The first time I did not know what was up. Ammunition? An emergency? No, they had ice cream for us, packed into freezer containers to keep it from melting, and boxes of fresh vegetables and lettuce! I remember the way our ARVN and Vietnamese Navy counterparts ate that ice cream until they had headaches and protruding stomachs.

I think that (*Vesuvius* "unreps") happened twice. No other supply ship captain ever even thought about, much less attempted, that kind of thing. The big supply ships generally were captained by Navy "airdale" (airplane pilot) captains ("four stripers"), who needed a "deep draft command" in order to be eligible for promotion to admiral. Because the airedales lacked any real ship handling experience or expertise, the Navy did not trust them with command of aircraft carriers or cruisers. Instead, the Navy gave these "admiral strikers" command of supply ships in which they could do less damage and by and large be supported by lower ranking officers and crew. These supply ship captains were so intent on the prospects of their promotions to admiral that we Brown Water Navy guys and our welfare never entered their minds. Only the *Vesuvius*, commanded by what Navy people call an "old salt," probably a Mustang (former enlisted), had the courage and the presence of mind to think of us. I'll always remember the USS *Vesuvius*, her captain, and her crew.

****

From time to time, we had a laugh or two at our OIC's (Munster's) expense. Lt.(jg) Donald Douze reported aboard about halfway through my tour. He was a bit on the chubby side, with his blond hair buzz cut and acne scars on his puffy cheeks. His best features were eyes that were pale blue, the color of ice cubes. We seldom saw those eyes, however, because Douze slept while others of us were awake. In turn, he always was awake while others slept.

Douze was no beach blanket lightweight. He was exceedingly smart, a geek who had studied chemical engineering. He would stay up until 4:00 A.M. every night, reading scientific journals and engineering magazines his mother sent to him from the States. Then he would be sent out on patrol at 7:00 A.M., by which time the Vietnamese summer sun would be branding iron hot. Douze would fall asleep a few hundred meters from shore. Munster detested Douze, thinking him a rank incompetent, bordering upon the dysfunctional (in Munster's lexicon, the rest of were merely incompetent). After Douze had made two attempts at patrols, Munster assigned Douze to administrative duties (of which there were none). Douze never went out of our little compound again.

One evening meal Munster sat at the head of the mess table while Douze sat at the foot. Three of us (other officers) sat on either side.

The meal served that night consisted of chili on mounds of white rice. Douze shoveled it down, which was easy to do because it tasted very good, but about halfway through the meal Douze stopped. His pale blue eyes glazed over.

Suddenly, Douze began vomiting. Bad enough you say, with chunks of masticated rice and chili being heaved onto the table from which we had been eating, with that foul, sour stench of stomach acid permeating the air. But it was worse, for Douze was a projectile vomiter: the big red kidney beans in the chili were the projectiles. The beans flew from Douze's mouth two meters across the table, like bullets from a machine gun, hitting Munster's fatigues and, I think, his face, as well as the plate from which was eating. My colleagues and I had to kick each other under the table to distract one other, to suppress our laughter.

Munster looked as though he had swallowed a razor blade. He was angry and disgusted. He dropped his napkin on the floor, stood up, spun on his heels and left without a word.

Three days later Douze was transferred. I never saw him again.

****

We had very American meals when eating in our compound (C Rations in olive drab tins while on patrol but good food in quarters). We had Department of Defense "Four Way Beef," which included steaks and roast beef. We had generous stores of cigarettes, beer, ice cream now and then, snack food, and more, with only fresh fruit and vegetables absent. Simultaneously, the military actively discouraged us from sampling the local food, on the grounds that Vietnamese food could make us sick. To bring the message further home, information officers embellished the warnings: we were told that Vietnamese cuisine made ample use of dog and rat meat.

Munster never did redeem himself for all the cheap shots and verbal punishment he handed out that year I spent under his command. But, once or twice, he did surprise us.

We had a piece of echo sounding equipment which we could mount on the bow of a Yabudda. Those primitive sonar rigs could detect solid objects under water; it could also act as a depth finder.

Well, the depth finder went down, wouldn't work at all. Munster had us send out a CASREP (casualty report) to everyone but his brother, just as they do in the big time Navy. We notified Nha Trang (Coastal Surveillance Center III Corp), COMNAVFORV in Saigon, the Seventh Fleet, Navy Supply Center in the Philippines, Navy Supply Corps in Washington D.C., CINCPAC (commander-in-chief, Pacific) in Hawaii, and countless others.

Lambert, our technician, took the device apart. He gave me a part number for the component that had failed. I pointedly asked Lambert to check again. He came back to me with the same part number. So I gave Munster the part number, scribbled on a scrap of paper. Munster caused the communications guy to send out a second CASREP message, detailing more on the failure and including the part number.

Two hours later Munster called me in. The Navy supply depot in the Philippines, 500 or more miles away, was air lifting the part in from Cubi Point Naval Air Station. Six hours later a twin engine Navy airplane appeared over Phan Thiet Bay. We floated below on a Yabudda junk, ready to retrieve the package. The pilot made two passes over us at an altitude of 500 feet, waggling his wings. On the third pass, out of the airplane popped a small parachute that floated a waterproof package down to the water's surface.

I thought "what a waste." We never did use that echo sounding device much anyway. We could do without it, leaving it inoperative, but I kept my mouth shut. Munster loved to play big time Navy, with his CASREPs, distress signals, supply planes, and on and on. I guess he thought all the dramatic messages and communications kept his name in front of the powers that be, or were, that is, the admirals.

We got back ashore, took the package back to our compound, unwrapped it, and gave the part to Lambert. Five minutes later Lambert re-appeared, this time with a red face and a sheepish grin. "Wrong part."

"Jesus Leroy. How can that be? We checked and double checked."

Lambert led me to his work bench in one of the plywood huts. The new part bore the number I had written down. The written number matched the malfunctioning part Lambert had removed from the depth finder. But the new part was twice as big and bore no resemblance to the part on the fritz.

"It don't fit. I don't know why but it's not the right part." Lambert shook his head.

Ordinarily, this situation would have placed me in severe difficulty. Munster would blame it all on me. I would get a lecture, one lasting an hour or more. I would be assigned extra duties, including patrols, for days and weeks to come.

But it was worse, for we had sent a distress signal and the support people had responded, with great alacrity, on December 25, Christmas Day. We had pulled supply clerks, ground personnel, communications officers, pilots, crew chiefs, and a half dozen others away from their holiday routine and their Christmas dinners, for nothing. Although military were away from their families, they still had the day off and celebrated Christmas as best they could.

I thought that this mistake was the biggest of my year's tour, so egregious that Munster might attempt to have me relieved for cause, probably sent home, cashiered and disgraced. Munster was that kind of vindictive person.

I went right in, blurting out to Munster that tens of thousands of dollars had been spent and Christmas routines disrupted, all for naught, to bring us the wrong part. The replacement part would not work, no matter how we tried. And it was my fault.

I can say it was the only time in the year I knew him when the Munster truly was magnanimous. "Obviously, you were working from an outdated supply manual. They've changed the part numbers and probably the design of these things. Ours is an old one anyway. Don't worry about it."

I could not believe my ears but, just in case, I got out of there as fast as I could. I grabbed a book, heading for my best hiding place, lest Munster have second thoughts. And for a fleeting moment, the first since I had been a kid, I thought "there must be a Santa Claus," even in Vietnam.

****

Munster also considered himself to be quite the combat warrior. This attribute did not cause us as much pain, as we seldom were presented with opportunities for nose-to-nose combat. But a few times we were. On those occasions, Munster stepped into the breach.

One of his first steps was a misstep. It was the first time we encountered (maybe) hostile fire. We were on patrol, close in to the beach in a secluded bay. I guess Munster thought he had seen a muzzle flash on the shore and he lost his cool. He began yelling, "Fire, fire." None of us had seen anything so we responded, "Where, where?" Munster screamed out, "In the trees, in the fucking trees." Well, it took us a few seconds before we could register, although "kill some trees" was Vietnam-speak for "fire at will."

We could and did bring considerable firepower to bear. We had both M-60 and .50 caliber machine guns, big WWII automatic weapons (Browning Automatic Rifles, or BARs), M-14s, and Thompson submachine guns. We cut loose. We mowed down stands of two-inch bamboo. We hit everything in sight. We kept up a barrage for what seemed like five minutes. When we quit, we were all panting for breath. I doubt whether Munster had seen anything, and undoubtedly we did great damage to our hearing. But we did like to shoot those guns!

A funny thing is that you cannot always tell when someone is shooting at you. If you are close enough, you may hear the retort of the weapon ("crack" for a rifle, "pop-pop-pop," like a string of firecrackers going off, for an automatic weapon). An observant person may hear nothing but see the muzzle flash, the explosion emerging at the end of the barrel of a weapon being fired. If you neither hear nor see anything, though, often you cannot tell you're being shot at until a bullet thuds into something solid around you (the side of the sampan, the little pilot house, etc.). I am told that you can hear a "whiz" as a bullet passes close by you but I never experienced that.

****

U.S. personnel always put down the Vietnamese (ARVN) troops. One joke making the rounds went like this: "The ARVN aren't so bad anymore. Used to be that when they encountered any sign of the enemy (VC or NVA) they dropped their weapons and ran. They're improving. They don't drop their weapons anymore."

Truth was that they ran the gamut. Some South Vietnamese troops were lazy, some were chicken, and some corrupt, but others were fighters. Vietnamese President Diem, and his ultimate successor, President Thieu, did not help. They kept the crack ARVN units, or many of them, close by Saigon (less than forty kilometers away) so that they, insecure, paranoid office holders, could call on those units for protection against suspected coups. President Diem kept a crackerjack Vietnamese Special Forces Unit, trained at U.S. expense, as his personal body guard, as did President Thieu after Diem (with a succession of incompetent generals and committees of generals in-between).

The Vietnamese officers were arrogant, condescending to their fellow Vietnamese, whom the officers regarded as country bumpkins, and mostly were corrupt. The ARVN units were chronically undermanned because of deserters and unauthorized leaves. The officers kept absent "ghost soldiers" on the roster and the payroll so that the officers could embezzle the pay, such as it was, the rations, and the supplies designated for the ghosts. As a result of ghosts, the undermanned ARVN units were not undermanned on paper—with the result that they seldom were re-enforced either, so they remained greatly undermanned in reality.

As I said, we had a Vietnamese Ranger battalion stationed in Phan Thiet. The Rangers were solid, brave troops who never shied away from combat. They went out on missions nearly every day, at least on those days their astrologer (necromancer) had cleared.

****

Another example of Munster's foolish combat escapades involved a Vietnamese gunboat (large patrol craft) which came into our province from time to time. We were just setting out from Phan Thiet on a night patrol aboard two Yabudda junks. It was on a Friday. The moon was full. We came up on the Vietnamese gunboat, trading fire with Viet Cong who were up in the sand dunes, all around where the Cham towers were (and still are), northwest of Phan Thiet town. The ARVN and VC literally were slugging it out toe-to-toe. We could see red tracers coming out of the sand dunes. That they, the Chucks and the ARVN Navy forces, could have destroyed priceless historical monuments did not seem to enter the equation.

We, the U.S, forces, could and should have slipped by, gone round the point, and on with our patrol. Munster, though, radios the Vietnamese gunboat commander that we would standby to assist. We groaned, saying to ourselves, "Now why did you have to go and do that for?

So there we lay, on the decks of the junks, suffocated by our body armor, which in those days was heavy and cumbersome (eight to ten pounds). It was hot, too. With the moon nearly full, we could see the gunboat, the dunes, and the Cham towers, or at least the shadows of them. The tension was palpable. Although we never did actually get shot at directly, we stayed there, ready to go in, for four, maybe five hours. I remember that Friday night as one of the most stressful, indeed scary, of my year in Vietnam.

I guess that as a military guy you want a leader who has a bit of the combat warrior mentality but not someone who puts you needlessly at risk. Most times Munster was the former but on occasion he could really stress us out with his Audie Murphy imitations (Audie Murphy, later a movie actor, was the most decorated soldier in World War II).

****

The last time I saw Munster was when we came home from Vietnam. As we walked into the airport passenger terminal, we were surrounded by flags draped over the railings, like bunting on the Fourth of July. A small Navy band was playing. A welcoming committee of Navy officers awaited us.

There, standing immediately in the foreground, were Munster's wife, his daughter (may be six or seven year old) decked out in a pink dress, and his son (maybe nine or ten), fitted out in his dark blue Cub Scout uniform. Beyond them were the Navy brass, a couple of admirals and other high ranking officers. Munster was first or second through the door. He seemed to be heading right toward his family members who all had big smiles on their faces, especially happy on this joyous and festive occasion. At the last moment, he swerved around wife, daughter, and son, making a beeline straight for the admirals and began shaking their hands. He ignored his family, a butt kisser to the last.

After I came back from Vietnam, I kept in contact with several of those with whom I served and kept in close contact with a couple of them. In fact, we still get in touch from time-to-time. By contrast, I do not care and in fact strongly hope that I never see Munster again. I, and I think the other officers who served under him, have for Munster nothing but the withering disdain that an officer holds for another who has failed to win the respect (not affection, but respect) of subordinates who served under him.

5

Ninety-Nine Percent Boredom, One Percent Terror

They make the mountains burn. It's [napalm] not pretty exactly.
It's astonishing. It fills your eyes. It commands you.

—Tim O'Brien, *The Things They Carried* (1990)

They also serve who only stand and wait.

—John Milton, *On His Blindness* (1667)

AIRPLANE PILOTS DESCRIBE FLYING AS ninety-nine percent boredom, one percent terror. For modern day commercial pilots, it's 99.99 percent, punctuated by very small moments when they must confront emergencies. My combat duty in Vietnam was like flying an airplane, at least the way flying used to be. I am certain that actual combat of the kind Marines and Army soldiers did is much more terrifying but I and the guys with whom I served basically did the ninety-nine percent boredom, one percent terror thing.

My very first episode of terror came the third day I was in Vietnam with the first junk I searched. On a sunny early May day, we had ventured out from Phan Thiet to the lane close-in to shore where the coastal passenger and cargo shipping traffic moved up and down the coast of Vietnam. The senior enlisted guy sighted an older, dirty, unkempt sampan moving within the caravan of smarter, mostly steel hulled, vessels heading up and down the coast. We hailed it to stop, which it did, and we moved smartly up and along side of it.

Vietnamese fishing junk.

My enlisted guys and I prepared to board the junk. We fixed the two vessels fast together with a mooring line we attached to the junk. Frank Gagne was behind me with a weapon (we had M-14 rifles, the precursors to the Colt M-16s which became the dominant U.S. weapon in the war). Sam Houston, I believe, was behind Gagne, with a sawed off shotgun, which made no sense at all because Houston, who was small, could not at all see around Gagne, who was big. I had a .45 caliber pistol but holstered, which did me no good at all.

I hopped aboard the Vietnamese sampan. It was a calm day so the sea was flat. The two vessels were not bobbing up and down. Gagne followed me. I checked in the small shelter on the junk's deck: a woman and two small children were inside. I pushed aside a bundle of clothing. Nothing amiss there. I went toward the stern, lifting up the wooden hatch to the engine compartment. The compartment contained a smelly, two-stroke engine. Nothing out of the ordinary there.

By this time I was relaxed, rocked back on my heels, feeling pretty comfortable at this boarding and searching stuff even though it was my first day on duty and my first junk. I lifted up boards to check a cargo compartment and, beneath it, the bilges. Nothing there. I moved forward to a second compartment, talking over my right shoulder to Gagne as I lifted up the boards to peer into the bilges. There was a Vietnamese man (a teenager really) with an AK-47 pointed straight at my chest. I was flatfooted, my weapon still holstered, and my body completely blocked out Gagne's line of sight and therefore his field of fire.

I cannot say that my complete life passed before my eyes. I do remember thinking, quite calmly, "I'm dead." But I wasn't. I stepped aside. Houston came up. He and Gagne motioned the kid up to the deck, grabbing away his weapon as he stepped toward them. Once they had the AK-47, the three of us let out big sighs of relief, relief that we had really screwed up and gotten away with it.

Turns out that the Vietnamese kid did not have any ammunition. I don't think that he was a VC. I think rather that he and his father or uncle were black marketers who had stolen or bought a quantity of assault rifles. We confiscated their sampan, turning them, the assault rifles and the sampan over to the Vietnamese National Police in Phan Thiet.

From that day forward we took steps to choreograph our movements. "If you fail to plan, plan on failure," Navy instructors had taught you. After that incident, we planned. We rehearsed and rehearsed. One member of the boarding party would quickly move out wide where he had a fairly open field of fire. The second boarding party member would do the same, but to the other side. We had to be especially careful that we did not block each other's line of sight.

Coast Guard WPB boarding and searching a junk.

We imposed upon ourselves a "sterile cockpit rule" such as commercial air pilots use: no unnecessary talking or jabbering until we completed our search. We talked about it and did dry runs until we had honed our boarding procedure to a fine point.

In the year that followed several similar incidents occurred, when we found suspected VC hidden in bilges, beneath decking. We did much better. We were prepared.

Night-time patrols were a different matter. Instead of boarding and searching junks, we went up and down the coast to do surveillance on any shore-based suspicious activity and to intercept any shipments of arms or war materiel, which would most probably occur under cover of darkness. For these patrols then, we had no lights whatsoever.

On cloudy nights, or when there was no moon, the darkness would be near absolute, like "midnight in the garden at Gethsemane," eerie, spooky. One moonless night we were motoring along at a fast

Nightime boarding of an offshore trawler. *Left to right:* Sam Houston, Frank Gagne and the author.

clip (five or so knots for us). Everyone was resting save me and, I think, Caldwell. Ahead of us I saw a red dot appear. I had the tiller in my hand. I pulled it all the way toward me, swinging the rudder to the left and the Yabudda's bow to the right. I then pushed the tiller back, nearly all the way to the left ("meet her" in nautical terms) to get the swing off, and then some, so that in turning we would not slide sideways, broad-siding whatever was out there.

Three or four meters away, in the darkness, we felt more than saw a presence, which slid down our port side out into our wake. "Man, that was close," I said. It hit us what we had seen: the glow of a cigarette end as one of the fisherman in the junk took a puff. Only that tiny red glow had saved us from an accident that could have maimed or killed several persons.

This kind of thing happened often at night. Many Vietnamese fishermen had a lantern in their junk but a large minority did not. On some nights, the number would be not insignificant, as scores of junks and sampans would be out night fishing.

In the morning, as we motored out on patrol we would listen to Armed Forces Radio from Saigon. We actually did listen to Adrian Cronauer, who Robin Williams played in the movie *Good Morning Vietnam*. We heard the Beach Boys, the Temptations, Little Anthony and the Imperials ("Shimmy, shimmy coco pop, shimmy shimmy bop, sitting in a native hut...") as we laid on the deck motoring out to begin our patrol. Once on station, field discipline required us to turn the portable radio off but for the first thirty or forty minutes we listened to this wacky disc jockey and the music he played. "Good morning, Vietnam. It's hot—hot enough for crotch pocket cooking." It was exactly as the movie depicted; the radio show, the rock n' roll, and Cronauer never failed to boost morale.

Another moment of sheer terror came from weather rather than the enemy. In monsoon season, September or early October I think, we motored up through our patrol area in very rough five to seven foot seas. Rain squall after rain squall enveloped us. Visibility was less than half a mile. Everyone hung on for dear life as the junk's bow crested each wave, slamming down into the trough beyond, and repeated the maneuver, over and over. We were soaked through, miserable, woodenly going through the paces, getting bruised and banged up as the junk's gyrations threw us against the little pilot house, trying to get the patrol over with. I had somehow lost much of my religion since arriving in Vietnam, but I was praying then. "Give unto me a break (in the weather), Oh Lord."

As we reached north of Cu Lao Cau, the island where the Japanese scuttled their Southeast Asia fleet after World War II, and which helped mark the north end of our patrol area, we started to execute a 180 degree turn, to return to the barn. With a following sea, we would rush southward, back to Phan Thiet and to our compound, out of the nasty, cold rainy weather. We could dry out, warm up, have a drink or two, eat heaping amounts of hot American food, read a book, watch a movie, or have a nice long sleep. Only trouble was that we made it only halfway, through the turn that is, not back to our base.

We were trapped in the trough, or in successive troughs as the waves, which seemed to be getting bigger and bigger, rolled relentlessly on. Our junk had only a single diesel engine. We did not have the power to push through and complete the turn.

We were worse than caught. We had a roll indicator on the side of the junk's pilot house. The indicator pendulum swung over to indicate successively greater rolls—thirty-five degrees, then forty degrees, then forty-five degrees, a fifty degree roll! As each wave pushed us over, and we rolled, soon we were looking straight down into green ocean water. We hung on with any hand hold we could manage. We were going to capsize unless we did something fast. Our junk was a mile or more offshore. Certainly some of us, maybe all of us, would die.

I don't know who suggested it but we all moved to the stern of the junk. Our collective weight caused the stern to stay down so that the single propeller could bite into the water. It worked. Slowly the junk began to turn again. We powered through the waves and out of the trough to resume our patrol, now on a southerly direction. We had a following sea to speed us back to our temporary home. It was another example of ninety-nine percent boredom, punctuated by moments of sheer terror. It was terrifying in general to go out on the ocean in small vessels during bad weather, but caught in the trough was a particularly frightening episode.

We never found weapons in quantity again but in boarding and searching we found plenty of black market and smugglers' goods, draft dodgers, persons without required identity cards, and, occasionally, a suspected VC. We always had with us two or three ARVN petty officers, who could speak both Vietnamese and some English.

They directed who would be detained. Some ARVN petty officers would cause the "arrest" of numbers of people while others left everybody, or most everybody, alone.

We would cram the detainees into the bilges of the Yabudda, with a meter or so of headroom. When we returned to base, we would follow our Vietnamese counterparts' directions as to disposition of the detainees, which invariably was to turn them over to the National Police, at least for initial processing. At the end of some missions we would turn over eighteen to twenty people; at the end of others, two, one, or none—the number depending upon which ARVN Navy petty officers had accompanied us.

Later, not then, we got a glimmer of the true facts. VC, we were told, perhaps in a bit of hyperbole, preferred to be captured, if they were captured at all, by the ARVN, who would just execute the suspects on the spot. The less preferred alternative was to be placed in the custody of the National Police. I am not sure what we could have done differently had we known the true facts (taken fewer prisoners?) but the inhumanity many Vietnamese exhibited toward other Vietnamese has always been troubling to me.

****

We also had forms of excitement other than boarding and searching sampans. Plying the waters of our province with some frequency was a small (150 feet long) tramp steamer, the *Zipper*, which flew the French tricolor. The vessel was always dirty, the hull streaked with rust. The officers and crew all looked like Humphrey Bogart in *The African Queen*: dirty strap t-shirts, beards, cigarettes dangling from the corners of their mouths.

Everyone up the chain of command was convinced that the *Zipper* re-supplied both the Viet Cong and the NVA. According to our orders, because she was French flagged, the *Zipper* could not be boarded, at least forcibly. Higher ups wanted to avoid even the semblance of an international incident.

We could try to make things difficult. If we could get aboard the *Zipper* peaceably, we could investigate. So we had a standoff. We would put one of our much smaller junks alongside the *Zipper*. The skipper would turn the larger vessel sharply across our bow, shouldering us aside. The *Zipper's* crew would treat us with Gallic contempt, jeering at us. We would try again, and again, in what was a campaign of harassment. We would often do this exercise in rough, gray weather when we would roll and buck through the heavier seas. I often wondered why the *Zipper's* crew did not pour hot boiling oil on us, or at least douse us with a fire hose. The exercise probably relieved the boredom for them as well as for us.

Trying to board the *Zipper* was excitement but of the manufactured sort. Genuine excitement was calling in an airstrike, which I had several occasions to do. At the very north of our patrol area, Highway One ran next to the sea, on a narrow shelf between the ocean and a 300 meter hill, or small mountain. The VC always would attempt to occupy the highway, closing it down for several hours.

High on the hill, to deter the VC from capturing the highway, was a U.S. Special Forces camp. I never met them but I think nine or ten Green Berets ("Greenies") resided up there, some distance away from any other U.S. or ARVN military installation ("off the reservation" in Vietnam-speak). By reputation, the Greenies were arrogant and standoffish, regarding themselves as superior and maintaining a façade of mystery. But we saved their butts several times.

When the VC were feeling their oats, not only would they attempt to block Highway One, they also would mount a mortar or rocket attack on the Special Forces camp. On a few occasions, we were offshore watching matters unfold. On at least two of those occasions I (we) called in an airstrike.

Getting air support was convoluted, hampered by political considerations. We could not call for Air Force support directly. We were directed to make our requests to the Coastal Patrol Center in Nha Trang. If the watch officer there approved, our request would be forwarded to COMNAVFORV in Saigon. If the watch officer, or whomever else was in charge there, approved, they would forward the request, as approved, to the head honcho's office—COMMACV. From there the request would go the Air Force at Ton Son Nhut airbase close-by Saigon.

The entire process took approximately ten to twelve minutes. That delay would be unacceptable in many combat situations; we could live with the holdup here. Still, it seemed a pain in the butt.

We could hear the Air Force jets before we could see them. A military attack jet aircraft is at least ten times louder than a commercial or private jet, maybe even more. I always wondered how the aircraft got to where we were so quickly after the request had gone through the convoluted approval process. They came from Saigon, nearly 200 kilometers away, rather than, say, Phan Rang, which was much closer (a few kilometers away, actually). My best guess is that the Air Force had ready aircraft already in the air, or poised for immediate takeoff, at Ton Son Nhut. Whatever the case, we could hear the jets coming long before we could see them. Then they would appear, five to six miles to the south of us, flying low, coming out over the coastal mountains and then above the water.

They (I think they were F-104s, Lockheed Starfighters, and there were always two of them) flew right at us, offshore half a mile or less. The jets would have our position (map coordinates) from the request we had sent. As the pilots approached us the leader would ask for "pigeons," which was the bearing to target. In the jets would swoop, no more than 150 feet above our heads, sound rattling the fillings in our teeth, and once directly over our heads the planes would bank sharply toward the target. They would follow out the radial we had given them ("pigeons"), out from us toward the bombing target.

All of this time the jets and we (I) would be talking on the radio. I would be nervous, jabbering, not always understandable. The pilot of the lead aircraft, on the other hand, talking with me, would be detached, almost drawling as he extracted further instructions from us. Aircraft pilots of all stripes, commercial and otherwise, must attend a special school to teach them how to speak calmly to those of us in the back or on the ground.

Napalm, jellied gasoline that burns to 2,000 degrees Fahrenheit when it ignites, is nothing more than applied "bathtub chemistry." A little known fact is that when they were able to do so the North Vietnamese and the Viet Cong used napalm as well, destroying entire villages and U.S. infantry positions in the South.

I know that napalm is a cruel and indiscrete weapon (it sucks air from lungs and turns human flesh and bones to ashes) that human rights and other advocates would ban for all time. North Vietnam's use of napalm does not change these facts.

During the Vietnam War, anti-napalm activists commenced shareholder and other campaigns against Dow Chemical Co., the U.S.'s principal (only) supplier, to attempt to force Dow to cease manufacture of the product. Dow continued to manufacture the substance, despite increasing shareholder campaigns not to, and even though and in spite of the fact that it was unprofitable to do so. That is all somewhat in the abstract.

In the here and now, napalm explosions were a sight to behold and useful as well, at least to us. The aircraft released the bombs containing napalm. As the bombs hit the ground, halfway up the hill, a giant orange cloud unfolded, with dark grey tinges at the top. The orange cloud, seventy to eighty meters high, unfolded further, rolling up the hillside, toward the crest and toward the aircraft which had dropped the charges, and upward, several hundred meters in the sky. Smoke would begin to emerge from the ball of flame, spiraling slowly upward several hundred additional meters. The aircraft at that point were thundering sharply upward, seemingly toward the vertical and the clouds. A napalm attack could be terrifying but awe inspiring at the same time. It gave the officer on the ground (me) the giddy illusion that somehow he was in control of these machines and the show of power and might which they could unleash.

And it worked, at least in these instances. The napalm attacks by jet aircraft always caused the mortar attack to cease and the Viet Cong to retreat. The VC might try an attack or a diversion five or six weeks later, but invariably we were done for that day. With the Air Force, we had done our job, protecting the Special Forces camp and the Greenies one more time.

Mortar attacks upon the Special Forces camp were serious affairs. On a couple of occasions, we had VC mortar attacks on the compound in which we lived, as we had minutes after my arrival on my first day in Phan Thiet. These mortar attacks were more haphazard, random, and less serious affairs than the attacks on the Special Forces camp. When a couple VC were able to sneak into Phan Thiet, one of the things they would do is fire a few rockets or mortar rounds at our compound and then run like hell.

Nonetheless, we would take cover, diving under tables and whatnot. Now I knew that when I obtained my discharge that I wanted to go to graduate school, most specifically, to law school. So I had to arrange to take the Law School Admissions Test (LSAT), a three to three and a half hour multiple choice test. I would need a test score in order to apply to law school. Because I was in Vietnam, I had to arrange for a special one person testing center. I got Mike Benzing, a Naval Academy lieutenant senior to and stationed with me, to agree to act as the test proctor.

I think I paid a $40 fee to take the test. The Educational Testing Service (EDS), which devised and administered the test, or at least used to, paid Mike a $90 fee for acting as proctor, which Mike generously split with me. So I think that I may be the only, or one of the very few, test takers who ever made money taking the LSAT, or any EDS (Educational Testing Service) examination, for that matter.

So, this time the mortar attack occurred as I was about halfway through the admissions test. Mike and I dived under the table. The attack ended almost before it began, and we were back on our feet. At that point, Mike said, "Clock is back on." This was very unfair. My number two pencils and my papers had scattered onto the floor. I had to pick them up and get re-organized before I could begin where I left off. I protested but when it came to any official duties, military or otherwise, Mike always was a hard ass.

I have always thought that my LSAT score would have been ten to fifteen points higher but for the Viet Cong. As for Mike, good cop (I made $5), bad cop (I lost 5 minutes), I guess.

****

Closer again to actual combat were evacuation missions, which we were to accomplish several times. Just to the north of our patrol area was a beautiful, sandy stretch of coast known as Con Na beach. There, too, Highway One ran next the sea. There, too, the VC would attempt to blockade or otherwise close down the highway, Vietnam's only north-south link. Just above the road was a small Vietnamese fishing village. I don't even remember the name (Con Na?) and the village is too small to be on any of the maps.

When the VC went on the rampage, our orders were to evacuate the fifty or so people who lived nearby the military action. There would be gunfire (lots of it but not directly at us) and jets overhead. U.S. Army helicopters would be firing rockets into the hillside. In the midst of this cacophony, we had to shepherd people, all dressed in black pajamas and conical straw hats (*non bai tho*), to our Yabudda junks, which would be close in to shore, in half a meter of water. Many of the Vietnamese were old. Most did not understand the instructions we shouted out. It seemed obvious to us but many of the Vietnamese were bewildered, not understanding what we expected of them, namely, get aboard and get the hell out of there. They seemed to hesitate before wading into the surf and out to the junks. Intemperately, we would pull them, and push them, trying to expedite the whole process.

These evacuation missions were among the most stressful assignments I had in Vietnam. True, the VC never shot at us, but we always labored under the fear that the VC would discover what we were doing and start shooting.

I suppose that my combat, or near combat, experiences taught me several things. One was what an undeveloped and primitive country Vietnam was in 1966. That seemed to hold true for the Vietnamese themselves, or at least the ones we saw on the coast and in villages: fisherman who did not make fast a line we threw them, allowing themselves to be pulled into the sea, or families and old people who dawdled and seemed to play dumb as fire fights raged on above us.

Two, was the French influence, which was strong and which we saw both with the *Zipper* and the availability of good baguettes and coffee (*ca phe*) on every corner, even in a backwater such as Phan Thiet. The French had, after all, ruled the country as a colony from the 1860s to 1954, during which time the effect of their culture was strong and pervasive.

Three, was that the experiences devoid of actual, hard-core combat experiences, those involving foul weather, misguided motor attacks, boarding tossing trawlers offshore, accidental misfirings, or other physical dangers, could be nearly as stressful, in a few instances as dangerous, as actual combat with bombs and explosions. In the last line of his sonnet, *On His Blindness*, John Milton wrote that "they serve who also stand and wait." I'm not sure that holds for all the instances I have described in this chapter but it was true for many of them.

6

Random Reminiscences

The theft from PXs and American warehouses was so extensive that not only cigarettes, whiskey, hair spray and other consumer items but rifles, ammunition, helmets, and flak jackets were for sale on street corners. Whole consignments of furniture, typewriters, and fire extinguishers disappeared without a trace.

—Stanley Karnow, *Vietnam: A History* (1983)

[Visitors to Vietnam] will every now and then come across the not especially appetizing spectacle of a couple of natives carrying on a pole between them a nice fat dog prepared for some village banquet.

—James Bradley, *The Imperial Cruise* (2009)

THEY SAID THAT YOU COULD BUY ANYTHING at Saigon's Bring Cash Alley. I don't know whether that was true. I never made it to Saigon during the year I fought in the War. In fact we were forbidden to go there. Saigon, its pleasures and its fleshpots were for staff officers, intelligence types, and the brass.

Smuggling and black marketeering were not solely the province of the Vietnamese. U.S. military also were active participants. The biggest money of all to be made was in currency arbitrage. The prohibition on all unnecessary travel to Saigon was to combat it, as was the payment to us of our wages in script rather than greenbacks.

Arbitrage is the taking advantage of price differences that may arise between markets. An arbitrager would do so by buying at low price in one market, selling at a higher price in another, taking advantage of the temporary price imbalance between markets. For example, if Starbucks shares were selling in New York for $25.00 and in Hong Kong for $25.50, the arbitrager would buy in New York while simultaneously selling in Hong Kong. Modern, nearly instantaneous communications and the widespread use of computers have eliminated many opportunities for arbitrage that used to exist.

Vietnam in 1966-67 was ripe for arbitrage plays, especially in the currency (then the *piaster*, now the *dong*), as there were few, if any, computers in those days (at least in private hands). If a currency trader had greenbacks, he could buy Piasters in Saigon, go to Danang, or Hue, or wherever, and sell them for a profit. He would go back to Saigon, this time with more money, and repeat the process.

In Phan Thiet, we had stationed with us a senior Army advisor (a senior sergeant, an advisor to the ARVN Ranger battalion) who had, as others had done, brought with him to Vietnam a grubstake of greenbacks. The sergeant disappeared every occasion on which he stood down from duty, allegedly to engage in currency trading. Over his year in Vietnam he turned $50,000 US into $150,000 US ($200,000 into $600,000 in today's dollars).

The Army sergeant cum arbitrager did it by traveling all over Vietnam. How could he have done that? Phan Thiet was in the boondocks, or nearly so, certainly off the beaten track. We had a short dirt airstrip, partially paved with Perforated Steel Plating (PSP). Two engine Air Force C-123s Fairchilds would land there to re-supply us but the strip was too short to accommodate bigger, four engine Lockheed C-130s. Also those C-123 flights were intermittent. So I always wondered how that sergeant got enough hops (upcountry, down to Saigon, and so on), at least enough hops to make the money that he did through arbitrage.

I found out thirty years later, while building a house in Gig Harbor, Washington. The next-door neighbor was a retired Air Force colonel who had served in Vietnam. He flew smaller propeller driven and jet passenger and cargo planes up and down the country. He told me that he and his crew and other Air Force crews as well used to stop all the time in Phan Thiet. Enterprising Vietnamese fishermen would go out to the airstrip, selling lobster and other seafood delicacies to the American airmen, who evidently passed through quite frequently. The U.S. airmen also would give a hop to any service person standing by. Accompanying the lobsters, the Army sergeant would ride to a busier airbase, from which he could get hops all over Vietnam. I could think of many worse ways to spend your off-duty hours.

****

Another revelation came to me not thirty years, but six months later. We were supposed to be silent while on patrol, at least while we monitored the coastline of Binh Thuan province. A barking dog would have given us away and thus by implication pet dogs were forbidden.

But we got a dog a la Sherlock Holmes that did not bark, in the night or otherwise. He was of medium size, black with white markings, much like a border collie. We named him "Tomb," after the nickname we gave our sleeping quarters. He was a frisky, friendly but obedient sort. Against regulations, we took Tomb on a couple of patrols with us—but then one day he disappeared, not to be found anywhere. We were saddened but went on with our duties.

Six months later I was walking down Phan Thiet's main street (which also is Highway One). Along came a Vietnamese farmer with twenty or more ducks trussed up by their feet and tied to the small cargo carrier over the rear wheel of his bicycle. This was a common sight. A farmer could be taking twenty-five chickens, or three live pigs (in a basket or wire cage) to market, all on his or her bicycle. A block later along came another Vietnamese. On the back of his bicycle was a tall, circular wire cage. In the cage were three small to medium size dogs, dark blond or yellow in color. They were going to market.

All at once the penny dropped. I knew what had happened to Tomb.

Vietnamese ate dog. I don't know then whether it was a delicacy or not, although subsequently many U.S. servicemen have told me that it was, and is, as many Vietnamese believe that consumption of dog meat increases sexual potency. *Thit cho,* dog meat, appeared on many Vietnamese restaurant menus, back then and now. *Canh cho,* dog meat stew, was a favorite. Of course, that would give fits to PETA members here in the States, but I think that PETA members are against many things, eating dogs (and cats too) included.

I ate dog once. We visited an ambush site outside a Vietnamese village. The ARVN generally were friendly; they liked to kid us and each other and otherwise joke around. The ARVN there were cooking dog meat. They dared me (made me) eat a bite, which I did. I have no memory of what it tasted like, the texture, etc. I guess I have blocked it out of my memory, another horror of war.

****

We coastal patrol forces even tried a couple of ambushes, or armed patrols, ourselves. Of course, we had no business doing that, in the main because the Viet Cong could run circles around us. We had not been trained to do any such thing as ambushes. Nonetheless, we would land a shore party of nine or ten who would do an armed walk-through of a coastal village. I suppose the idea was a show of force to intimidate the local Charlies.

Perforce we must have done the opposite. Here were these big Americans, several inches taller, fifty pounds heavier, and ten shades lighter in skin tone than the Vietnamese, who were small, slight, and darkened by near constant exposure to the sun. These American big devils would slowly walk through carrying big, ugly automatic weapons, frightening the women, the children, and some of the men, or at least generating resentment. I think of Gagne, who was 6' 5",

76

carrying a Browning Automatic Rifle, an ammunition belt slung around his neck. He prided himself on his warrior image (Rambo was much later but that was the idea), as we all did. We scared these people, who mostly wanted to go about their lives. We probably did as much for the VC side as our own (maybe more). Fortunately, after we did these armed patrols a couple of times we stopped. I would like to think that we wised up but I think we more or less stumbled out of what we had stumbled into.

In the preface, I said I was not a hero. I remain confident of that assessment but I did come close once.

One summer morning we assembled a fleet of Yabudda junks. We loaded a company of ARVN rangers from the battalion stationed in Phan Thiet. We were to take these troops about twenty-five klicks north, where a free fire zone stretched along an expanse of coastline filled with large sand dunes, fronting the ocean. Once we landed them, the rangers were going to go up over the large sand dunes, conducting "reconnaissance in force" beyond the beach and the dunes, where it was thought some VC might be.

So under a bright blue early morning sky, with animal cracker shaped clouds off on the eastern horizon, a line of junks, seven or eight total, each laden with eight to ten soldiers, came out of Phan Thiet Bay, turning northward. I don't remember having much to do. I lay there on the deck, letting my mind run free. When we got to the staging area, I came out of my reverie, much like waking from a summer nap, standing up now but still feeling lazy and sluggish. Our junk, maybe the third in line, milled about ("hove to" in nautical terms), waiting for the other vessels to pull up near us.

For some reason, some of the rangers were to transfer from our junk to one of the others. The two junks came together, side-by-side, to facilitate this but they were bobbing up and down, unevenly. One of the U.S Army enlisted advisers went to leap from our junk to the other. He missed, falling into the open sea.

The sergeant was not a strong swimmer. Moreover he was wearing a heavy pack, filled with who knows what—ammunition, hand grenades, claymore mines, I don't know. He struggled to stay above the surface. He was gulping down a lot of sea water as his head and mouth bobbed below the surface.

Everybody started yelling. No one did anything. I had been a lifeguard at a swimming pool when I was in college. I was a fairly strong swimmer. I didn't think twice. I jumped in to the water. I swam around to the rear of the floundering trooper, grabbing him under the armpits. I treaded water to keep us afloat, but only for a few seconds. A Navy guy, it might have been Bones Caldwell, or VD Donner, threw us a line which the sergeant took. The junk's crew rapidly hauled him aboard. I swam three or four strokes over to the Yabudda, climbing aboard. The incident was over in a less than a minute.

"I shoulda gotten rid of the pack," the Army guy said, as a prelude to thanking me. "I tried to get it off," he offered, by way of thanks. I was standing there in a tee shirt and fatigue pants (long before camouflage BDUs), soaking wet.

"What a half-assed thing to do," the Munster chimed in. "Why did you try to hold him up? Strip that haversack off his back. It's heavy. You dumb ass."

"You gotta be fucking kidding me. You see what I just did and you're giving me shit about it?" I said. We had learned that the Munster would back off if you stood up to him—better also to lace your reply with profanity for emphasis.

Munster was irritated because he had not done it himself. In his mind's eye, he pictured himself quite the action hero.

Now, technically, I have always maintained I was entitled to a medal, specifically the Navy and Marine Corps Medal, given for actions leading to the rescue of another sailor or Marine in non-combat conditions. But my commanding officer, the Munster, maintained that I didn't do anything, at least worthy of a commendation and citation for a medal. He would not put me in for any decoration.

I am certain that if Munster had done what I did he would have put himself in for a medal—the Silver Star or Navy Cross, no doubt. But for me, nada. I should have milked it for more, with some struggle and thrashing in the water. Instead, the whole rescue effort was over in a flash.

As it was, I missed my chance at a small iota of bravery, or at least recognition for it. That I had not been recognized stung, like a paper cut, or worse, but not much worse.

One last water borne story, or immersion in water, recollection. I was what the Navy then graded as a Class C diver, trained to use SCUBA but not hard hat or more serious forms of deep sea diving. I think I had two afternoons' orientation at Pearl Harbor, where the Pacific Fleet had its dive school.

In Vietnam, we had Navy issue SCUBA gear—air tanks with two hose regulators (most modern gear uses a "single hose regulator," consisting of hose, regulator, and mouth piece). One of the enlisted men, Spencer Moak, and I were the certified divers in our group, so it fell upon us to play "Sea Hunt" (a 1960s television show).

When our group had left our patrol craft in unsecure locations, such as anchored overnight or on a mooring buoy in Nha Trang harbor, the underside of the hulls had to be checked before we returned to patrol. The reason? The danger that during the night the VC might have attached explosives (an underwater bomb) to the hull. It also had to be occasionally done in secure settings as well (say, the swift boat base at Cam Ranh Bay, or Phan Thiet harbor) to remove fishing nets from propellers and shafts. Fishing nets and fish traps were ubiquitous in bays and inlets along the Binh Thuan coast. Running over them, fouling a patrol craft's propulsion equipment, was a hazard for us, especially when on a night patrol, while the destruction we wreaked I am sure more than tweaked a fisherman's nose or two.

This underwater duty, to check the hulls of multiple patrol craft, fell upon us. Moak and I hated it, for several reasons. First, as I remember, it always took place early in the morning, 6:00 or 6:30, at first light, and it always was cold. Where we were was a tropical place, but I remember both the air and the water as being frigid—not meat locker cold but goose bumpy cold. Perhaps our blood had thinned from our time in that warm locale, or perhaps it was because we were so nervous, or perhaps it was a combination of both. Maybe it was just plain cold.

Second, it was dangerous. We never found a bomb or explosives of any kind but there always was that risk, one of which we remained acutely aware. We also had no clear idea what we would do if we found anything. Radio the Army MPs, or the Coastal Patrol Center, I suppose, but the uncertainty ratcheted up our anxious state.

A clear and present danger was fish nets. As I said, we found and had to cut those away all the time. The fear we had was that some idiot above, on the boat, would start the engine while we were down there, underwater. Turning propeller blades would slice us up but good.

The third fear was sea snakes. In those waters there floated on the surface large olive and yellow snakes, two meters long, thicker than a fire hose, and butt ugly. Reputedly, sea snakes, one of which we encountered perhaps every other day, were poisonous. I never found out for sure, but did not need to as I never wanted to come near one, poisonous or not. I don't like snakes.

Again, as with explosive charges, we never encountered a sea snake while we were diving. I think it was too early in the morning for them. The snakes seemed to appear in the warmth of the day, lolling on the surface of the ocean, drifting with the current, catching the sun's rays.

I always had a big lump in my stomach, becoming cotton mouthed as time approached to put on our scuba gear and go into the water. Except for once, on the Great Barrier Reef in Australia, I haven't been scuba diving since my Vietnam days.

These episodes illustrate that many of us in combat and combat related activities encountered hazards and dangers even when the VC or NVA were not shooting at us, or probably even in close proximity.

These dangers were nothing like those faced by Marines and soldiers, who had bullets whizzing about them, wounding and killing them or others with whom they served.

But recounting these duties and the risks we faced re-enforces my belief that we earned our hostile fire pay ($65 extra per month each month you were in-country) each and every one of the twelve months for which I received it. I may not have been a hero but I earned the pay, as well as the medals and campaign ribbons for my year in Vietnam, as did the guys with whom I served.

Others, besides those who fought, earned their pay as well. I am thinking of the heroic efforts supply and medical support troops always provided, in this case Air Force personnel from Clark Air Base in the Philippines.

****

Gagne, my big, rugged enlisted colleague, was on patrol with us in the extreme northern reaches of Binh Thuan Province, far from our base in Phan Thiet. He had been complaining of stomach pains but over a few hours the pains became more severe. Lucky for us our medical corpsman, Desjardins, had gone on patrol with us, which he used to do from time to time, probably to relieve boredom. Desjardins examined Gagne, swiftly arriving at a diagnosis of acute appendicitis. We should get Gagne to a medical facility as soon as we were able.

Our medical support usually came by helicopter, from Cam Ranh Bay, with evacuation to the Army hospital there. But we did not have a hand in determining that; we merely reported our emergency to the Coast Surveillance Center in Nha Trang. Very quickly the watch there reported back to us that this time evacuation would be by Air Force flying boat, to the Philippines, in five hours.

Four and half hours later, flying low, came a twin-engine, high wing flying boat (no floats like a seaplane; it would land on its hull).

While the aircraft circled, the pilot requested that we lay down a slick to mark a landing area. We began a long slow turn to port, smoothing the water's surface a bit, but we were too small to lay down the slick a larger vessel would. Once we had marked out an area as best we could, the flying boat came in for a landing, stopping about 200 meters north of us.

The Air Force pilot turned and taxied his ship (literally a ship at that point) south. He stopped about fifty meters away from us. A large side door in the aircraft fuselage popped open. Out came a yellow inflatable life raft. Next, out came two muscular Air Force paramedics, dressed in wet suits, who climbed into the raft. They paddled the raft over to us. Gently, but swiftly, they took a prone Gagne into the raft. With barely a word, they paddled swiftly back to the flying boat, stowing Gagne, themselves, and finally the raft back inside.

The pilot gunned his engines, turned the aircraft around, and taxied a few hundred meters. He turned the plane again, into the wind, revved his engines for a long minute, and began his takeoff roll. Impeded by the water, the plane seemed to gather speed glacially. We wondered if the pilot would make it airborne at all. Suddenly, "vroom—whoosh," punctuated the air as vapor trails shot out the back of the airplane's wings. The Jet Assisted Takeoff (JATO) bottles had kicked in. In the blink of an eye, the airplane's speed seemed to triple. The airplane nosed skyward, leveled for a few hundred meters, and then climbed steeply, banking sharply to the left and toward the Philippines. We watched the plane climb but it was soon out of sight. The entire episode, from first sight of the aircraft until it disappeared in the clouds, took less than ten minutes.

Often when we medevaced troops, or otherwise transferred them to Temporary Additional Duty (TAD) we never saw them again. But rough and ready, his appendix removed by Air Force surgeons, Gagne was back with us in a few weeks, ready and eager for his next patrol.

My most pronounced memory, however, was not Gagne's return

but the tremendous backup we received from behind-the-lines support units. Although we never got a Bob Hope or other USO show (not even close), we received ice cream and vegetables from the Vesuvius; obtained a part airlifted to us from the Philippines on Christmas Day; had a sick trooper airlifted out in a matter of hours by a crackerjack Air Force crew; and received supply and evacuation countless times by the Army guys from Cam Ranh Bay. Although much is made of inter-service rivalries and turf battles, and military related screwups, at least in the pressure laden environment of Vietnam, the other services (Coast Guard, Air Force, Army) and branches of our own (Navy) always came through—*always*—swiftly and many times at personal risk to the soldiers, sailors and airmen doing the job.

****

One last memory was a land-based one: Christmas and New Year 1966. Both my sister and my mother sent care packages. My sister, I remember, sent a large size "Little Orphan Annie" Playboy comic book. My mother, like mothers everywhere, sent some books, some fudge, and other food, and some handkerchiefs. Maybe my mother, a librarian, thought that someday I would write *Blowing Your Nose in a Combat Zone.*

In Phan Thiet was an orphanage for Vietnamese children, run by a Christian organization from the United States (Presbyterian, I think). We (eight or ten U.S. combat troops, those who wanted to go) went there for Christmas Eve, with a few gifts for the children and food purloined from the U.S. commissary (a couple of canned hams, Number 10 cans of vegetables). The orphanage had a Christmas tree. We gathered around it, singing Christmas carols: "Silent Night," "Oh Come All Ye Faithful," "Little Town of Bethlehem." What I remember most, though, was that for some reason we sang "Auld Lang Syne," what I have always thought a New Year's Eve song. It was as warm and cheery a Christmas as could be hoped for a group of lonely guys, 7,000 miles away from their families. All these years later what sticks in my mind about that night is the line, "We'll drink a cup of kindness, dear, in days of auld lang syne."

****

On New Year's Eve we were on patrol. To paraphrase, it truly was "a dark and stormy night." On New Year's Day, the U.S. Navy tradition is that the officer who is Officer of the Deck writes a poem in the ship's log, marking the end of the old and the beginning of the new year. We had only Yabudda junks rather than ships but we observed the custom.

It fell upon me to write the poem, which went something like this (you can look up the original in the U.S. Navy Archives):

We're here to protect hot dogs, apple pie, and motherhood,
But more than that we look out for our brotherhood,
Each to each we are bound,
No one will be shot or drowned,
So little do I or my mates have to fear,
It truly is a Happy New Year.

We came off patrol about 3:00 in the morning. We gathered our weapons, radios, and other gear, making our way silently to our quarters. I doubt whether anyone other than the few of us, and perhaps a clerk back in Washington, D.C., ever read that corny poem. The next morning we all slept in. When finally we awoke, it was January 1, 1967.

7

Two Homecomings

Coming home after a long absence in the war zone is a strange experience, like you just re-entered the earth's atmosphere from outer space and you know that things have changed.

—Nelson DeMille, *Up Country* (2002)

We [Vietnam veterans] would not return to cheering crowds, parades, and the peeling of great cathedral bells. We had done nothing more than endure. We had survived, and that was our only victory.

—Philip Caputo, *A Rumor of War* (1977)

NAVY AND ARMY PEOPLE WITH WHOM I SERVED were all pretty loose. On second thought, though, they all were decidedly compulsive in one respect: every one of them was a numerologist with respect to the length of his Vietnam tour. "I've got 119 days plus a wakeup," one guy would say. The next might offer, "I have 211 plus a wakeup." I never saw anyone maintaining a calendar but everyone seemed to have that number (plus a wakeup) at the ready for anyone who would listen.

For some reason, I got sent home a week early. I served 11 months, 23 days, 4 hours and 20 minutes. I had it down, and still do to this day, to the last minute. So no need existed to factor in a "wakeup."

I hitched a ride on a small U.S. Navy minesweeper which took me north to Cam Ranh Bay, where I was processed for my departure from Vietnam. A day later I boarded a DC-8 charter, which flew first to Hawaii, where it refueled, and then on to Travis Air Force Base east of San Francisco.

After a few days in California, I put on my Navy dress blues, splendid (I thought) with two rows of campaign ribbons, representing the medals I had received (how do those generals and admirals, who never served in combat, get all those rows of medals and campaign ribbons? For a year in combat I managed only four medals). I had telephoned my mother with my flight number and time. I was eagerly awaiting a celebratory homecoming.

I was relatively new to flying on commercial airplanes. The Continental flight attendants guessed (I think) that I was just back from Vietnam. They pampered me the entire way. Their special treatment buoyed me still higher.

It was all downhill from there. I arrived home in the Midwest at 5:00 in the afternoon. From the top of the air stairs (no jetways in those days, at least in smaller airports), I saw neither my mother nor any other member of my family waiting for the plane. "Caught in rush hour traffic," I thought.

So I waited half an hour, then forty minutes. From a pay phone, I called my mother's house—no answer. I called my older sister's house—same thing, no answer. I called my oldest brother's house— no answer yet again (there were neither cell phones nor voice mail in those days either). The bloom was starting to come off the rose.

I made my way down the airport concourse, walked across the terminal lobby, went into the lounge, and took a seat at the bar. The bartender served me. I nibbled at my drink, biding my time when I would call family members again. Out of the corner of my eye, I noticed coming from a table in the room's dimly lit recesses a middle-age, balding businessman, dressed in a pin striped suit.

He was drunk. No introductions, no hello's. He must have noticed those ribbons on my chest. He lit into me, "Baby killer. You guys should just lay down those guns and quit. You f-u-c-k-e-r."

So it was not to be—not only no celebratory homecoming but no gin and tonic either. This was still 1967. I had no idea the antiwar feeling had already become so strong, permeating places like Dayton, Ohio, although I was to encounter that anti-war hostility many times over in the ensuing months. I got the hell out of there.

I left my drink and I left the bar, deflated and defeated. I thought that I would collect my luggage in the baggage claim area. I could take my bag and sit on one of the benches outside. It was April—beautiful spring weather, warm breezes. I could call my mother or my brother a little while later.

My luggage consisted of one medium size suitcase and a tax free liquor cartoon holding four bottles of booze, including two bottles of Jack Daniels bourbon. Now, in Vietnam other service men took photographic slides or color prints. I had a small, hand-held movie camera with which I had taken Super 8 movies. Because my suitcase was stretched full to the limit, I had stuck the movie reels (developed) down the sides of the tax free liquor carton.

I claimed my luggage. I had walked but twenty feet when the bottom of the carton, which somehow had gotten wet, fell through. Four bottles of liquor dropped, three of them smashing on the floor, breaking. More importantly, or sadly, the movie reels drooped onto the pools of bourbon and gin on the marble floor. The alcohol in the puddles of booze ruined my movies.

A skycap approached me. He looked up into my face, "Broke your JD, did ya?" I wanted to cry. I probably did cry.

Many who came home from a tour in Vietnam had lousy homecomings, or at least anticlimactic ones. By contrast, they say that Civil War veterans' homecomings were all anticlimactic, as were the remainders of their lives, for a different reason. Nothing could top what they had seen with their own eyes in that war or the relief they felt when it was over. They spent the rest of their days around courthouse squares in Wisconsin and Illinois, reminiscing about their experiences. Even as they grew old, they were heros to their fellow citizens, young or old, of their town, of their state, and of the entire nation.

Nothing, I felt, could have been worse than our homecomings. We Vietnam vets were the opposite of the veterans of other conflicts such as the Civil War, WW II, Iraq, or Afghanistan. We came home as anti-heros. Sometimes even our own families did not show up to welcome us home (although in truth all that had happened was that my mother got the date wrong).

The best thing for a Vietnam veteran to do upon returning to CONUS (Continental United States) was to put his military uniform in the back of the closet, or the bottom of the steamer truck, and closely guard the fact that he had served in the Vietnam War. If you revealed your Vietnam service to anyone other than family and a few close friends, you ran a considerable risk that you would be belittled, criticized, or condemned.

The return home also produced utter and profound culture shock. I had left an environment in which guys wore colorful striped Beach Boys or Kingston Trio short sleeve shirts, with button down collars, khaki pants or white chinos, and penny loafers. It was almost a uniform. Girls wore A-line skirts and blouses with Peter Pan collars and circle pins. A year later I returned to hair everywhere—long shoulder length hair (or longer), pony tails (on guys), mustaches, beards, facial hair of all kinds. Tight bellbottoms replaced chinos, bellbottoms of all varieties, with rips, tears, and paint stains. Guys and girls wore necklaces. Peace pendants hanging from the neck had begun to appear. A lot of people smoked dope. Respect for authority, or for one's elders, had not completely disappeared but everybody (young that is) seemed prone to question assumptions and long held beliefs, about everything. The amazing thing was that these changes seemed to have taken place in just a year, the year I had been gone.

Many parents and friends of returning Vietnam veterans observed how quiet many of the returnees were. They ascribed that quiet and reserve to the horrors of war that these young men had seen, too terrible to forget, flashing back in their minds time and time again. Undoubtedly, that was true for some.

But for others, including me, reality was different. *One*, in Vietnam you just did not talk that much. You might have gone on twenty-hour, thirty-hour or longer patrols without speaking to anyone else or uttering five words. Coming back home, you had lost much of your ability to speak.

Two, though, if you had not lost the ability to speak you had lost much of your vocabulary. I once estimated that my active vocabulary had decreased by forty percent during my year in Vietnam.

Three, what substituted for words of all and various kinds were "four letter fillers." You did not open your mouth for fear that what came out would send your mother or sister into a swoon. I remember hearing a senior enlisted guy telling a younger soldier that he had reached his limit: "Three 'fucks' in one fucking sentence doesn't make any fucking sense." Truth be told, in Vietnam it sometimes did.

Four, it was just the shock of it all. Only twelve months before, we had left an orderly, predictable world only to return to one that had turned upside down. Most of us (many of us, but not all) quickly adjusted, but the deadening impact of all that had changed was very real.

Five, in many quarters, as I said, we felt despised. In *A Rumor of War*, Philip Caputo writes the following:

Hawks had an almost clownish view of the Vietnam veteran as a drug-addicted, undisciplined loser, the tattered standard bearer of America's first defeat. The Left drew an equally distorted picture of [the veteran] as, at best, an ignorant hardhat with a gun, at worst as a psychopath in uniform. In the eyes of the antiwar movement, each [War veteran] was the incarnation of what it considered a criminal policy.

I had a second homecoming of sorts four months after my first one. I mustered out of the Navy, driving cross country to start law school four days later. Wrapping myself in an old sleeping bag, I slept in national parks where I could roll under the car in case it rained. I subsisted on a loaf of Wonderbread, a pack of American cheese and half a gallon of orange drink. Although I had left the service with twelve months of hostile fire pay in the bank ($65 per month), had banked all of my base pay (which was tax free for the period you were in Vietnam), and had "sold back to Uncle Sam" sixty days leave (the maximum), I was paranoid about paying for law school. I was the fourth of four children whose father died when I was in college. My mother was a retired librarian who could not help financially at all. Even though I had a half scholarship (Chicago Title & Trust Foundation Scholar), otherwise I would be on my own paying tuition, books, and living expenses while attending an expensive private university (Northwestern).

John F. Kennedy's view of history was that "Victory has 100 fathers; defeat is an orphan." For a veteran returning from Vietnam, it was like that or worse—even much worse.

I was one of two returning Vietnam vets in my class of 165; one of the first two to attend that law school. The other guy, Bob Fry, had been an officer in the Marines. He had part of his hip shot away. He walked with a cane. He was a true hero, so most of my classmates left him alone. Besides, he was married; other than at class time, Bob went home to be with his wife and was seldom seen around the law school.

So I quickly became the target of opportunity. Moreover, I made the mistake of living in the graduate student's dormitory, midst all the other first year students. Everyone, and I mean everyone, was against the War, except for me. The War and the things I had seen were too fresh in my memory. I was still digesting my experience while trying to get the school year off to a good start. I tried not to think about my positions on the War, or recall what I had done, not done, or seen in Vietnam, reserving memories and judgment for later. Moreover, I suffered some of the symptoms of what Philip Caputo referred to as *combat vertanitus*: "…an inability to concentrate, a childlike fear of the darkness, a tendency to tire too easily, chronic nightmares, an intolerance of loud noises—especially doors slamming and cars backfiring—and alternating moods of depression and rage." Those symptoms made it difficult for a first year law student to adjust and to study.

But my fellow students could not leave me alone. They would wake me at 11:30 or midnight to debate the War. Students would come from two floors below or three floors above. I would be forced to sit in a straight back chair while anti-war advocates, up to twelve of them at a time, circled me, asking questions and shooting down my answers. It was a scene straight from *The Manchurian Candidate*.

I was still mildly in favor of the Vietnam War but had no strong convictions. I therefore did not know what to say—so I would bait my antagonists with tales I made up as I went along. "Take an old Vietnamese lady and stuff a live hand grenade in her mouth. The top of head will blow straight up, twelve to fifteen feet into the air." Now I never saw anything like that. Further, I doubt whether anyone else did either. But my fellow students turned inquisitors would go ballistic. "Let me at him," "Filthy bastard," "The electric chair would be too good for you."

Another line of questioning might be, "How could you shoot old people, women, and children?" "That's easy," I would say, "you just lead them less than you would a running man" (paraphrasing Michael Herr's *Dispatches*). Now I never harmed a hair on a single Vietnamese head, that I know of, but again the cries would go forth, "Dirty bastard…." The assembled students, all of whom thought themselves anti-war activists, would begin arguing amongst themselves. I would slip out of the room, going back to sleep, this time behind a locked door.

At times, I felt a subliminal pull back toward Vietnam even though I had no real desire to go there. I was not alone, as I later discovered. Again, Philip Caputo: "[V]eterans…felt a strange attachment to Vietnam and, even stronger, a longing to return." My attachment was exacerbated by my surroundings, filled as it was with young twenty-two year olds:

> This desire to go back did not spring from any patriotic ideas
> about duty, honor and sacrifice….It arose, rather, from a recog-
> nition of how deeply we had changed, how different we were
> from everyone who had not shared with us the miseries of
> the monsoon, the exhausting patrols, the fear of a combat as-
> sault….We had very little in common with them. We did not
> belong to [the civilian world] as much as we did to that other
> world where we had fought (Philip Caputo).

My single ally was Professor Harry Reese, my advisor and civil procedure teacher. He was a good ally to have because, on information and belief, it was Harry Reese, rather than the courtly Dean John Richie, who ran the law school. Short of stature, and a chain smoker, Professor Reese was dubbed "Harry the Rat." Harry was famous for wearing the same costume five days per week—black suit, crisp white shirt, and a black tie—but never a hat, overcoat, or gloves. In those days, Chicago had at least three brutal cold snaps each winter when the temperature would fall to minus ten, staying there for three weeks. Nonetheless, we students all had seen Professor Reese walking in from the parking lot, or navigating down an icy street, with nary a protection against the cold.

As I entered law school, not only the students but the faculty were openly and vociferously anti-war. Before my very eyes, in a matter of months, law professors went from pin stripe suits, suspenders, white dress shirts, and foulard ties to hippie wannabe costumes: Levi's, work shirts, work boots, and red bandanas tied around their necks.

Faculty were outspoken about their opposition to the War as well, even in class, sometimes cancelling class altogether in order to attend antiwar rallies in downtown Chicago.

As the only veteran squarely in everyone's sights, I was lost in the midst of all of this; but Harry Reese, ordinarily not user friendly to law students, took me under his wing. He saw to it that I received invitations to several cocktail parties and receptions held at the law school. He gave me ample, and good, advice on how to approach law study and on course selection.

Why? Because unknown to my fellow students, like me, Harry was a Navy guy, a war veteran, and a small town Ohio boy (I was raised on a farm until I was thirteen). Raised in the small Ohio town of Waverly, at nineteen or twenty Harry had left Ohio State University to join the Navy during WWII. He flew fighters as a carrier pilot in the Pacific Theatre of Operations (PTO). When he had mustered out of the service in 1945, and finished at Ohio State, Harry attended Harvard Law School, where he finished high in his class.

I appreciated Harry's solicitude for my predicament as one of the first returning war veterans and his friendship and advice. But I found out about his Navy service only several years later (Harry did not readily give out details about himself).

His war service also explained one other quirk. Professor Reese was a very enlightened person, who tirelessly promoted diversity in the law school and who always, or almost always, conducted himself as the gracious gentleman. The one exception was his inflexible and sometimes rude attitude toward Japanese people. He could not abide them. If he was in a receiving line greeting students, or new faculty, or practicing lawyers, and a Japanese American approached, Harry would turn his back, or step out of the receiving line, or both. His animadversion toward Japanese was palpable, and most peculiar. I suppose that the Japanese treatment of American and other prisoners of war, including downed fliers, had left Harry with a blind spot.

But in my first year back from fighting in Vietnam, and my first year in law school, the supposedly enigmatic Harry Reese reached out and helped me immeasurably.

After my first law school year, my fellow students lost the deferments that had once been given automatically to any full time student. The Selective Service then instituted the draft lottery system. The race was on, at least for those with low to mid range draft numbers (say, 1 to 120 versus 300 to 365). The race was to get a further deferment, get into an ROTC unit so that if you had to go at least you would be an officer, or get into a reserve unit whereby you would only spend six months active duty, followed by six years in the reserve or National Guard—anything to lessen your chances of being sent to Vietnam. Unlike today, when reserve units make up much of the backbone of our forces in Afghanistan or Iraq, with thirty-five- and forty-year-old men and women serving several tours, in those days service in the reserves was practically a guarantee that you never would be called upon to go to Vietnam, let alone serve in actual combat there.

Out of 165 law students, sixty had to drop out because of draft pressures. But fifty-nine of those got into reserve units. Only one, Marvin Feingold, got drafted. Now, Marvin was anal-compulsive but his compulsivity was always aimed in the wrong direction. He was the only student I know who had obtained and read all his first year books the summer prior to his first year. Big mistake. Because when he tried to read them the second time, when it really counted, his eyes would glaze over: it was "deja vu all over again." Marvin would not be able to recall a single thing when the next day's class discussed something out of the book.

Like Donald Drouze in Vietnam, Feingold would sleep while everyone else was awake, to be awake while everyone else was asleep. He would fall asleep over his books early on in the evening, while we were studying. Around midnight, just as everyone else had ceased studying and was going to bed, Marvin would awaken. He would then stay up all night, or most of it, poring over law texts. Then, when classes began the next morning, and we all were awake, Marvin would fall asleep once more, missing most everything that went on in class and often class itself. Well, Marvin got drafted and served three years in the Army as an enlisted man.

Most people got deferments. There were seventeen women in the class who were not subject to draft pressure. Every one of the remaining students, eighty-six (eighty-eight less Fry and myself) got deferments, mostly on medical grounds. For example, one friend had bad knees, so he flunked his draft physical and did not have to serve.

Other cases were not so straightforward. To evade being drafted, another friend stole letterhead stationery from the office of a professor of orthopedics at Northwestern University School of Medicine. He read medical books and got a medical student to help him, forging a letter describing a congenital hip defect. He spent an entire night with his roommates taking turns pulling and twisting his leg so as to inflame his hip joint. With the letter, a limp, and an x-ray, he obtained a deferment. He did not have to serve. In a few days, he was as good as new.

Those not quite so creative consulted a draft avoidance lawyer, euphemistically termed a "selective service practitioner," mostly by themselves to ennoble their specialty. These lawyers had a whole bag of tricks but they had to vary and coordinate their use of various tricks, tactics, and strategies. If the Selective Service found any one "out" from the draft showing up too frequently, they could and sometimes did amend the regulations to eliminate the loophole. For instance, it was a not-too-well-kept secret that the two federal judges in Puerto Rico either were against the War, or did not take failure to report for induction cases seriously. The two judges would find defendants guilty but sentence them to one hour in the lockup.

Now draft registrants would always retain their home town draft board where they had registered upon turning eighteen, but they would be ordered to report for their draft physical at the induction center closest to where they lived. So someone from Kansas who lived in San Juan, Puerto Rico, would be ordered to report for his physical in San Juan rather than in Kansas and would be prosecuted in Puerto Rico if he failed to report. If too many draft avoiders moved to Puerto Rico, however, either President Nixon would put some additional conservative judges down there, or the Selective Service would change the rules. Draft avoidance lawyers had many arrows in their quiver but had to vary the use of them.

One arrow from the quiver was to recommend obtaining an obscene tattoo, say, on the heel of the saluting hand ("F*** You"). Another was to get braces on your teeth. Both obscene tattoos which could not easily be covered, or the presence of orthodontic appliances on teeth, were grounds for deferment. If those or other tactics began to be used too frequently, the risk was that the government would re-write the rules.

In *The Things That They Carried*, Tim O'Brien describes how he nearly crossed a river from Northern Minnesota to Canada so he could avoid the draft (after a week of indecision, he chose not to). But if you had the foresight, and $10,000-$12,000, you could hire a lawyer who, if you contacted him or her in time, probably could get you out of the draft. You didn't necessarily need to go to Canada, although many did.

I never saw or heard of bribes being paid to get out of induction, but it came close. Under the Selective Service System, the ultimate, or penultimate, authority was the local draft board, a panel of three older, distinguished citizens who as a collective were the repository of ultimate power. Every community had a draft board.

As the War continued, with casualties and protests mounting, many draft boards encountered great difficulty in finding replacement board members. A friend told me that his draft board had recruited his father, a prominent corporate executive. The existing board member met the father for coffee one rainy Saturday morning. They took their takeaway coffees to the car which the board member parked on a side street, where he tried to convince my friend's father to serve. No overt promises were made, but the implication seemed clear: Bruce, my friend, would get a deferment of some sort if his father served several years on the draft board.

Churchill stated that the "first casualty of war is truth." That certainly was true of Vietnam. Night after night ABC, CBS, and NBC news programs reported "kill ratios" of ten, twelve or fifteen VC or NVA soldiers for every American casualty. Later we learned that under General Westmoreland, the Army fudged or fabricated those numbers in any way they could, in outrageous fashion. Neil Sheehan's book, *Bright Shining Lie*, recounts the subtle untruths, including the exaggerated "body counts," told to Colonel John Paul Vann, a pioneering hero of the early war years.

The truth, though, went by the by on both sides, among those against the War as well as those who supported it. All of those young people I knew protested that Vietnam was an immoral war, an unjust cause, and even an unholy campaign. They may have convinced themselves that was so, but the real reason no one wanted to serve was, not only that they did not want to put themselves at risk, but they did not wish to see their lives disrupted one iota. I know that Samuel Johnson's dictum was that "Patriotism is the last refuge of scoundrels." But in days-gone-by, young people were known for possession of at least some semblance of patriotism.

Like most Vietnam vets, I do not begrudge those who did not wish to serve in Vietnam. I probably would not have wanted to go either, but I had no choice in the matter. I got sent. But as I grow older, it bothers me how much lying and hypocrisy there was about it.

There were risks, considerable risks. The Vietnam War Generation consisted of twenty-seven million men, more or less. Of those, 3.1 million served in Vietnam, but only 800,000 of those saw combat duty. Approximately 290,000 U.S. military were wounded; 58,000 were killed in the line of duty. If you went into the service during the war years, it was two-to-one odds that you would be sent to Vietnam. Once there, you had a one-in-eleven chance that you would be wounded; a one-in-fifty-three chance that you would be killed. Those are not good odds when betting on horses; those odds are too damned close when betting with your life. Many antiwar protesters did not say that. They argued that it was LBJ's war, or McNamara's war, or an immoral war, or an unjust war. Many (not all) of those young persons who evaded the draft seem like spoiled, dishonest rich kids.

Many protesters voiced distributive concerns. In *Fire in the Lake*, Frances Fitzgerald echoed these sentiments: "[The Vietnam War was] "a white man's war being fought by blacks, a rich man's war being fought by the poor, an old man's war being fought by the young." The statistics do not support those propositions, actually cutting in the opposite direction. For instance, 12.5 percent of those killed in Vietnam were black; the ambient African American proportion of the population is thirteen percent. Thirty percent of those killed were Catholic, the largest segment of which would be middle class; the ambient proportion of the population identifying themselves as Catholic is twenty-three percent. It, not the number of racial minority persons killed or wounded, is the biggest statistical anomaly of the Vietnam War.

The antiwar sentiment reached an apogee in Chicago, where I lived after I came home for good from Vietnam. The Democratic National Convention of 1968, which erupted in a police riot, marked in the minds of many the kickoff of the visceral, long-term antiwar movement. I lived a few blocks from Lincoln Park where the "Yippies" gathered for their own convention to nominate a pig for president. On a hot summer night I saw the Chicago police on three-wheeled motorcycles hidden in the bushes up a ridge in the park, east of the Yippie convention. Suddenly, the police rode down the hill into the crowd, like the U.S. Calvary, with a second policeman on the back of each motorcycle, wildly and wantonly swinging a baseball bat, seriously injuring protestors, many of which they then arrested and jailed.

Chicago became the center of the anti Vietnam War movement. U.S. District Judge Julius Hoffman and U.S. Attorney Tom Foran conducted a six month trial of the Yippie leaders which ended not only in guilty verdicts on the offenses charged but additional lengthy sentences of criminal contempt. This was the "Conspiracy Seven" trial, as the Yippie leaders turned criminal defendants (Jerry Rubin, Rennie Davis, Tom Froines, Abby Hoffman, Tom Hayden, Bobby Seale) became known. The we versus they, the youth versus parents, black versus white, the police versus young people, the murder of the Black Panthers, all filled the news headlines, raising the tension constantly in the air, exerting a pressure that you could reach out and grab.

In this milieu, I proved once again that I was not a hero, or at least a heedless one. One August evening my roommate Paul and I were walking toward the corner of Fullerton Avenue and Clark Street. We were on our way to a nearby bar for a beer or two. Now Paul was a very smart guy but a rash judge of people. Within minutes of meeting a dandy or parvenu at a party Paul would form a judgment, usually negative, and would need only the slightest provocation to express it ("You know, you're an asshole," for example). Paul could afford to do that—he was 6' 3", weighed well over 200 pounds, and had been a rugby player at Columbia, in New York, where he had gone to undergraduate school.

As Paul and I neared the corner, a pale blue and white Chicago police cruiser pulled up at the traffic light, in the curbside lane of Fullerton Avenue. The overweight cop riding shotgun had his window down. He looked at Paul, who had shoulder length hair and who also was nearest the street of the two of us, saying, "Get a haircut, kid." To which Paul, no shrinking violet, readily replied, "Fuck you."

I groaned, mouthing to no one in particular, "Oh no!" and began immediately looking for an escape route.

The other middle aged policeman who was driving jammed the car gearshift up into park, opened his door, and came around the rear of the police cruiser. As he did so, he drew his long black night stick from the holster on his belt. The other policeman, the one who had spoken was already out of the car, nightstick in hand. Combat veteran that I was, I was already looking for cover if not an escape route, most specifically a doorway in which I could hide.

Paul, cool as ever, proved why he later was to be first in our law school class two years later. Coming down the street was a handsome young couple, he dressed in coat and tie and she wearing a dress. Paul grabbed first the man, then took the woman by the elbow, saying, "I want you to watch this." The policemen stopped in their tracks, freezing for a few seconds. They then rammed their clubs back into their holsters and turned back toward their car, saying, "Fuck you, kid." Off into the hot August night they drove. Meanwhile, wobbly me, my knees nearly folding, rejoined Paul. We continued walking toward the bar.

Incidents such as that occurred all the time in Chicago and probably elsewhere. They may be mildly amusing but they also demonstrated how completely antiwar feelings and cultural shifts were polarizing the country in 1968. Everywhere you went it was thick and palpable, radically different from the America I had left behind in 1966. I came back a war veteran into a hotbed of sentiments and feelings I could not comprehend.

Time went by. After my return from Vietnam, I quickly turned against the War as well but for more practical reasons. First I felt that the U.S, defense establishment mucked it up, badly. When I first arrived in-country, there were 150,000 troops in Vietnam. When we came in off patrol with, say, ten prisoners, we made one report to our operational command, turning the prisoners over to the Vietnamese National Police. By the time I left, and there were then 450,000 men in-country (the number soon climbed as high as 505,000), we turned in five or more reports—on each prisoner! We practically had to count the tire treads on the soles of each prisoner's sandals. For every new person in the field, the military high-ups added five new intelligence types who would talk to you in low conspiratorial tones, or other desk jockeys who contributed not one scintilla to the efficiency of the war effort, but who thought that theirs was the most important job of all. Eighty-two percent of returning Vietnam vets, whether they agreed with the War or not, felt that they had been sent into a war which the politicians would not let them win.

Second, I came to the conviction that given the geography, the war effort was an impossible one. We built modern air bases every fifty miles. We dredged and enlarged or created from nothing sea ports along the Vietnamese coast. We had Special Forces and larger camps at every key point on Highway One but we could not, with 450,000 troops, even keep that highway open. Sir Charles could blockade it, even occupy it, seemingly whenever he wanted to. The VC could flee into Cambodia and into Laos where we could not aggressively pursue them. The VC dug tunnels right up to Saigon. North Vietnam kept its troops supplied via the Ho Chi Minh trail stretching for 800 miles through Laos and Cambodia. We could never close it down.

Third, and I came to this last, and much later: the Vietnam war was a civil war into which we Americans had no business intervening. When we discovered that, and discovered how venal and corrupt were the Diem and later Thieu administrations we propped up, we should have withdrawn. How I ultimately had that epiphany required a history lesson I never had before I went, together with increasing hostility in the environments which surrounded me, a young veteran trying to get a new life started.

Map of French Indochina, 1908-1954.

Half a Kilogram of History

A page of history is worth a pound of logic.

—Associate Justice Oliver Wendell Holmes, U.S. Supreme Court, 1926

Only by revolutionary violence can the masses
defeat aggressive imperialism and its lackeys.

—North Vietnamese General Vo Nguyen Giap, 1964

I KNEW VERY LITTLE OF THE HISTORY OF Vietnam before I went there. When we went through training, we had an afternoon briefing by an Army intelligence officer who seems to have fed us a bunch of irrelevant poppycock—good poppycock, but irrelevant nonetheless.

The Army major described the war as an effort to win the loyalty of the Montagnard tribe peoples who inhabited Vietnam's central highlands. Montagnard was a collective French term used for members of a number of colorful ethnic tribes (Black Hmong, "Flower" Hmong, Banhar, Dzao, Sedang, Taoi, Bur, Ba Co, Ca Hy, "White" Thai). Each group numbered 40,000 or so; there were at least fifty identifiable groups; collectively they amounted to approximately seven to eight percent of Vietnam's population. The Montagnards lived in long communal houses located in forest clearings along mountainous borders with Laos to the north and Cambodia to the west, and were known as fierce fighters. They did not like (detested really) the Vietnamese. They dressed in colorful hand-woven clothing, distinctive to this day, living separate and apart from rank-and-file Vietnamese.

Even when the War ended the North Vietnamese did not trifle with the Montagnards: everyone else in the South disarmed but the Montagnards kept their weapons.

The competing tugs and pulls exerted on the Montagnards of the Republic of South Vietnam and their U.S allies, on the one hand, and the North Vietnamese and the NLF on the other, may have been that week's or that month's news but it told little of the wider struggle or what the War really was about.

In 1861, the French occupied Saigon, then a village, and the surrounding three provinces, although French missionaries had been there for two centuries. The initial 1861 French annexation was soon followed by the annexation of three additional southern provinces, together with the naming of the French protectorate as Cochin China (1867).

The French missionaries, most specifically the Jesuits (the Rottweiler's of missionary work), had been in the country since early in the century, when the Japanese had expelled all foreigners, including the Jesuits, from Japan. Those priests and brothers then came to Vietnam. By 1858-59, ostensibly, the Jesuits in Cochin China needed protection; some had been imprisoned, others beheaded.

The Jesuits, the warrior caste of the intellect, famous for the rigor of their training and teaching, approached learning as a martial art. Their methods did not fit well with the Mandarins, high level civil servants who controlled the Vietnamese imperial court. The Mandarins exerted autocratic control over most aspects of Vietnamese society as well. In the early 1860s, the French sent a fleet of fourteen warships, headed by Admiral Pierre Paul Marie Benoit de La Gardinere. French ground troops had been in Vietnam since 1858. The French sent the reinforcements to protect the missionaries from the depredations of the "uncivilized" Vietnamese.

Europeans sometimes referred to the entirety of what today we call

Vietnam as Cochin China, but it was not until 1883 that the French coerced Vietnamese Emperor Hap Hoa to sign a treaty. The treaty established a French protectorate over what the Chinese formerly called "Annam," roughly the middle third of the country. "The Annamites were ripe for servitude," said a French colonial administrator.

Later, the French annexed the northern one third of Vietnam, known as Tonkin (a corruption of the original "Dong Kinh," where the great Vietnamese liberator Le Loi and members of his dynasty had their capital from 1426 to the 1800s).

Along the way, the French occupied and put in place colonial administration in Cambodia (1863). They named the combination (Cambodia and the three thirds of Vietnam) the French Indochinese Union in 1887. The French finally annexed Laos to the Union in 1893.

To this day, French influence is still evident, at times more visible in Vientiane or Phnom Penh than in Hanoi or especially Saigon. In the principal towns, tourists still find French restaurants. Vendors selling baguettes are on street corners. Although English now is the favored second language, and things French seemed to have become politically incorrect during the Dark Ages (1975-1992), today French has made a comeback. Professor Mark Ashwill in his book *Guide to a Nation at a Crossroads* finds that many young Vietnamese regard themselves as Francophiles.

In days gone-by (long gone-by), the Vietnamese chafed under French colonial administration, more so than did their neighbors, perhaps because the Vietnamese were industrious, eager to control their fate. In Southeast Asia, some say, "The Vietnamese plant the rice; the Cambodians watch the rice; and the Laotians just listen to it." The Khmers of Cambodia are also ethnically different than the Vietnamese—smaller and darker in complexion. Laos in particular is what many would term a "laid back place."

In 1904, the French put in place a colonial administrator named Paul Doumer, who later became president of France. It was Doumer who put Cochin China and Annam on a paying basis for his superiors and investors back home, but who in the process helped earn lasting enmity among local peoples. Doumer accomplished a positive cash flow by balancing the budget on the backs of the Vietnamese people, creating severe hardship, setting off generations of resentment and underground resistance:

• Doumer placed ruthless taxes upon staples such as salt or tea which the poverty stricken Vietnamese could ill afford to pay.

• Under Doumer, the French banned the fermentation and distillation of rice into alcoholic beverages (beer, wine, brandy), taking away from the people several principal pastime pursuits (making and drinking alcoholic potions).

• The French mandated the importation of expensive French wines and other French products.

• Doumer introduced to Cochin China the Brazilian rubber tree which led to the creation of huge rubber plantations throughout the country. French overseers brutally managed these plantations and the Vietnamese laborers on them.

• The French exploited native labor, not only in agriculture and domestic pursuits, but in high callings as well. The Frenchman who emptied trash containers made more than the Vietnamese university professor who taught Zola or Hugo to generations of Vietnamese students. As of 1903, the lowest paid Frenchman earned more than the highest paid Vietnamese. It was official French policy that it be so.

To be truthful, the French-Vietnamese affair was a love-hate relationship, albeit one in which hate eventually won out. On the love side, onward through the 1930s, many Vietnamese went to France for their education. Middle class Vietnamese spoke French, read

French novels, and affected French mannerisms and dress. They ate French food and spoke the language tolerably well.

By 1900, France had thirty-three colonies, second only to England's fifty (Germany had thirteen). While France's colonies (Algeria, Tunisia, French Guinea, Guadeloupe, Martinique, the Society Islands of Tahiti and Bora Bora) were neither as populous (India) nor as expansive (Australia) as England's, several were favorites of the French people and the French state. Vietnam was one of those. The French regarded the Vietnamese as their children, to be civilized and educated but also to be protected from themselves by their French parents.

In neighboring members of the Indochinese Union, however, far fewer native peoples benefited from French "benevolence." Tom Bissell, in *The Father of All Things*, notes that as late as 1960 Laos had only three Laotian engineers, two Laotian physicians, and one telephone per every 4300 Laotians, in a nation of four million.

French brutality began altering the love-hate balance with the Vietnamese. Colonial officials implemented "collective responsibility," much as the WWII German occupiers practiced against French villages found to have aided the French underground. The French would destroy any Vietnamese village found to have harbored guerillas, executing the village leader as well as other notables.

The French never practiced assimilation as the British did in India and other British colonies, raising up Indians and colonials to be police officials, advocates, judges, and colonial administrators. The French reserved all positions of note for Frenchmen. In Saigon alone, 20,000 Frenchman served as civil servants for the colonial regime. Of the Vietnamese admitted to the inner circle, most all were or had become Catholics, further alienating the Vietnamese Buddhist majority.

One Vietnamese extremely industrious and persistent in his opposition to the French was Nguyen Ai Quoc (Nguyen the Patriot), who in 1941 took on the pseudonym Ho Chi Minh (Bringer of Light, the most enduring of the thirty aliases he used over his lifetime). Ho

Chi Minh (1890-1969) led a struggle for independence and unification spanning four decades and thirty-four years.

Born in Hoang Tru, fourteen kilometers north of Vinh in central Vietnam, Ho was educated at the famous Quoc Hoc School in Hue. Despite a prestigious education, and a Mandarin father (both of which would have benefited him greatly if he had stayed at home), at age twenty-one Ho signed on as a cook and stoker aboard the French freighter *L'admiral LaTouche-Trevelle*. He left Vietnam on June 5, 1911. He did not return for thirty years. In 1913, Ho even lived in Brooklyn, New York for a year. Finally, Ho settled in Paris where he became active in Indochinese and Vietnamese affairs. He was a founder of the Vietnamese Communist Party, which went through many metamorphoses. Later the Vietnamese Communist Party became the Indochinese Communist Party. Still later the Vietnam Workers' Communist Party emerged, only to revert back to being the Vietnam Communist Party once again.

Ho reacted to the reports of increasing brutality by the French occupants of Vietnam, which fueled his increasing commitment to liberation. The French bombed villages; the Foreign Legion machine gunned whole populations. "[T]he figure of justice has had such a rough voyage from France to Indochina that she lost everything but the sword," Ho said in mild understatement.

The hands-on struggle for liberation began in 1941 when the Central Committee of the Indochinese Communist Party formed the Revolutionary League for the Liberation of Vietnam, naming Ho Chi Minh as its head. Ho had finally returned to Vietnam. Nothing happened immediately as the Japanese, as part of their Greater Asia Co-prosperity Sphere, had occupied Vietnam for the duration of World War II. An estimated two million Vietnamese died during the Japanese occupation. The Japanese confiscated the Vietnamese rice production, which historically had been plentiful, to feed its troops throughout the Pacific Theater. The Japanese thereby condemned millions of Vietnamese to die of starvation.

In 1945, after the Japanese evacuated, Ho Chi Minh's Viet Minh took control of the emaciated country, Emperor Bao Dai abdicated, and Ho Chi Minh proclaimed himself President of the Democratic Republic of Vietnam.

Ho was more of a nationalist than a communist, which may have been a reason for near constant name and organizational changes. Hoping for international, and particularly United States recognition of the Democratic Republic of Vietnam, in 1945, after the Japanese had left, Ho actually caused the dissolution of the Indochinese Communist party for a time. He never particularly liked the Soviets, even though he had spent time in Russia in the 1930s. He felt that Stalin and his aides condescended to him. Stalin once dismissed Ho Chi Minh's suggestion by saying, "Oh you Orientals, you have such imagination." Later, when an underling gave Ho some Marxist-Leninist broadside for his review, Ho tossed it aside, saying, "No peasant will understand this." It was rather Ho's successors, who after 1975, put Vietnam into "Marxist handcuffs," leading in turn to the excesses of ideology and the Dark Ages.

The French recognized Ho Chi Minh's 1945 government but only for a short while. Shortly thereafter, the French, and their victories allies, at the Potsdam Conference, gave the Chinese supervision of Japan's withdrawal from the north of Vietnam. They gave the British supervision of withdrawal from the south. The Chinese quickly had their hands full in their homeland, as the Kuomintang had to oppose Mao and his followers. The Chinese, thus, were not a problem, but the British were.

The British peacekeepers used 1,800 French troops to help them maintain order, opening the door for France to re-assert colonial rule, which it did, declaring Vietnam "a free state within the French Union." In fact, the French had never been totally out of power, for during their rule the Japanese left in place much of the French colonial administration. Flexing their re-found muscle, the French revived emperor Bao

Dai's reign, making him titular head of the new state. The United States clandestinely supported Bao Dai, the puppet, and his vices (women, gambling) with $4 million U.S. per year.

Ho, who had in 1946 publicly read to a crowd a Vietnamese Declaration of Independence (borrowing liberally from the U.S. Declaration of Independence, which Ho greatly admired), was more than upstaged by the French. They bypassed Ho altogether. Ho was to have no part in the government which took power after the Japanese left.

In 1946, the French bombed Haiphong, the large seaport 100 kilometers east of Hanoi, killing 6,000 Vietnamese. Thus began in earnest the first war for independence, which ended up as an eight year war of Vietnamese liberation lead by Ho Chi Minh. Ho relied on Vo Nguyen Giap for military leadership, as he did for many years. Bypassed as they had been by the French, Ho and General Giap rolled up their sleeves, forming a stalwart resistance force, the Viet Minh.

In 1954, General Giap finally surrounded the French base at Dien Bien Phu, a tear drop shaped valley in the mountains near the Laotian border, far away from any city or substantial town, surrounded by forested hills and then mountains. The French, under General LeClerc, hoped to lure the Viet Minh to a remote spot where the 13,000 French and colonial troops (Moroccan, Algerian, and Vietnamese as well as French) would crush the rebels. Instead, Viet Minh porters lugged antiaircraft and howitzer gun parts over muddy mountain roads. They reassembled eighty antiaircraft batteries, which along with the cloud overcast, neutralized France's air superiority.

Similar gangs of Viet Minh porters carried over the mountains parts for a number of howitzers, something the French strategists could never imagine the Viet Minh as capable of doing. Viet Minh reassembled the heavy guns in the mountains and hills overlooking the French fortifications. Learning that the Viet Minh had done what he denied they ever could do, the chief of French artillery (Pirot) committed suicide.

With 50,000 troops, their artillery, and high ground all around, the Viet Minh began a siege, digging tunnels toward the French lines and tightening the noose day-by-day. French aircraft dropped 3,000 French paratroopers to bolster the garrison. Despite the reinforcements, on May 7, 1954, the French surrendered, after a fifty-seven-day siege.

Upon surrender, the French evacuated to below the 16th degree of latitude. The Vietnamese rejoiced in the victory. Today every town or village in Vietnam has a prominent street named Dien Bien Phu, regarded as one of the most decisive military engagements of modern times.

Far away, in Geneva Switzerland, one day later (May 8), international powers convened a convention to deal with the Vietnamese "problem." Seven nations (Britain, Russia, France, the United States [as an observer], Vietnam, Laos, and Cambodia) participated. The August 1954 agreement designated the 17th degree of latitude as marking the line to separate the North from the South (the Ban Hai River), which later became the center line of the DMZ. The agreement further decreed that elections would take place throughout the entire country on or before mid-1956.

At the convention it was Ho Chi Minh who gave the most ground, something he always regretted:

- He agreed to the 17th rather than the 16th parallel of latitude as the line of demarcation.

- He signed on to a two year window for elections even though he and his advisors wanted six months.

- North Vietnam assented to a cease fire in the South even though the Viet Minh controlled large areas, thus nullifying at the peace table what the Viet Minh had won in hard fought actions on the battlefield.

China Premier Zhu Enlai lulled Ho Chi Minh into acceptance of the convention with assurance that as soon as the French left all of Vietnam would be the North Vietnamese's. Pham Van Dong, later the prime minister of Vietnam, always held the view that at Geneva

"China double crossed us." Numbers of North Vietnamese shared that view.

On behalf of the South, Ngo Dinh Diem refused to sign the Geneva document, calling the accords "catastrophic and immoral." In the end, only France and North Vietnam signed the Geneva Convention.

Ho Chi Minh and his communist government held sway in the North. In the South, Emperor Bo Dai proposed that he would be head of state and Ngo Dinh Diem, a politician from a prominent Catholic family in Hue, would be head of government. Instead of accepting Bao Dai's proposal, Diem deposed him, founded a new Republic of South Vietnam, and named himself as its president. When the time specified by the Geneva Convention came around, Diem refused to hold elections, then or at any time thereafter.

Vietnam seems a Catholic country, as a byproduct of the long French occupation. Today, even after the Dark Ages of vindictive communist rule, every town has a Catholic church while the larger cities have stone and brick European-style churches and cathedrals. Approximately fifteen percent of the population identifies itself as Catholic.

The dominant religion though is said to be Mahayana Buddhism, contrary to the Theravada Buddhism prevalent elsewhere in Asia. In truth, many Vietnamese adhere to what they term "triple religion"— Buddhism, Taoism (heavily pantheistic), and Confucianism (not a religion at all but a set of principles and guidelines for the conduct of one's life and place in the social order). The Vietnamese mix and match these strains as well as other beliefs. For instance, many Catholics revere their ancestors in a Buddhist way, returning to their ancestral home (*que huong*) for several days each year at Tet, the Vietnamese New Year.

But Vietnam also has many other sects, including Cao Daisim, founded in 1919, with its own pope and fairy tale cathedral in Long Than, ninety kilometers north of Saigon. The two million Cao Dai followers hold as near deities (signatories of the "Third Alliance Between God and Man") Dr. Sun Yat-sen, Nguyen Binh Khiem (a sixteenth century Vietnamese poet), and Victor Hugo.

Hoa Hao Reformed Buddhism was founded in the Delta in 1939 by Huynh Phu So, and emphasizes the personal, direct relation between humans and the supreme being. The sect also has two million adherents. During the 1950s and 1960s, more importantly, each sect (Cao Dai and Hoa Hao) had sizeable armies policing large areas of the countryside.

President Diem, and his shadow political ally, his brother Ngo Dinh Nhu, repressed the ebullience of all Vietnamese and of Buddhists in particular. The flamboyant Madame Nhu, the president's sister-in-law, substituted as a surrogate first lady, as Diem was a lifelong bachelor. Diem was also a fervent Catholic who had spent time in the United States, living in a Catholic seminary in New Jersey for a time. Diem also had become a protégé of Cardinal Spellman, the influential and powerful Catholic archbishop of New York, who talked regularly with and had the confidence of U.S. President John F. Kennedy. President Diem's older brother was a Catholic bishop in Vietnam with his see at Hue.

Madam Nhu, aka "the sorceress," aka "the Dragon Lady," held great sway in the Diem government, acting as the official hostess for her brother-in-law, President Diem. She acted as a forceful counterweight to the diffident president, badgering Diem's aides, allies, and critics with unwelcome advice, public threats, and subtle manipulations.

As with the Cao Dai and the Hoa Hao, Madam Nhu, too, formed her own army (of women), 2500 strong, outfitted with automatic weapons. She issued intolerant edicts based upon her own odd and restrictive view of Catholicism. The Vietnamese legislature rubber stamped laws against sentimental songs, dancing (anywhere, of any kind), divorce, cock fighting, boxing, the sale or use of condoms, brassieres with padded cups, spiritualism, and gambling. These sumptuary laws deprived Vietnamese people of the very things they liked and enjoyed in otherwise barren existences.

Simultaneous with press coverage of Madame Nhu's excesses, over-wrought by the Diem's maltreatment of Buddhists, Buddhist monks dressed in saffron robes doused themselves with gasoline, committing suicide by self immolation. Their martyrdom appeared on U.S. television news nightly. Madame Nhu fanned the flames by referring to the self-immolations as "barbecues." She exhorted Vietnamese to gather round the suicidal monks: "Let them burn and we shall clap our hands." The United States, which had been backing first the French and later the South Vietnamese, since the Truman presidency, felt compelled to act.

In October 1963, the Central Intelligence Agency engineered a coup d'état by the ARVN generals. Diem and his brother sought sanctuary in Saint Francis Xavier church (Cha Tam Church), the Catholic parish church in Cholon, Saigon's Chinese district, a church which may still be visited today. Under promise of a safe exile from the country if they "came in from the cold," Diem and his brother left the safety of the church, only to be murdered in cold blood by renegade generals while the armed personnel carrier in which they rode slowed to cross the railroad tracks. The assassination marked the beginning of a succession of low points in the American involvement in Vietnam (Madam Nhu survived, living in Rome, where she passed away on April 24, 2011, at age eighty-seven).

Perhaps to distract attention from the Diem assassination, in August 1964, the U.S. responded to attacks (one of which was later found to have been fabricated) by North Vietnamese patrol craft on two destroyers—the USS *Maddox* and the USS *Turner Joy*—patrolling the Tonkin Gulf, twelve to thirteen kilometers from shore. On August 2, the *Maddox* withstood an attack involving three torpedoes, two of which missed and one of which was a dud. The *Turner Joy* then came to the rescue. The attack on it, on August 4, may or may not have occurred, although many antiwar activists took the view that the Navy and Department of Defense fabricated the entire story of a second attack. The *Turner Joy's* crew members, to the last man, swore they were attacked, although subsequent research confirms that unique atmospheric conditions led to a radar readout appearance of an attack.

But the subsequent research was not done, at least back then. The *Turner Joy's* crew had less of a desire to deceive than a desire to affirm that an attack had taken place. Edwin Moise, in his book *The Tonkin Gulf and the Escalation of the Vietnam War*, paraphrases journalist terms by writing, "The story was too good to check."

On August 6, 1964, the U.S. Congress passed the Tonkin Gulf Resolution, authorizing the president to respond militarily in any way he saw fit, including the introduction of ground troops into Vietnam. The House of Representatives passed the resolution unanimously (461-0). In the Senate, Wayne Morse, the former dean of the University of Oregon Law School, and Earnest Gruening, Senator from Alaska ("Vietnam is not worth the life of a single American boy"), thought that the U.S. should not rush into anything. They voted "no" but the Tonkin Gulf Resolution passed 98-2.

The very next day, U.S. aircraft carriers moved into the Tonkin Gulf, adjacent to North Vietnam. From Yankee Station, those carriers launched airstrike after airstrike on Hanoi. Color photos of Navy fighters launching from U.S. aircraft carriers *Ticonderoga* and *Constellation* appeared in *Life*, including on the cover, finding their way into nearly every American home. Navy pilots flew sixty-four sorties in early August 1964, losing two aircraft, the pilot of one (Lt. Everett Alvarez) becoming the first of nearly 600 downed aviators to be imprisoned in North Vietnam.

In March, 1965, 3,500 U.S. Marines made amphibious landings at Danang, first to act as a garrison of the airfield to the west of Danang, later of the sprawling U.S. air base at Chu Lai, south of Danang. The Air Force unleashed "Rolling Thunder," with carpet bombing by B-52s from Andersen Air Base in Guam and later in Thailand, and "Operation Barrel Roll," which involved bombing in Laos and Cambodia that was never disclosed to the American people.

In Saigon, inept general followed inept general as president of the

"Republic" (General Duong Van Minh, General Nguyen Khanh). The generals' hold on power was so tenuous that they kept elite ARVN fighting units near the capital so that they could be recalled in case of a coup. So, while there were many and differing reasons for the ineffectiveness of South Vietnamese forces, one was that those with any proven track record could not be deployed more than forty kilometers from the capital.

Early in the War, ARVN troops under Air Marshall Ky, battled other ARVN troops under General Thi, killing each other for control of Danang and of I Corps. "With a government like that, and an army like that, in the country we were supporting," as early as 1965 Marine Lieutenant Philip Caputo concluded, "I knew that we could never hope to win the war."

The Vietnam War had begun, with an eager U.S, military, an enthusiastic, supportive U.S. population, a corrupt and inefficient ally, and a determined, vastly underrated foe.

9

The War Nobody Won

*I have asked… General Westmoreland what more he needs to meet
the mounting aggression. He has told me. And we will meet his needs.
We cannot be defeated by force of arms. We will stand in Vietnam.*

—President Lyndon Baines Johnson, 1967

*You can kill ten of my men for everyone I kill of yours.
But even at those odds you will lose and I will win.*

—Ho Chi Minh (Bringer of Light), 1966

*When we marched into the rice paddies… we carried, along with our
packs and rifles, the conviction that the Viet Cong could be quickly beaten.
We kept the packs and rifles; the convictions we quickly lost.*

—Lt. Philip Caputo, *A Rumor of War* (1977)

*Strong ropes inching gradually, day by day, night by night,
around the neck, arm, and legs of the demon, awaiting the
order to jerk tight, and bring the creature's life to an end.*

—North Vietnamese General Van Tien Dung, 1975
(Describing the NVA preparations for final conquest)

WHY WERE WE (THE AMERICANS) THERE? Why did we stay there?
Why did we stay there after President Richard Nixon's 1968-69 prom-
ises of "peace with honor?" What was the cost to the United States?
To North Vietnam? To South Vietnam?

For the United States, the Vietnam War had three stages:

• Fighting, 1965-1967.

• Fighting while negotiating, 1967-1970.

• Negotiating while fighting, 1970-1973.

The South Vietnamese government fell two years after the U.S. completed its withdrawal from combat, crumbling completely in 1975. Saigon itself fell on April 30, 1975, forever symbolized by an NVA tank breaking through the fence, advancing across the Presidential Palace lawn. Vietnam, North and South, thereafter entered the Dark Ages. In 1978, Vietnam adopted the anti-capitalism laws, forfeiting all privately owned property and businesses to the state.

In the War years, 1963 to 1975, 58,000 U.S. men and women died in the War. The North Vietnamese and the Viet Cong suffered a total of two million deaths, the ARVN approximately two million more. Before Saigon fell, two to three million Vietnamese left their homeland. After the fall, another million persons escaped by sea (the "boat people"). An additional 500,000 escaped overland, through Cambodia and Laos. When the government condemned private businesses, another 500,000, many of whom were "overseas Chinese," left the country.

In a country of forty-two million, which Vietnam then was, approximately ten percent of its citizenry lost their lives. All told, through death or emigration, the country lost nine million plus, or slightly more than twenty-one percent of its inhabitants. The South, which contained about sixteen million people at the time, lost six million, or more than thirty-seven percent, of its citizens.

As is true in many wars, all of this cost was the result of a series of misunderstandings. U.S. presence in the first place and the beginning escalation of the War were instances of the tail wagging the dog.

With Vietnam the tail was anti-communism. Following World War II, the United States had backed Chang Kai Chek (the "peanut" to U.S. General "Vinegar Joe" Stillwell), who, rather than fighting, hoarded the military supplies the U.S. provided. After the war, Chang Kai Chek's Kuomintang government fell to the ragged forces and communist party lead by Mao Tse Tung, despite those mountainous supplies of weapons, ammunition, and other war materiel flown in the U.S over the "hump" and trucked in on the Burma Road. By 1948, Chang Kai Chek and his followers had fled to the island of Formosa, which became the nation we know as Taiwan, routinely referred to as "Free China." Once again, the U.S. had bet on the wrong horse.

The waves of anti-communism set off by the rapid fall of China reached their zenith in the early 1950s with the witch hunts under Senator Joseph McCarthy and the House Committee on Un-American Activities. Thousands of Americans were blacklisted because they had read a pro-communist book while in college, or for no reason at all.

You cannot underestimate the width and the depth of the anti-communist sentiment that ruled this country in the 1950s, even after Joe McCarthy's disgrace and death. As a child, I was forbidden from ever mentioning any political leaning of either my mother or my father. In fact, my father, who worked for the government, never would disclose the slightest political leaning or inkling to his four children.

President Kennedy, President Johnson, Secretary of Defense Robert McNamara, the Joint Chiefs of Staff, Secretary of State Dean Rusk, senators, members of Congress, and citizens all saw the activities of the Viet Cong, Ho Chi Minh, and the North Vietnamese as the newest frontier for the much dreaded expansion of communism. The U.S. calculus was that we had to fight the National Liberation Front (Viet Cong) and the North Vietnamese because they were Communist which, Tom Bissell tells us, "...was necessary because Soviets and Chinamen were Communist, trying to take over the entire world and using Vietnam as a staging ground." Dean Rusk echoed those sentiments: "[This] is a civil war that has been captured by the Politburo.... It is part of an international war. [W]e have to look at the struggle in terms of which side we are on. [H]o Chi Minh is tied in with the Politburo...."

Compounding the misunderstanding on the U.S. side was the American "can do" spirit. Winston Churchill wrote that the American "national psychology is such that the bigger the Idea the more whole-heartedly and obstinately do they throw themselves into making it a success. It is an admirable characteristic, provided the Idea is good." It is less than admirable if the idea is bad, as it was in Vietnam.

As World War II had demonstrated, the American nation could accomplish anything to which it dedicated itself. It was not colonialism per se but an outgrowth of America's "Manifest Destiny" of the 1830s and 1840s. Manifest destiny supported a belief by many Americans in their obligation to export their benefits to less privileged nations. We were extending American ethics and political realities as an antidote to totalitarianism. We called it "nation building." President Lyndon Johnson spoke for the nation when he said, "We fight for values and principles rather than territories or colonies."

Manifest destiny, which had not died, a fervent belief in American exceptionalism, and deep-seated conviction of that the communist cartel was engaged in a plot to take over the world, a ploy that had to be stopped, combined to make nearly universal a belief in the need for war.

On the North Vietnamese side, the American efforts were viewed as nothing more than those of neo-colonialists, dragging up memories of over 100 years of exploitation by the French. Actually, among Americans especially sensitive to North Vietnamese charges of neo-colonialism, the U.S. went overboard in upholding the integrity of the South Vietnamese government and military, which in reality were corrupt, inefficient, and totally lacking in integrity. Charitably, their leader, Nguyen Van Thieu, was once described as "South Vietnam's tough, soft spoken, intelligent, perpetually dapper, and moderately crooked president." His appearance gave a "sheen of legitimacy to what deeper down was a thoroughly corrupt government."

Both sides misunderstood the true state of affairs. The American leaders completely misunderstood the situation. The North Vietnamese, led by Ho Chi Minh, were nationalists first and second, perhaps even third, intent on reunification of North and South. They were "communist light," only as a fourth or fifth consideration, communists of convenience. They had an abiding suspicion of and dislike for China, dating from China's occupation in 200 AD of Vietnam for a thousand years. The Vietnamese willingly accepted Chinese aid but neither Chinese advice nor China's brand of communism. They would have never let the Chinese in, as the U.S. feared that the North Vietnamese might have done if the U.S. escalated the war. The same held true of North Vietnamese attitudes toward the Russians, whom they also disliked.

Similarly, the North Vietnamese were mistaken. Among Americans and their leaders, there existed an acute distrust for the imperialistic motivations which flourished among the nations of Europe at the end of the nineteenth century. Imperialistic intentions and neocolonial aspirations were never, ever in American consciousness.

In the War's early years, the South faced only the guerilla tactics of indigenous Viet Cong. To distance villagers from VC terrorist tactics, the government moved them into heavily fortified villages, called *Khu Tru Mat or* strategic hamlets. Quickly these became Potemkin villages, and worse. First, their construction aroused resentment, as ARVN troops would impress 13-14,000 Vietnamese who, free of charge, were to build a village capable of housing 3-4,000, with the excess left out in the cold, despite their labors. Second, strategic hamlets removed farmers and field workers long distances from the rice paddies they had to tend each day. Third, Viet Cong cadres, which were underground anyway, moved quietly to the fortified strategic hamlets with the others, where the VC gradually resumed their brutal tactics.

Then, gradually, in 1966 and later, the NVA troops begin progressing down the various fingers of the Ho Chi Minh Trail, infiltrating at a rate of 20,000 troops per month.

General William Westmoreland, the tall, straight-backed South Carolinian who headed U.S. Forces in Vietnam, often was referred to as the "corporate general." His strategy was to hold no territory but to conduct offensive sweeps (search and destroy missions) through the largely denuded countryside. With superior U.S. technology (helicopters, night vision goggles, smart bombs, etc.) allied forces would achieve superior, even astonishing, "kill ratios" of 10-1, 12-1 or 15-1, which they actually did achieve. But in devising his strategy, Westmoreland failed to take account of the tenacity and stubbornness of Ho Chi Minh and the North Vietnamese leaders, who not only could and did offer up a seemingly limitless supply of soldiers but who also were prepared to continue doing so even if it took twenty-five or thirty years to wear down the Americans.

Westmoreland's answer was more—more of everything. U.S. troop strength reached 550,000. That was not enough. After the Tet Offensive of 1968, Westmoreland formally requested 206,000 additional troops, which would have bought U.S. strength to 756,000 men and women in-country by May, 1968. To his credit, President Johnson (LBJ) turned Westmoreland down. Not too long afterward, General Creighton Abrams replaced Westmoreland.

LBJ, often portrayed as the villain in all of this, also turned down the Joint Chiefs of Staff, who wanted:

- The go-ahead to use tactical nuclear weapons against North Vietnam.

- A green light to invade Cambodia, Laos, and North Vietnam.

- Permission to bomb the dikes holding in the Red River, which would have unleashed titanic floods on Hanoi and surrounding areas, killing hundreds of thousands of North Vietnamese civilians.

- All-out bombing of VC and NVA R & R areas, training camps, fuel depots, power plants, and industrial areas.

- Activation of U.S. military reserves and use of those troops in the war effort.

- Mining of Haiphong Harbor (which eventually did occur in May, 1972).

LBJ was a politician, not a statesman. He believed he could horse trade his way through anything, or most things. He approved of enough to appease the Hawks, those in favor of the war, if only to obtain their continued support for his Great Society and War on Poverty initiatives (The Office of Economic Opportunity (OEO), Model Cities, The Legal Services Corporation, VISTA, Head Start, Job Corps, and others).

Yet President Johnson held the line on all-out war efforts (invasion of North Vietnam, activation of reserves, etc.) in order to appease the Doves, whose approval also was critical to the Great Society. He ordered continuing resources and an expansive, but limited, war effort, to keep the Hawks satisfied and the Doves quiescent. LBJ played both ends against the middle, as he had learned to do as a Texas politician. But he always had firmly in mind a line beyond which he would not go, despite Westmoreland's and the Joints Chiefs' entreaties.

LBJ never learned that a politician's virtues can become a statesman's vices. A statesman blunders when he attempts to play both sides at once, or against the middle; a politician gets re-elected that way. Then, too, LBJ's advisors did him no favors. Subsequent to the war, several wrote that they followed the Goldilocks principle: give LBJ a soft choice, a hard choice, and the one in the middle (which they favored), LBJ could be counted on always to choose the latter, which he would find "just right."

In my mind, the turning point in the Vietnam War came with the Tet Offensive, which began on January 31, 1968. Tet, the most important holiday of the Vietnamese calendar, takes place over five days. Traditionally, all Vietnamese return to their family villages and family homes, where they see aunts and uncles, cousins and grandparents, eat copious meals and pay homage to their ancestors. In 1968, ARVN (Army of the Republic of Viet Nam) commanders granted leave to eighty percent of more or their soldiers, who journeyed to visit their families. The Viet Cong and NVA entered into a cease fire, as they always had for the period of the holiday.

Then, at 3:00 A.M.on January 31, 1968, Viet Cong infiltrated 100 villages, towns, and cities in South Vietnam. Undermanned ARVN garrisons offered little resistance. In bigger towns VC commandeered radio stations, telephone exchanges, key bridges, and highway and railroad junctions. In some towns, such as the Imperial Capital of Hue, the Viet Cong settled down for a long occupation rather than the hit-and-run tactics for which they were known.

The offensive's purpose was to provoke an uprising of South Viet-namese. Instead, it was met by no reaction among South Vietnam's citizens: "No uprising, only silence." Militarily, as well as politically, the Tet Offensive also was a disaster.

ARVN and U.S. casualties were 9,000, while the Viet Cong lost 90,000 men and women. Tet marked the end of the VC as a signifi-cant fighting force. Thereafter the War became almost exclusively an NVA endeavor. Viet Cong leaders, who the North Vietnamese cal-lously cast aside in the post-war years, mark the true demise of the Viet Cong as beginning with tremendous VC losses in Tet.

Instead, the effect of Tet was most acute back home, in the United States, an effect the North Vietnamese never thought about, much less intended or banked upon. Television news showed hours of cov-erage, as U.S. Marines stormed the Citadel and the Imperial Palace in Hue. Marines fired clip after clip of M-16 rounds over the Citadel's brick walls and around corners. Despite helicopter assaults, rocket attacks, and machine gun fire rained down upon them, the Viet Cong held the Purple Forbidden City, the inner most inner sanctum, until February 24, when the ARVN finally lowered the NLF flag. The vast grounds of the Imperial Palace were totally destroyed.

What swayed U.S. public opinion the most took place on the morning of February 1, 1968, in Saigon. South Vietnamese had captured a young Viet Cong, perhaps twenty or twenty-one years of age. He was dressed in a checked shirt and shorts. The police brought the young man, made memorable by a shock of dark hair standing straight up upon his head, to the Chief of Police, Colonel Nguyen Ngoc Loan. Exasperated by the crumbling order all around him, the skinny, balding Loan raised his right arm and hand, which held a small caliber pistol. With no hesitation, Loan fired point blank into the temple of the suspected VC, who winced, crumpling to the roadway, dead. Over and over the scene played on United States television. The effect was palpable. In an hour, or a day, or a week, millions of Americans turned against the War. However biased or prejudiced they may be, Americans have an inbred respect for human life and for fundamental fairness. Both sentiments were utterly trashed by that defining moment, which tipped sentiment, leading eventually to an avalanche of feelings against further U.S. involvement in Vietnam.

The brutality of the Viet Cong, who ripped children's arms from their sockets and murdered village headmen, was nowhere more demonstrated than by their conduct during the three weeks they occupied Hue. During the Tet Offensive, the Viet Cong murdered over 12,000 Hue civilians, Vietnamese and foreigners alike: missionaries, doctors, nurses, school teachers, aid workers, shopkeepers, any person thought to have a leaning toward the South Vietnamese government. Historical revisionists airbrush Viet Cong and NVA atrocities, downplaying them as a series of isolated incidents, but they were no such thing.

By contrast, while involving much smaller numbers of people, atrocities committed by U.S. troops receive continued attention, in the history books and elsewhere. The latter is as it should be: the mark left by mass atrocities, whether in Vietnam, Ruanda, or Serbia, should be indelible, particularly for U.S. forces who should be held to the highest standard. The former is not. It should not be quickly forgotten that the Viet Cong especially rank among the most brutal, callous mass murderers of history.

Shortly after Hue had been re-captured by the U.S. and the ARVN, the U.S. began to negotiate with North Vietnam. LBJ turned down Westmoreland's escalation requests. On March 31, LBJ announced that he would not serve a second full term as U.S. President ("I shall not seek, and I will not accept, the nomination of my party for another term as your president"). The U.S. and South Vietnamese began an intensive Pacification Program ("Win the hearts and minds of the people"), designed to leave Vietnamese in their native villages but ameliorate the conditions which had caused them to sympathize with the NLF in the first place. Surreptitiously, the CIA began Operation Phoenix, to remove (eliminate) the last vestiges of VC influence in the villages and towns.

The North Vietnamese continued to pour men and supplies down the Ho Chi Minh trail, which the U.S. and South Vietnamese never could shut down, despite carpet bombing missions by B-52s from Guam and Thailand and repeated forays by U.S. and ARVN ground troops. The NVA detoured through Laos and Cambodia, where, fighting a limited engagement, U.S. ground forces could not go, either in pursuit or to block tendrils of the Trail (small contingents of Special Forces, known as "Daniel Boone Squads," secretly went into Laos and Cambodia through much of the War but never in anything like the force needed to interdict traffic on the Trail).

NVA troops moved down the Trail during rain storms and under cloud covers which neutralized U.S. air superiority. The NVA reinforcements moved under the triple canopy of the jungle. Where spaces were open to the sky, the NVA rigged camouflage cargo nets to approximate jungle canopy. They marked caves as hiding places; they dug "spider holes," one-man vertical foxholes that protected against all but direct hits. NVA troops learned to take cover when they heard the buzz of a propeller driven U.S. spotter plane. The Cessna over-flight was certain to be followed by saturation bombing fifteen to twenty minutes later.

By and large, though, in 1969-70, the Vietnam War entered a lull, with U.S. and ARVN forces in control of more countryside than they ever had been. The Pacification program seemed to be working. The VC had ceased to exist as a threat.

Entering into this picture was Richard M. Nixon, elected U.S. President in November, 1968, and Henry Kissinger, Harvard Professor turned National Security Advisor (later to be Secretary of State). The U.S. electorate voted Nixon in on his promise to end the Vietnam War, to achieve "Peace with Honor."

Richard Nixon was a fundamentally dishonest man, who would do anything, promise anybody or anything, lie to vast audiences as well as to individuals, all in order to get himself elected to high office. Despite his public statements, he toyed with the use of nuclear weapons. He thought seriously about bombing the Red River dikes around Hanoi.

More than half of the U.S. servicemen who died in Vietnam died *after* Richard Nixon took office. The War dragged on for six and a half years after the American people voted for Nixon and his "Peace with Honor" slogan, four of those years with U.S. ground forces fighting and dying.

Henry Kissinger, who cultivated an image of himself as the ultimate diplomat and negotiator, proved to be a Prussian at heart, an inept lackey of Richard Nixon. Author Tom Bissell concludes, quite correctly, that "[I]n fact only one species of humanity seemed to emerge with consistently full sails after dealing with Henry Kissinger: Asian communists."

The Vietnam War should have ended, for the U.S. at least, in 1969, 1970 at the latest. Instead, in May, 1970, Richard Nixon sanctioned the U.S. invasion of Cambodia. In 1972, American war planes mined Haiphong Harbor. Hundreds of thousands more died, year by year, until the final North Vietnamese offensive, ending with the fall of Saigon on April 30, 1975.

THREE TASTES OF NƯỚC MẮM

10

Unanswered Questions

Vietnam is still with us. It has created doubts about American judgment, American credibility, about American power... throughout the world. It has poisoned our domestic debate. So we paid a price for decisions that were made in good faith and for a good purpose.

—Former U.S. Secretary of State Henry Kissinger (1984)

[I] had a small role in organizing the [1972] antiwar demonstration [near] Paris Island... [T]he featured speaker, Dr. Howard Levy, suggest[ed] to the few young enlisted Marines present that if they got to Vietnam, here's how they could help end the war: roll a grenade under their officer's bunk while he was asleep. [F]ragging... was becoming more and more popular with the ground troops who knew that this war was bullshit.

—Pat Conroy, *My Losing Season* (2002)
[Finding Levy's suggestion "outrageous."]

TWO OF THE HIGHEST COSTS OF OUR INVOLVEMENT in Vietnam were, first, the loss of 58,000 lives and, second, the deep rift in our society. Why were we in Vietnam, especially when our involvement evoked such bizarre, even treasonous, reactions such as Dr. Howard Levy's (see above quote) in the domestic sphere and the loss of credibility and respect in the international one? If we were not wholly committed, why did we not pull out early, much earlier than 1973? Why did we stay so long, at such a high cost to our national psyche and such a cost in lives?

The U.S. involvement began to wind down in 1970 with troop withdrawals from Vietnam, but in fits and starts. Wisconsin Congressman Melvin Laird had succeeded Clark Clifford as Secretary of Defense. He and U.S. commanders were fed up with a South Vietnamese government and military that tried to assert themselves by defying the Americans even in disputes that resembled quarrels between a parent and an adolescent. The U.S. had lost patience with the Vietnamese who consistently tried to "free ride" on U.S. efforts. We began pulling our troops back to the Vietnamese coast, assigning them to garrison and support rather than active combat roles.

At home, in the U.S., the demonstrations grew larger. In April, 1971, 250,000 marched in Washington D.C., led by John Kerry, who later became a United States Senator and the 2004 Democratic presidential candidate. Kerry dressed in worn fatigues. Peter, Paul, and Mary sang "Where Have All the Flowers Gone?" from the Capitol steps.

Secretary Laird coined the term "Vietnamization" for the withdrawal of U.S. troops from combat roles, leaving the fighting to the South Vietnamese. On the ground, General Creighton Abrams, who had replaced the ramrod- straight William Westmoreland, supported the change in direction, sending a message to the South Vietnamese that no longer could they depend altogether on the U.S.—our patience was reaching the breaking point.

From time to time, President Nixon revealed his true self. Privately, he told advisors that his biggest mistake had been "not to bomb North Vietnam from the start." He sent Vice President Spiro Agnew out as the administration's attack dog. Agnew termed demonstrators "nattering nabobs of negativism" and "an effete corps of impudent snobs."

Frustrated by his own and Kissinger's inability to negotiate with the North Vietnamese, and by other factors such as the U.S. Senate's rejection of two of his Supreme Court nominees, Court of Appeals Judges Haynsworth and Carswell, on April 30, 1970, Nixon announced the invasion by U.S. and ARVN troops of Cambodia (the "Cambodian Incursion" as it was officially called). Demonstrations and riots erupted throughout the U.S. , shutting down colleges and universities. In May, 1970, called out to quell student demonstrations, Ohio National Guardsmen killed five students at Kent State University. Republican Governor James Rhodes had called the demonstrators "worse than Brown Shirts" (Benito Mussolini's fascist supporters in 1930's Italy). Polarization of the U.S. accelerated, typified by Governor Rhodes's comments and Nixon's intransigence.

Ex-Alaska Governor Walter Hinkel, Nixon's Secretary of the Interior, publicly objected to the war. Nixon fired him. Nixon announced that "under no circumstances will I be affected" by demonstrations. He commandeered television prime time to rally support of the silent majority, a term he had coined: "My fellow Americans, I ask you for your support. Let us be united for peace. Let us be united against defeat. Because let us understand: North Vietnam cannot defeat or humiliate the United States. Only Americans can do that." Secretly, he relished his Patton role, the military figure throughout history Nixon most admired. As mentioned earlier, Nixon even toyed with the idea of using tactical nuclear weapons.

Candidate Nixon ran on a sacred pledge to end the war. Eighteen months after he took the oath of office, in many ways he had greatly expanded it. In Nixon's first year of "seeking peace," 10,000 more young Americans died in Vietnam.

Fortunately, cooler heads prevailed. Laird set a target of a reduction to 260,000 U.S. troops in-country by December 31, 1971. Not only the Doves (George McGovern, Frank Church) but the Hawks (John Stennis, Scoop Jackson) and the moderates (Hugh Scott, Charles Percy, Mike Mansfield, William Fulbright, Jacob Javits) of the U.S. Senate came out publicly against the war.

Nixon and Kissinger remained frustrated. They had finally decoupled the twined notions of a military and a political settlement.

The United States would attempt to achieve a military settlement with the North Vietnamese. The Americans and the North Vietnamese would leave for later resolution (another day, another place) a political settlement, which might presumably include some form of power sharing, to the government of South Vietnam and the National Liberation Front.

Kissinger, however, had written in his scholarly work of the virtues of "linkage," the opposite of de-coupling, in diplomatic negotiations. The linkage he would introduce here, though, would be with Russia and China, whose support was absolutely essential to North Vietnam's war effort, not linkage with North Vietnam. He would "link" continued U.S. cooperation with various Russian and Chinese desires with a request for continued Russian and Chinese pressure on the North Vietnamese to come to the bargaining table and, once there, to make concessions.

Nixon and Kissinger were buffaloed. How could they continue to be re-buffed by North Vietnam, which would not even come to the bargaining table? "I can't believe that a fourth rate power like North Vietnam doesn't have a breaking point," Kissinger said.

What they never could contemplate was the rigidity of the North Vietnamese and the complete lack of control over them that the Russians and the Chinese had. The North Vietnamese were, according to Kissinger, "fiercely, and at times, counterproductively willful." Illya Gaiduk, in *The Soviet Union and the Vietnam War* (1996), wrote that "The Vietnamese communists turned out to be unreliable and selfish allies who often caused difficulties for their Soviet comrades." The North Vietnamese constantly badgered the Russians for more missiles and equipment. Meanwhile, Soviet citizens living in Hanoi were poorly treated, kept under constant surveillance. China and Russia, as pretenders to leadership of the worldwide communist and revolutionary movements, it turns out, had no influence or sway over policy in North Vietnam or the direction of the War.

The Chinese were predisposed against unlimited aid to the North

Vietnamese anyway. Chairman Mao Tse Tung took a very cautious approach to Vietnam. He wished to prevent the War from expanding to the point where it might require direct Chinese participation. He was preparing to launch the Cultural Revolution; he needed the Red Army's help to do that. Second, he wanted to avoid a conflict in Vietnam like the one in Korea in which the Chinese had absorbed horrendous casualties. Third, planning for the 1972 visit of President Richard Nixon to Beijing and the thaw of relationships with the West were well underway. Chairman Mao did not wish to derail or sidetrack that in any way, including by helping the North Vietnamese wage war, effectively against the U.S.

The North Vietnamese played the Chinese and the Russians against one another to get necessary arms and materiel but listened to neither. The United States and Henry Kissinger never seemed to grasp that.

Le Duan, Pham Van Dong, Nguyen Giap Vo, and the other leaders who came formally to power following Ho Chi Minh's death in September, 1969, viewed defeat of the U.S. as a sacred duty, never a matter for compromise, much less for capitulation. Finally, Kissinger came to the conclusion the opposite of which William Westmoreland had reached: the U.S. could never outlast the North Vietnamese, winning a war of attrition. In boxing terms, North Vietnam was a fighter "who punched far above its weight." Kissinger redoubled his efforts to bring the North Vietnamese to the negotiating table.

Kissinger and Le Duc Tho, the gray, austere, aloof North Vietnamese negotiator, first met in a private house in a Paris suburb on February 21, 1970. Thus began a marathon negotiation. To facilitate it, Nixon went on U.S. television to announce that U.S. troop strength had decreased to 340,000, with a further 90,000 to be withdrawn by spring 1971.

Nixon's announced concession moved Le Duc Tho not one iota. It was not until two years later, in October 1972, that Kissinger and Le Duc Tho reached an agreement in principle: Kissinger dropped a

U.S. demand that there be a mutual withdrawal (U.S. forces and NVA troops); in a leopard spot settlement, the NVA troops could maintain control over those areas they controlled at settlement. In turn, the North Vietnamese made a tiny concession. They dropped their demand for President Thieu and his government's immediate resignation, probably secure in their knowledge that Thieu and his government would fall soon after the U.S. left anyway.

Nixon wished to conclude the peace agreement prior to the November 1972 elections, at which time he would stand for re-election as president. Again, the North Vietnamese and Le Duc Tho balked. At that point, ever the closet warmonger, Richard Nixon ordered the infamous Christmas Day bombing of Hanoi (Operation Linebacker II, Dec. 18-29, 1972; 3,000 sorties flown).

It worked, although countless other, less drastic measures undoubtedly would have worked as well. The North Vietnamese returned to negotiations on January 8, 1973. The United States and North Vietnam signed the Paris Accords between them nineteen days later, on January 27. The U.S. began the immediate withdrawal of its remaining troops. Exchanges of prisoners began. A month later, in February, 1972, Nixon made his historic trip to Beijing and China.

Within a year of the Paris Accords, an estimated forty percent of the ARVN troops had deserted. Corruption ran rampant throughout the ARVN ranks. Vietnamese quartermasters demanded bribes from field commanders for food and ammunition. Vietnamese field officers demanded payments before they would call in medical evacuation helicopters or air strikes. ARVN generals functioned as corrupt warlords, domineering, pillaging, and doling out patronage in the geographical areas President Thieu, in return for the generals' loyalty and support, had assigned to them.

In the United States, Watergate and the improprieties of President Nixon and his administration quickly took over newspaper headlines and television evening news. In disgrace, President Nixon became the first U.S. president to resign from office, on August 9, 1974. It had been a scant eighteen months since his triumphal visit to China and Mao, a little more than that since the Paris Accords had achieved "peace with honor."

There was no peace, really, for the Vietnamese. President Thieu and his Vice-President, Air Marshall Nguyen Cao Ky, made the mistake of ordering military operations against the pockets of NVA then in place in South Vietnam. Thieu and Ky awakened if not a sleeping giant then a very determined one.

During 1974, the North Vietnamese retaliated. They planned a decisive final offensive. They invaded South Vietnam on January 7, 1975, with 120,000 NVA troops spilling across the DMZ to join NVA soldiers already in the South.

Danang was the first major city to fall, on March 24, 1975, liberated by female NVA soldiers. Hue fell less than a week later, on March 30, 1975. Brave ARVN commanders and their battalions or regiments made stands here and there but had no protection on their flanks. As the ARVN came under attack by the advancing NVA, perforce they fell back toward Saigon.

Vietnamese President Thieu resigned on April 21, 1975, leaving for Taiwan on April 25 (he settled in Orange County, California). Panic seized Saigon. Hundreds of thousands of Vietnamese, those who had any connection with the government or the military, sought to flee, along with their families. Tens of thousands more non-Vietnamese (U.S. civilian government, relief agency, and other NGO employees) also sought to exit the country.

The U.S. Navy stationed ships close-in off the South China Sea coast, 100 kilometers east from Saigon. Principal among those ships were the USS *Princeton*, the USS *Denver*, and the USS *Iwo Jima*, vertical envelopment ships each capable of carrying a regiment or more of U.S. Marines, with a fleet of helicopters to transport those marines to trouble spots on shore. A fleet of seventy to eighty helicopters from those ships evacuated U.S. civilians and Vietnamese military and civilians around the clock, for a number of days. Manned by Navy and Marine pilots, CH 53 Jolly Green Giant and CH 46 Sea Stallion helicopters made round trip after round trip between the ships and the roof of the U.S. Embassy building. The last photograph before Saigon fell, though, is of a smaller UH1- B Huey helicopter, attempting to rise into the air with would-be refugees hanging onto to the helicopter's skids.

Saigon fell, South Vietnam ceased to exist, and the War ended on April 30, 1975.

Why had the United States stayed so long? Why had the U.S. not withdrawn sooner, when the futility of the war had become apparent as early as 1969? Everyone has their own view but many, including myself, lay the fault exclusively with Richard Nixon and Henry Kissinger. One, Nixon would do anything, say anything, tell one lie to one group and another lie to the next group. "Peace with honor" and his intention to seek it were blatant lies.

Second, "peace with honor" was the worst kind of lie, not only at odds with but the exact opposite of truth. Nixon, and Kissinger with him, were closet warmongers. Had it not been for public opinion in the U.S., influenced by anti-war demonstrations, Nixon and Kissinger might have turned Vietnam into a conflagration of all Indochina, with nuclear weapons used and millions more wounded and killed.

Third, Nixon and Kissinger were inept. They never were able effectively to bargain with the North Vietnamese. In return for what were token concessions, Kissinger and Nixon gave in (folded) completely, which perhaps would have been acceptable, if it had happened in early 1970. They wasted over two years and countless American and Vietnamese lives for nothing.

Fourth, Nixon and Kissinger never analyzed why, of the some thirty nations who had supported the War (Australia, New Zealand, Korea, Philippines, Thailand, et. al.) in the beginning, none ever increased its commitment as the War dragged on. Several significantly lessened theirs, despite explicit U.S. requests that they not do so. They refused because they had come to realize that the conflict was a civil war rather than the first stage of a communist takeover of the region. North Vietnam represented no threat to the other nations of Southeast Asia. The domino theory was a bankrupt idea. Nixon never seemed to have picked up on that at all.

Nixon and Kissinger help set the stage for Vietnam's withdrawal from the world stage and concomitant entry into the Dark Ages—a time that saw murder and execution of its citizens, imprisonment, re-education camps, the forfeiture of private property, the Vietnamese invasion of Cambodia, wars with China, and a downward spiral of the standard of living, making Vietnam one of the earth's poorest nations and creating a downright nationwide surliness that lasted until the late 1980s.

The passage of time after Ho Chi Minh's death and the complete stalemate in the War and in negotiations to end it allowed the doctrinaire Marxists to ascend to power, with a small group of inflexible ideologues taking Vietnam backward in time and through wave after wave of human anguish.

It was to a country emerging from these Dark Ages, at the beginning of *Doi Moi* ("renovation")—with a new constitution granting religious and economic freedom (1992), the cessation the United States trade embargo (1994), and official U.S. diplomatic recognition (1995), but still with one of the lowest per capita annual incomes on earth ($235 USD per person), that I returned in 1995.

TASTE TWO

A NAVY VETERAN RETURNS–1995

11

Ho Chi Minh City

I have been waiting here [outside the Presidential Palace]
since early morning to transfer power to you.

—General Duong Van Minh (Big Minh), at the
Surrender of South Viet Nam, Saigon, April 30, 1975

There is no question of your transferring power.
You cannot give what you do not have.

—Colonel Bui Tin, North Vietnamese Army,
in reply, at front entrance of Presidential Palace

IN JUNE, 1995, TWENTY YEARS AFTER THE fall of Saigon, I was pinned down in Bangkok, Thailand. In days gone by, Bangkok City was not a bad place in which to be pinned. But with rises in standards of living, many Thais had moved to the capital city. Many had used new incomes to purchase automobiles, motor cycles, and motor scooters. Noisy *tuk-tuks*, three wheeled motor scooter passenger conveyances, were everywhere, pestering pedestrians, whom the *tuk-tuk* drivers could not believe would walk.

Bangkok was a city choking on itself: hot, crowded, gridlocked with automobile traffic. While I was there, a second traffic policeman died from lead poisoning due to inhaling leaded gasoline fumes. At major intersections policemen directing traffic wore gas masks.

Once you figured it out, you knew that fast travel around Bangkok was by cigar boats, up and down the numerous canals that criss-cross the city. The canal water was so polluted with oil, human waste, and garbage, that cigar boat passengers would raise side curtains to eye level before the boat left the boarding platform. No one wanted even one drop of the foul water to touch their skin.

My destination was Vietnam, which had recently emerged from the Dark Ages during which the ruling North Vietnamese had walled the country off from all international contact, since 1975. In 1994, the U.S. Clinton administration removed the embargo on trade with Vietnam, instituted in 1979 by President Jimmy Carter to sanction the Vietnamese for invading Cambodia. More recently, on July 11, 1995, the U.S. had established full diplomatic ties with Hanoi. Tourists were beginning to trickle into the county (10,000 in 1996).

They could trickle in, though, only on the day specified on the visa they had earlier obtained. Mine, costing $92 US, read June 2. I had to spend six days in Bangkok before I could fly to Saigon, re-named Ho Chi Minh City (which South Vietnamese, for the most part still defiant, call Saigon).

I was excited to re-visit and see, for the first time really, a country where I had spent a year of my youth. I was not disappointed. Every misadventure that could befall a visiting tourist befell me. I spent fifteen days travelling with complications, worries, and concerns every single day, but I had a great time.

Bangkok to Saigon is a one hour flight, an uneventful over flight of Cambodia, lying between the countries of Thailand and the southern portion of Vietnam. I remember red flat earth below me as we flew on to Vietnam.

The Thai Airways Airbus landed at Tan Son Nhut, the sprawling airfield close-in by Saigon. Ton Son Nhut has always done triple duty, U.S. airbase, the civilian commercial airport, and the site of the U.S. armed forces Vietnam headquarters ("Pentagon East"). It had been a busy, busy place.

In 1995, two things struck me as I rode in on the taxiing aircraft.

One was how deserted the airport was. We were the only airplane in what once was a beehive, the deserted air of which now stood in stark contrast. Second was that many of the accoutrements of war were still there.

Most haunting were the revetments, partially buried concrete half pipe type structures to house fighter aircraft, protecting them from the Viet Cong mortars and rockets which rained on the airbase two to three nights a week all through the War. Then, during the War, the revetments were sandbagged and guarded. Each held a Phantom jet or an F-l04. By 1995 they were empty, blackened with mildew, but still there—fifty-five, sixty or more of them.

The concrete apron was bumpy, probably not repaired since 1972 when the American combat forces left. When the aircraft stopped, the ground crew rolled air stairs up to the airplane—no telescoping jetway as found in most airports by that time.

The terminal building was wooden—straight out of the movie Casablanca. Passengers entered a large room, empty but for four daises, each manned by a uniformed immigration officer. A distinct air of neglect, even abandonment, and musty damp pervaded the place. Beyond the immigration area was a glass wall through which I could see a single baggage carrousel—no porters, no baggage carts, no sign boards, nothing else in sight.

When my turn came, with the bored and indifferent gesture common to border police everywhere, the immigration officer waved me aside. I had a photo of myself in my passport, another on the visa I had obtained from the Vietnamese authorities in Washington, DC. But I needed a third, which I guessed would go to the security or the immigration police, two of the several branches of Vietnam's ubiquitous police force.

I knew of this third photo requirement before I left Thailand, and I had one. The difficulty was the third photo was in my suitcase (really backpack with a suitcase handle) which (presumably) was in the next room. I could not go there because I had not yet been admitted to the country.

"Double Pay on Double Bay" say Australians, referring to a ritzy harbor suburb in Sydney, a popular ferry boat tourist destination. Well, in Vietnam, it was "Quad Pay in Hue" (pronounced Whey), or something like that. Everywhere in Vietnam the tourist had to pay up to six times what a Vietnamese citizen paid. Often admission to museums or historical sites was free for the locals while tourists and foreigners had to pay up to $6 U.S.

Right there, in Ton Son Nhut air terminal, thirty steps into the country, I had to pay $30 U.S. for a head shot, taken with a Polaroid camera and costing no more than a $1.00. And nothing but U.S. dollars would do; no Vietnamese *dong* thank you. I did not mind the higher tariffs once in a while, but after a time the constant rip-offs got to me.

I passed through immigration into the baggage claim area. My baggage was the only item left on the carrousel. The suitcase had been broken into. The little lock was snapped off; my shirts, underwear, socks, and books were strewn about. The thief had not taken much, if anything of value, mainly because I had camera, travelers checks, diary, pens, and all other utensils of value in my daypack, kept by my side at all times.

So, two misadventures under my belt in my first twenty minutes in Vietnam, I sallied out of the arrivals terminal to be met by a blast of warm humid air and a cacophony of shouts from taxi drivers, hotel touts, and car service drivers. As is my wont, I pushed my way through the milling, pushing crowd, stepped off the curb, and started down the road to Saigon.

I could have walked to central Saigon, which is only five kilometers or so from Ton Son Nhut. But my destination was the cyclo stand, about 100 meters down the way. Cyclos were unique to Vietnam but the means of conveyance was wide spread throughout Asia.

Other Asian countries (and as a novelty some U.S. cities as well) have pedicabs, passenger two-wheelers pulled by a bicycle and rider (three wheels altogether). With cyclos, the bike and rider push the one- or two-passenger compartment rather than pull it.

There are thousands of cyclos in Saigon but the government does not permit them near the airport, probably because they are too inexpensive, not enough of a gouge on the tourist for the government's taste.

Restrictions on the cyclos also could be plain old mean-spirited punishment of the sort the North Vietnamese government liked to dish out to South Vietnamese on a regular basis. Overwhelmingly, cyclo drivers are ex ARVN—infantry officers, Vietnamese Air Force pilots, and the like. After the war, the North Vietnamese permitted ARVN enlisted men (those who were not executed, and many were) to return to their jobs and their villages. But ARVN officers, at least of the rank of captain or below (the higher ups—generals, colonels, majors either escaped or were, with no exceptions, executed), went to re-education camps. After completion of their multiple year prison terms, ARVN officers were not permitted to occupy any job of substance or to return to native towns and villages. So, in Vietnam you found former university chemistry professors pulling weeds in rice paddies, or high school teachers sweeping streets. Former ARVN tank commanders or fighter pilots pushed passengers around in cyclos, earning a few dollars per hour. The waste of human capital was stupendous.

The North Vietnamese, vindictive bullies, did worse after the War ended. They bulldozed ARVN military cemeteries. When they could not bulldoze entire cemeteries, they desecrated the graves of former ARVN officers and their families. Those actions were slaps, nay, punches, nay, haymakers in the face, especially to Buddhists but also to other Vietnamese for whom visits to ancestral and family graves had deep religious significance.

I hired a cyclo driven by a fifty-year-old ARVN vet, hopped in, and directed him to take me to the Rex Hotel, the "American Generals' Hotel," in the city center. As the city had grown to five million, the sprawl had reached to the airport and beyond. But as with developing counties everywhere, there were few automobiles. Many pedestrians walked in the street with their backs to the traffic. There was a swirl, with motor scooters, bicycles, and small trucks (but few cars), replacing the ox carts that had been there thirty years before. Trash, paper, and plastic tumbled along on the ground.

The Vietnamese, at least those in the south, are pleasant people—polite, good natured, and helpful. Beneath the placid Buddhist or Catholic exterior lies a certain industriousness and a short fuse. It has been said, "Your average Nguyen [there are only 300 surnames in Vietnamese, approximately half of which are Nguyen] is polite until you piss him off."

I waved my cyclo driver over to a roadside stall selling cold drinks. June 2 was a hot day so I thought I'd buy drinks for myself and the driver. I was unfamiliar with the currency, though, and I gave the driver a 50,000 *dong* bill ($20 US back then) when I meant to give him 5,000 *dong* to give to the vendor. Not a word was said; I only found the discrepancy later in my hotel room. I am certain that after he left me off the driver circled back to split the booty with the woman selling drinks. So much for one vet to another, I guess, although extreme poverty had something to do with it too.

So through this kaleidoscope we (my driver and I) went. Vietnam in 1995 was a totalitarian police state. You could never tell that from the streets of Saigon (as compared to Hanoi). Nearly everyone was going out of their way to break some law or regulation—drinking in public, walking in the street, blocking traffic, running traffic lights, sleeping in the parks, jaywalking, spitting, and on and on. Central Saigon was filled with lighted billboards and blinking neon advertisements, mostly then for French, Korean, or Japanese consumer products—Sony, Panasonic, Mitsubishi, Peugeot, Hyundai, and, of course, Coca Cola. The Vietnamese people may not have had any money, yet, but it was clear the multinational corporations were banking on the Vietnamese standard of living rising soon.

The cyclo took me to the Rex where my travel agent had booked me. Early on in the War, the street level of the Rex housed the Abraham Lincoln Library, reputedly a CIA front. Later during the War, the REX functioned as the Bachelor Officers Quarters (BAQ). The generals, admirals, and senior staff lived there (a military saying was that "I'd rather have a sister in a brothel than a brother on the staff"). Those of us in the field had a high degree of contempt for staff and intelligence officers and the high life they lead, compared to the rest of us. The Rex was the symbol of all that and I, twenty-nine years later, was staying there.

I left my luggage in my room, taking the elevator to the fifth floor rooftop bar/restaurant for lunch and a beer. These rooftop bars were notorious watering holes where senior officers, staff types, and press corps mingled. There were three in a few block area: the Rex, the Continental (the bar was known as the "Continental Shelf"), and the Caravelle, a story or two taller than the others. Many staff and intelligence "pukes" finished their alcoholic evenings on the Caravelle rooftop, watching the pyrotechnics as the VC mortared Ton Son Nhut, a few kilometers away.

When in Saigon, an American tourist could do all the war stuff ("Cong World," as sometimes it is known). Or go to Vung Tau, Nha Trang, etc. ("R & R World"). The former presidential palace, ugly and functional, had become a museum (Reunification Palace), surrounded by spacious grounds. You could pass the former U.S. Embassy, the state oil company, from which helicopters plucked the last refugees on April 30, 1975, but you could not go in. You could venture from Saigon up Highway 22 to the VC tunnel labyrinth at Cu Chi. I did none of that stuff. I was there to see the country, not the War. I would start with Saigon.

Dominant impressions gained in my 1995 visit to Vietnam were my newly-found surprise at how beautiful Vietnamese women were;

The "Continental Shelf"—journalists' watering hole during the War.

how dishonesty and petty crime permeated many aspects of the place; disgust at the gouge of the foreigner and especially the tourist by the government; and the black marks the Russians left, which, seemingly, they have done everywhere they have ever been.

Sunday morning I took a run to Van Hoa Park, near downtown. Inside the park walls were scores of Vietnamese playing badminton in the morning cool. At one point during the Dark Ages that followed the War, the repressive and dictatorial North Vietnamese Politburo dictated that everyone in the country arise at 6:00 A.M. or earlier, to go into the road or street and perform physical exercise. Maybe the crowd in the Saigon park was a hangover from that.

After a shower and breakfast, I set out to see the city. I walked a few blocks, then hailed a cyclo. The driver took me to Cholon, the large Chinese suburb, and the Binh Tay Market there, which goes on for blocks and blocks. I visited the St. Francis Xavier Church (Cha Tam Church), where the Ngo bothers sought sanctuary before they were assassinated in 1963, many say with the connivance of the American CIA.

But I was burning up. I wore shorts and a short sleeved shirt, fully exposed to the burning sun as I rode in the cyclo. I asked my driver to go back to the Rex so I could put on long pants and a long sleeved shirt. The driver, though, pulled up two blocks short of the Rex, explaining by gestures that the center of the city, where the Rex, the Continental, the Caravelle, the colonial opera house, the French Hotel de Ville, post office building, and Notre Dame Cathedral stand, is a "no go zone" for cyclos unless they had a special license. My driver could get into serious trouble with the police if they caught him in there, which they were highly likely to do, as the doorman at the Rex would probably call them. This silly regulation seemed another of the countless efforts by the government to gouge the tourist, getting them to spend more money.

The women in Saigon, I found to my surprise, were absolutely beautiful. Thirty years before I was used to weather beaten women, with skin dark leathery from constant exposure to the hot tropical sun. Universally they dressed in black pajamas, with conical straw hats. Often, half their teeth were missing, with the remainder, if they had any, and their gums stained red from chewing betel nuts. Many rural and blue collar Vietnamese chewed through the day to achieve a mild narcotic effect. Their black cotton pajamas were ill fitted, with the pant legs and shirt sleeves too short, exposing more rough skin and cheap sandals. Women who from the age of their children could not have been older than their late twenties looked to be in their late fifties or early sixties.

I am certain that I saw slender, more attractive Vietnamese women back then, too; but even at younger ages the effects of relentless sun and the other elements on their skin had begun to show.

Saigon was a revelation to me. I did not see more than two or three women wearing the *ao dai*, the traditional form of Vietnamese dress, with the high Mandarin collars on long silk blouses split up the sides and matching loose pantaloons worn beneath. Traditional *ao dai's* made slender Vietnamese women seem more spirit than flesh.

I did see, however, slender young women in Western dress with long black hair, delicate features, and beautiful skin, pale and fair but healthy looking too. I was so taken with the young women's beauty that one day I went past the Cathedral Notre Dame, stopping behind a tree next to a stop light. When the light turned red, I popped out to photograph young women on bicycles, or motor bikes, going off for their lunch hours, as they pulled up to the crosswalk. Many of the women wore a suit or other jacket, backwards, to shield their arms and necks not only from exhaust and road dust but from the noon day sun. Others wore opera gloves, covering their arms up to the elbows. Preserving their beautiful skin from the ravages of exposure to the sun had the highest priority. Narrow brimmed straw hats with a rose pinned to the front seemed the fashion.

More than any other, the sight of these beautiful young women brought home to me that, at least in South Vietnam, a new generation had taken over. The War is forgotten, nonexistent even in the consciousness of these young people, who were not born or were toddlers when the war ended. North Vietnam and Hanoi are different stories, strikingly so, but here in the South no one brought up the War anymore.

****

The Russians were in Saigon and elsewhere, from 1975 to 1980, until the Vietnamese kicked them out. I have travelled to many counties in which the Russians once had a substantial presence: the republics of the former Yugoslavia, Hungary, Slovakia, the Czech Republic,

Cyclos, still the major form of transportation in 1995.

Poland, Lithuania, Latvia, and Estonia. Everywhere they once were the Russians were actively disliked. In some places where Russians refuse to leave, such as the Baltic States, the criticism was vocal. The Russians were coarse, unfriendly, and clannish. They never learned the local languages or otherwise attempted to blend in. Of course, in Vietnam the dislike was mutual: because Vietnam was closed, repressed, backward, and economically undeveloped, Russian advisers begged their superiors to assign them to duty in Africa rather than Vietnam.

In Vietnamese, the derogatory word for foreigner, *Lien Xo*, actually means "Russian." Three, four blocks maybe from the city center, towards the Saigon River, are symbols of the Russian legacy. The symbols are ten to twelve story apartment blocks, constructed by the Russians, then a mere fifteen years old and already crumbling. Large pieces of concrete have fallen off. The exterior walls are coated with thick black mildew. Red streaks of rust run down the buildings' sides. Russian engineers and construction crews must have had no pride of workmanship whatsoever.

Until 1980, when the Vietnamese government threw them out, there were approximately 10,000 Russian advisers in Vietnam: structural engineers, architects, sanitation engineers, hydrologists, medical doctors, civil engineers, road building contractors, construction foremen, etc. The Russians spent upwards of $1.5 billion per year ($1.5 billion exactly in 1979) to rebuild the country. The Russian technicians, a head taller and ten shades lighter skinned than the Vietnamese, were rude, unfriendly, and coarse, as has been said. The Vietnamese summed up their attitudes toward the Russians with shorthand: they referred to them as "Americans without dollars."

****

Back to crime and my third (or was it fourth?) misadventure. Later on Sunday I was walking toward my hotel in Saigon, a block and a half away, surrounded by Vietnamese, over whom I towered by nearly a foot (I am 6' 2"). I came to a place where a sidewalk vendor sold *pho*, Vietnamese noodle soup. These portable restaurants, common in Asia, have plastic chairs, a tiny plastic table, and a large soup cauldron. They take up sidewalk space, forcing any crowd on the sidewalk to funnel down to navigate around the al fresco restaurant. As I fit into the narrow opening, I felt rammed from behind by a bicycle. I turned around to fend off whomever was walking the bike, which turned out to be two nine- or ten-year-old boys dressed in Sunday best (white shirts, pleated pants, etc.). As I pushed them away, I felt not my pocket being picked but the absence of my wallet.

I turned, facing again forward. Then I saw the dip. She was a middle aged Vietnamese woman in a brightly colored blouse and blue pants, walking obliquely away from the crowd and out into the street. I broke loose from the crowd, ran out, bear hugged her, and lifted her off the ground, meanwhile yelling, "My wallet, my wallet!" I had gotten her— foiled the attempt at robbery of a tourist.

Immediately, a Vietnamese man began yelling in English, "Here, here." I was worried not so much about losing money but credit cards, driver's license, etc. I let the thief go so I could get my wallet back. I retrieved my wallet, then looked around. The entire pick pocket team, the boys and the dip, was gone.

The woman had taken only my U.S. money, about $75. She had left intact a wad of Vietnamese *dong*, equivalent to about $75 U.S. All the credits cards and the like still were there. A number of Vietnamese commiserated with me, several telling me in quite good English that pick pocketing was an all too frequent occurrence in Saigon, one for which they profusely apologized.

I reported the incident to the hotel, who bought a limousine around to take me to the police station. Hotel staff insisted that I file a police report, as the authorities had declared an all-out campaign against pick pockets. The hotel sent a translator with me. She and I painstaking filled out the police form but the policeman sat in the back of the room, smoking cigarette after cigarette (Vietnamese smoke like chimneys), not interested in the slightest.

The other displeasing lack of order came from the beggars, all children, who will not leave a tourist alone. I have been to India, had Gypsy beggars try to embrace me and pick my pocket in Seville, in Budapest, and in St. Petersburg. Nothing was as bad as were the children beggars of Saigon. They grabbed your arm, pulled on your pants leg, surrounded you in numbers like swarms of locust, made you feel afraid to sit on a park bench. The only way to avoid them was either to stay inside of hotels and restaurants or to keep moving. It was curious. Most places I went in Vietnam I was surrounded and followed by numbers of Vietnamese, many of them children, for whom I was a great curiosity. But they never begged. It was only in Saigon.

Sunday evening I took a nap. I awoke to hear noises outside. I pulled up the curtain to peak outside. There were thousands of Vietnamese, parading past the hotel, many arm in arm. They paraded up the street half a block, turned at the ornate Hotel de Ville, went down the other side of the boulevard, turned left into Le Loi, and around a circuit, until they came back to the hotel again. Although Saigon is a city of five million, each week "Saigon Sunday Night Fever" takes place, just like the *paseo* in a small Spanish or South American town. It goes from 10:00 in the evening, sometimes lasting until 4:00 A.M. Monday morning. It's kind of endearing. Young people see each other and mingle. Older couples stroll, seeing many of their friends. *Chay long rong* ("living fast" is the literal translation) really means cruising, and they do it every Sunday night.

The people of Saigon were generally friendly, more capitalists than communists, free spirited, mostly Buddhist with a significant and influential Catholic minority. They were friendly to foreigners. They would not rat you out to the authorities if you broke a minor law or regulation, as Vietnamese in the North would do. The Southerners actively disliked their government, which they viewed as totalitarian, xenophobic, corrupt, inefficient, vindictive, and anti-South, but they love their country.

Saigon, the symbol of the South, did not seem overly dirty, certainly not decrepit at all, but not overly clean either, like Singapore was. The buildings were four or five stories in height, square and squat, with arcades at street level. The center had a good deal of French colonial architecture but the French influence was not as strong as it was, and is, in the provinces or in Phnom Penh, the Cambodian capital. Most of Saigon was non-descript with mildew and peeling paint in quite a few places. The city had some charm but it was filled with pick pockets, child beggars, hustlers, and touts. Because the latter were beginning to get to me, I decided that it was time to move on.

12

East to Nước Mắm City

All that talk about "liberation" twenty, thirty, forty years ago, all the plotting, and all the bodies, produced this, this impoverished, broken-down country, lead by a gang of cruel and paternalistic, half-educated theorists [the Politburo].

—Former NFL Colonel and *Time* Correspondent Pham Xuan An, 1991

Now the region seemed dead, a desolate, impoverished place. Yet there was hope, for "a country does not simply die. Its inhabitants renew themselves, and the eternally fertile land will give up its treasures to those who know how to process them."

—Ian Buruma, "Phnom Penh Now," *Travel and Leisure*, 2003 (quoting Xavier Brau de Saint-Pol Lias, nineteenth century French traveler in Indochina)

IN MANY DEVELOPING COUNTRIES THERE are not one, or even two, but three tiers of public transportation.

Most frequently at the bottom are the public buses, in 1995 Vietnam what were called the "Torture Buses," 1920's Renaults, ancient vehicles which had been in service for the seventy years since the French brought them over. As with any motor vehicle, the components first to rust out were the radiators. Because Vietnam walled itself off from the rest of the world for many years (the Dark Ages), Vietnam had little foreign exchange. So the Vietnamese never were able to purchase replacement parts for their busses and trucks or replace the radiators which, if you will excuse the pun, had evaporated.

The Vietnamese came up with a solution, albeit not an ingenious one. To the tops of buses, and on top of the cabs of over-the-road trucks as well, the Vietnamese welded fifty-five gallon oil drums. Then, every twenty kilometers or so along Highway One, Vietnamese transportation authorities built, or caused locals to build, water towers, much like the towers train locomotives used in the days of steam. The trucks and buses formed long lines at each of these watering stations. Once the drum was filled, off the buses and trucks went, with a constant stream of water flowing from the roof-top drum down through the engine, cooling it, and then running out onto the road. Every developing country has fleets of similar buses (in Central America the "chicken buses" are brightly painted old U.S. school buses) but the engine cooling systems used in Vietnam were unique. While the systems worked, the constant stopping and lining up for water made progressions up and down the country, slow as they were, slower still, painfully so.

The top of the line in transportation, I suppose, are commercial airplane flights and express passenger trains. In 1995, the Vietnamese had just instituted a Ho Chi Minh City-to-Hanoi train, dubbed the "Reunification Express," making its first runs about the time I got there, but I know little or nothing about the Reunification Express. I do know that later I took a local train from Danang to Hue. It took seven hours to go 105 kilometers.

By 1995 Air Vietnam flew throughout the country but it had few, if any, Vietnamese pilots. All those pilots capable of flying big airplanes had been in the Republic of South Vietnam's Air Force. As a result, when the war ended, the North Vietnamese captors sent the pilots off to re-education camps (prisons), to be followed by work in a rice paddy or driving a cyclo.

In the 1970s and 1980s Air Vietnam flew Ilyushin and Tupelov aircraft. Those Russian planes have the worst safety records in the world, in any set of hands. Until the mid '80s, the sets of hands were those of Russian crews. Later they were French. One United Nations lawyer I know told me about flying into Hanoi in an aged Russian airplane. He swore he could see the ground below through cracks in the fuselage. I am sure that by 1995 air transport had improved but I wanted to see the country, not fly over it in an airplane. Anyway, air transportation was expensive.

Which brings us to the intermediate form of travel. In many Asian countries in which I have travelled there exists a travel underground, consisting of mini-buses, vans, and similar passenger conveyances which go throughout the country. I once rode a van from Lake Toba, in the north of Sumatra (Indonesia), to Bukitinki in the south, fourteen hours for $25. I have paid for rides over long distances in Malaysia and in the Philippines. The seating may be crowded, eight or nine passengers plus driver, but it beats being crammed in with people, pigs, and chickens on the busses, it is much faster, and you see the country.

The *Lonely Planet Guide* for Vietnam pointed me to the Sinh Café, on the fringe of downtown (01 Le Loi Street) Saigon. I went there to reserve a seat on the van going to Nha Trang the next day, a 450 kilometer trip. I would get off at the halfway point, Phan Thiet, for a fare of $15 USD.

You meet all interesting sorts in these cafes and on the vans, rendezvous points for budget travelers. I met an Irish guy teaching English in Korea who travelled every chance he could. An attractive Dutch woman was on holiday from her work as a television producer in the Netherlands. An English guy, who had spent twelve years marketing deodorants for Proctor & Gamble, was beginning his second year of travel. He would keep going until his money ran out. A Dutch engineer had him beat. He claimed to have been on the go for six years. He had a beard down to his waist, which tended to prove it.

The only American I met during the entire trip I met on the van—a Californian, trying to combine exotic travel with business. His ultimate goal was to reach the highlands, around Da Lat, and farther in the North where farmers raised coffee. His objective was to explore the feasibility of bulk shipments of coffee beans to the U.S. He seemed prescient, far ahead of Starbucks or Green Mountain.

At 7:30 A.M. the following morning we departed Saigon. Thirty kilometers or so north of Saigon we came to the huge American military bases at Bien Hoa, a large airfield, and then Long Binh, the Army headquarters post. These sprawling bases had also been the indoctrination center for new U.S. infantry arrivals, and home of the Big Red One, the First Air Calvary, with whom we had operated in 1966-67. Long Binh once housed 50,000 U.S. troops. In 1995, the big base's chain link fences were still there, rusted and falling over in places. Little else was visible.

Soon thereafter, a Michelin rubber plantation came into view. It occupied both sides of the highway, one of many rubber plantations the French built, but in Vietnam War terms referred to as "the rubber plantation." The rows of rubber trees went for kilometer after kilometer of highway. Scores of square miles were covered with straight, neat rows of rubber trees going off in the distance as far as the eye could see and beyond. The appearance was sinister but at the same time innocuous, like the gingerbread house in Hansel and Gretel. During the War, the Vietcong had infested the place. Neither the ARVN nor the Americans could root them out. The Australians fought a major battle there.

My reverie brought back memories of Sam Streeter, of Brookline, Massachusetts, a graduate of tiny Beloit College in Wisconsin. Most of us, as I said, were scared, hesitant even to wander about Phan Thiet (where we were stationed), let alone the countryside. Streeter was different. He was a bit older, and much braver. He arrived after I did, to be an advisor to ARVN infantry forces. Early on, Streeter bought a motorcycle which he kept chained under lock and key in a Vietnamese farmer's shed. When off duty, Streeter would start up that motorcycle and off he would roar. Then one day Streeter did not come back.

We knew he had not gone west, where there were no roads. He probably had not gone north either. The VC dominated the north of our province. Even twosomes and threesomes did not go there. You only went there in force. So that left the south. He could have gone down Highway One almost to Saigon, hooking a left to Vung Tau, the beach resort (there is a direct highway now). Or he could have gone to the honky tonks outside the Bien Hoa airbase and Long Binh Army post.

We speculated that the VC in the rubber plantation had gotten Streeter. We never learned the truth—so Streeter became an MIA (Missing in Action). By the early 1990s, approximately 3,000 American MIAs remained unaccounted. It was the North Vietnamese's willingness to help render further accounts on MIAs that constituted the first olive branch (an MIA office opened in Hanoi in 1992), thawing relations between Vietnam and the U.S. By November 2001, that number had dwindled to 1,948, according to the Library of Congress MIA Database, and to 1,666 by the latest count (2012).

Of course, among VC and NVA, the MIA account stands at over 300,000 but the efforts to track down NVA MIAs seem neither persistent nor strenuous.

We quickly came to Phan Thiet. The Vietnamese driver let me off on the main street, which is Highway One, north of the bridge. He could not believe I was going there—no tourists did. Phan Thiet was several commercial blocks along Highway One, north of the bridge over the Phan Thiet River, and several commercial blocks along Highway One, which bent slightly back toward Saigon and the west, south of the bridge. A second bridge crossed the river two blocks farther inland. None of the side streets (in fact none of the streets except Highway One) were paved—all were hard packed sand. Besides the bridge, the principal landmark was a water tower decorated to resemble a pagoda, with a tile roof and gardens around the base, next to the river.

In 1995, Phan Thiet had one hotel, on the main street, back south of the bridge. I went there. It was full. Out in the sand dunes northeast of town, toward where the Cham towers were, the Japanese were rebuilding an old French beach resort, with the main attraction to be an eighteen hole golf course. The Japanese architects, their engineers, and a few of the principal investors were in town, so the ten or twelve room hotel was full.

The hotel's proprietress, a middle aged Vietnamese lady, directed me to a guest house, back across the bridge, north a ways, and two blocks down a side street. I slung my pack on one shoulder and hiked over there. The guest house, much like a medieval cloister, had a central veranda with doors facing onto it. The guest house had rooms to rent. I booked one, putting my pack into the room. I think I paid $6 USD. I set out to explore the town where I had been twenty-nine years before.

Not much seemed to have changed. The few three story buildings included the hotel and a Catholic church along the waterfront. Although unpaved, the streets were clean, much cleaner than in Saigon.

I decided first to explore the north side of town. Very quickly I accumulated an entourage. For the two days I was in Phan Thiet, a dozen or more people, some children some adults, followed me everywhere I went. I got the usual "Hello, where you from?" They also called me *lon* (big) or *dai* (long) for big or long nose. I have a nose that is larger than some, smaller than many, but longer than the average Nguyen.

The more adventuresome of my Vietnamese followers wanted to touch my nose. More than a few of my companions, who largely were hairless, wanted to rub the hair on my arms.

Everyone wanted to practice English. I walked along for some time with a young fellow who explained that he worked at the airport. Apparently Air Vietnam had one commuter flight a day from Phan Thiet to Saigon.

I walked to the northern and eastern extremities of town, out where the Japanese were building the golf course. Ahead I could see the sandy beach and the northern sweep of the bay stretching nearly out to infinity, with Hai Long village in the distance. To the side, on my right, I could also see Vietnamese every few meters, at the surf line, their backs to the ocean, their conical straw hats in place, squatting down.

Many of the people had no toilets in their dwellings. They did their business in the ocean. The fiction was that other people, on either side of you, were invisible to you, just as you were invisible to them. But I wondered. How is it going to go down with Japanese, French, and other foreign tourists when, standing on the tee, they see numbers of Vietnamese defecating in the surf, thirty meters away?

I walked back into town along the north side of the river. Once this had been the expatriates' quarter, while local people had "hootches" across the river, to the south. The large homes with verandas and blue tile roofs were unkempt. Their white stucco walls were smeared with black mildew but the houses were occupied, not decrepit. It struck me that long ago, even in the 1920s and 1930s, there had been a foreign presence even in a remote backwater such as Phan Thiet.

What also struck me was the absence of automobiles. Transportation was by bicycle, cyclo, or bullock (water buffalo) cart. Twenty nine years before there had at least been some cars—Peugeots, Citroens, Renaults, even the occasional Ford and, of course, American military jeeps. Now, after nearly three decades of communist rule, there were none.

One hallmark of rank-and-file Vietnamese always has been that they are industrious (again, "The Vietnamese plant the rice, the Cambodians watch the rice, the Laotians just listen to it"). I found evidence that substantial numbers of persons in Phan Thiet, a provincial capital, were unemployed or underemployed, I guess because they lacked outlets for their innate industriousness. The evidence was the ubiquity of movie houses with mid-day crowds in them. These movie houses were more like smaller circus tents than brick-and-mortar theaters, with side curtains up to chest level. The insides were dimly lighted, not wholly dark. I could see into the several I passed by in Phan Thiet. Each was full, or nearly so, with movies running. Now with the absence of televisions, let alone VCRs, I could see people flocking to these movie houses in their free time. But these were packed at 11:00 A.M. on a weekday. My guess was that if there had been sufficient jobs, the movie tents would not have been so crowded.

The Vietnamese government claimed that Gross National Product had been rising at seven percent per year since 1990 but it must have been from next to nothing. In 1995 per capita income was only $235 USD per year, one of the lowest reported anywhere. Even in 1995 the World Bank placed the poverty line at $2,000 USD per capita income per year. Vietnamese were far below that.

After some time spent seeking out things I had remembered from Phan Thiet in 1966, in heat that melts an American or European, I fixated on having a cold beer. I found that in a city of 80,000 not much in the way of refrigeration existed. After inquiries at several places, I settled for the local mineral water (Vinh Hao, Spring Water) over ice, health risk be damned. The few times I have gotten sick while travelling I can trace directly to a drink over ice, which had been made with the local, unpurified water. This time I risked it again but did not get sick.

That night at dinner, which I had at the Phan Thiet Hotel, I did find refrigeration. When I ordered a beer, though, it took forever. When the waitress served it, the beer was only slightly chilled. The hotel had refrigeration but not a lot of it. When someone ordered a beer, the Vietnamese stuck a warm one in the refrigerator or freezer for ten minutes, then served it to the customer.

The south side of Phan Thiet was a maze of narrow lanes, with upper stories protruding out over the walkways, like a medieval city.

A narrow crack of sky was visible above. I wandered through, coming out south of the river, on the magnificent beach stretching out for kilometers, to point Ke Ga in the distance, marking the southern extremity of Phan Thiet Bay. The locals were drying small fish on straw pallets spread out in the sun.

It truly was one of the grandest beaches I have ever seen, until you look closely. Up on the beach, at the high water mark, was a ten meter wide bank of junk plastic and Styrofoam. It wasn't there 29 years ago. Today it was, but not visible from farther away because most of the junk was clear or translucent plastic: milk containers, plastic bags, or bread wrappers. And there the junk will stay because the plastic will not biodegrade in a hundred years, or more. The beach resembled the town dump, or a sanitary landfill before it's bulldozed over. Revisiting those beautiful beaches of Binh Thuan had been a goal of mine for decades. Seeing up close what a deplorable condition the in-town beaches had come to was one of the bigger disappointments of my trip.

I went to a Catholic church that faced the beach. The church had a deck on its flat roof. I climbed up there. I was able to see out over a wide swath of the ocean front. I met an older man in a beret who spoke some English and French. We spoke for a while.

One influence that was less evident in 1995, or had to some extent become politically incorrect, was the French. In 1966, we communicated with a patios of French and Vietnamese. We sprinkled conversations with *beaucoup* this or *beaucoup* that or *voulez vous?*, badly pronounced but understandable. *Xin loi* ("Sorry about that") is one Vietnamese phrase that has stuck in my mind.

By 1995, no one under forty understood French or, if they did, would not speak or admit to it. By contrast, older Vietnamese people, at least educated ones, did not seem to care, speaking French freely. But the French influence in Vietnam was fading, much faster than in Phnom Penh (Cambodia) or Luang Prabang (Laos), cities in which

I have been where there still are French restaurants, automobiles, and smatterings of the language.

On my way back through the narrow walkways between the hootches was a *nuoc mam* factory. There were many but at the one I visited, I turned through a double doorway into a large open space which turned out to be the factory. Corrugated plastic skylights let in sunlight from above. On the concrete floor were several large wooden vats. It must have been a down time because the smell was not too bad. Anyway, this attractive middle aged Vietnamese lady struck up a conversation with me. Why was I in Phan Thiet? I told her, which then incited her to drag me further into the place. One of the workers, it seems, a guy about my age, was an ex Viet Cong. He proceeded to pull up his shirt, showing me his bullet wound from the War. He described to me how all through the war there were many VC just four or five kilometers outside of Phan Thiet. The lady seemed to be quite excited about this meeting of old foes. For some reason, though, I was not. I was polite but I really did not want to talk about the War. I made some agreeable noises but got on my way as soon as I could.

At night in Phan Thiet, a single light bulb was visible only on every third or fourth block. No street lights existed. You sensed rather than saw pedestrians and bicyclists moving about you. With no moon, the blackness was so thick, so heavy, so velvety, you felt as though you could take the night in your hands and wring it like a wet T-shirt.

The candlepower of a city of 80,000 was less than that in a U.S. high school gymnasium on a Friday night. I had a small backpacker's flashlight, a Mini Maglight, which I carried with me as I walked to dinner.

Before dinner, I had spent a couple of hours practicing English with the young policemen who also stayed at my guesthouse. As I said, everyone in Vietnam wanted to learn English. English was very difficult for Vietnamese because their own language was a tonal one. Vietnamese could give any word six meanings depending upon the register in which they spoke. With six different tones at hand, they did not learn how to pitch English, which by and large has only a single tone, without first conversing with a native speaker, like me, learning by trial and error how to pronounce English words.

The guest house in which I stayed was a haven for the city's policemen, many of whom lived with their families in the villages out in the countryside. During the week, they slept, five or six to a room, at the guest house, going home on the weekends.

It was funny. Here in pajamas, with toothbrushes sticking out of their breast pockets, were these friendly souls, barely more than teenagers it seemed, earnestly practicing their English language skills. By day they wore uniforms, carried pistols, directed a much sterner visage at the populace, and affected an authoritarian stance.

Repeatedly the policemen and I practiced English greetings, words, and phrases. Then, when I could go on no more, I excused myself to go to dinner. They clamored about me, wanting to know when I would return.

After my warm beer and dinner, I took my little flashlight, walking the five to six blocks back down the side street to my guest house. My new friends waited up for me. We practiced English for another hour or so until some of them, and finally I, drifted off to our rooms. By 11:30 I lay on the bed, in my room, lightly sleeping.

The guest house owner, a friendly man of fifty, raps on my door. I get up and answer. He gestures for me to get my passport. "Come to the front entrance archway," he gestures. I pull on a T-shirt and some shorts. A blast of warm air hits me as I go out of the room into the dark night.

I am met by two uniformed policemen coming my way. They meet me outside the door to my room, backing me up back and then back once more, into the room. The two police pull up chairs. I sit on the edge of the bed. The police, who presumably are immigration police, which every Vietnamese town or city of any size has, proceed to interrogate me.

The police want to know why I am in Phan Thiet, especially because no tourists come here. By a salute, by firing an imaginary rifle into the air, and by writing "1966-1967" on a scrap of paper, I explain that I was here in Phan Thiet during the Vietnam War. They understand and seem to accept that.

The immigration police next point to my landing card, a copy of which is in my passport. They take the position that because on my landing card, in the space "address while in Vietnam," I had filled in "Rex Hotel, Ho Chi Minh City," I have no permission to be anywhere else. Because I filled out the card the way I did, I do not have legal authority to be anywhere else in Vietnam but the Hotel Rex.

I smile, remind myself to go with the flow, not to turn hostile. Mentally I prepare for a trip back to Saigon should one be necessary. I point out that the bottom of the landing card states that upon reaching any new destination the visitor to Vietnam must register with the local police or present landing card, visa, and passport to each new hotel. As best as I am able I point out that the statement implies that visitors to their country can and will move about, away from the address written on the card filled out at the airport.

The thin, almost gaunt, police officer who questioned me had one of those pinched and perpetually frowning faces, with high prominent cheekbones and a large forehead. His eyes were narrowed, focusing on me. The middle of the night interrogation, however, was surprisingly non-threatening, a surrealistic flavor to it, like an academic debate. The debate was hampered because with our English, French, and Vietnamese we probably had only 150 words in common. Nonetheless, we went on.

The guest house owner sits on the bed with me, as does his friend, a fellow I had met earlier in the evening. The policeman holds his cigarette with his middle fingers, in the French or European fashion, rather than between index finger and thumb, the American way. He blows smoke up in the air, or turns his head away from my face while he exhales. The friend puts his arm loosely around my shoulders, in the Vietnamese way (Vietnamese are physical with those whom they know). At times everyone, save me, is smoking a cigarette.

After an hour, the police tell me that I must come to security police headquarters the following day. They are confiscating my landing card, my $92 visa, and my passport. The guidebooks say this is all to be expected. Immigration police regularly find irregularities in tourists' papers, requiring hefty fees ($50?, $75?) in U.S. dollars to pay for "corrections." I don't know what got my dander up but I decided I wouldn't, and didn't, pay the bribe, allowing them to leave with my passport, which I dislike ever leaving out of my sight.

My ace in the hole may have been that earlier I had befriended those policemen who were staying at my guest house, practicing English with them. The landlord must have told the immigration police that I had been patient and helpful. Next morning when I went to pay my bill the guest house owner had my passport and documents which he returned to me. I think too that by remaining at my side during the interrogation the night before, the owner and his friend had prevented any open solicitation of a bribe and had signaled to the immigration-security police that I was an OK sort of guy.

My bill paid, I went up to the corner where, as with every other block on the main street, a vendor was selling fresh baguettes. I bought one and also a bottle of fruit juice (*nuoc ep*, literally water from squeezing or pressing an object) for my breakfast. Then I began my search for a car, driver, and guide who could take me into my patrol area of twenty-nine years before.

THREE TASTES OF NƯỚC MẮM

13

MOTORING SOVIET STYLE

There on the road, standing near [was] an old jalopy, a beat up
Lada with a broken windshield ... [The Turkmen] beckoned to me.
He introduced me to the driver, a small, sad looking man in a dirty sweater.
"Five dollar," the Uzbek said, showing me five fingers. I paid and, doors
banging, springs cracking, tires bumping, we began to race across the
[countryside], the drizzle streaking dust on the cracked windshield.

—Paul Theroux, *Ghost Train to the Eastern Star* (2008).

I QUICKLY FOUND WHAT MUST HAVE been the only tour guide and
driver in Phan Thiet, in a tourist office several doors off the main
street, on the other side of the river. Tran Van Lee, the guide, was an
older (middle aged?) man wearing a short sleeve white shirt, dress
pants, socks and sandals, with a healthy head of hair, tall for a Vietnamese, perhaps 5' 8" or 5' 9". The white shirt and black dress pants
combination was the standard form, in fact the only form, of male
business dress, seen on thousands of males in Vietnam as you headed
northward from Saigon. It reminded me of the Society of Mary Brothers who taught me in high school.

Mr. Lee was having his morning coffee. "*Chao Ong,*" I greeted him.
Ong is an honorific meaning "Mr." or "Sir." It would be rude (mildly)
only to say, "*Chao*" (hello, or good day), without an honorific suffix.

Mr. Lee did not check his calendar or anything. When I said I
wanted to try to visit my old patrol area, and then be taken to Nha

Trang, he said yes immediately, sending for his car and driver. We agreed on a price, $35 I think, and we were good to go.

The driver, Thuy, was young, also tall, and skinny, dressed in a threadbare sweater. He was friendly but did not say much, because he did not speak English very well. His car, an old Czech model (a Tatra?), was big, black, boxy, glistening with polish but with dents here and there. It spewed out oil smoke, which tripled in volume as the car climbed hills. The seats were overstuffed, plush, decorated in a red plush fabric midway between velveteen and corduroy. I sat in the back.

We started out north, then turned right onto the provincial road running through the area of the Cham towers, above the sand dunes north and east of Phan Thiet and then along the beaches fronting on Phan Thiet Bay. Very quickly we were out of town, the blue sky expansive and the landscape of high sand dunes with ancient brick towers, evocative.

Immediately Mr. Lee began an attempt to dissuade me from visiting my old patrol area. There were no roads or, at best, sandy tracks into much of the province, he argued. Besides, the drive to Nha Trang would take much of the day. Mr. Lee wanted to get started in that direction.

I insisted that we push on, which we did but only for fifteen minutes more. We came along to Hai Long, a village of 500 that sits in the lee of a hook (a small peninsula) out into Phan Thiet Bay. We were ten kilometers or less from Phan Thiet itself but we had gone back three centuries. Hai Long had no electricity. Palm trees waved in the breeze, shading portions of the village from direct sunlight. The only mode of transportation was by bullock cart, of which we saw a dozen. The water buffalo pulling the carts snorted and salivated as we passed by them in the car. Pedestrians walked leisurely along, stopping to visit with one another in the road, as there were no other cars or trucks. We got out of the car, standing underneath a spacious and clear bright blue sky. After five minutes were ready to go again, for although it was a picturesque spot there was little else to see or do. We could go no farther east, or so I was told, as the road ended there. So we turned around.

We headed back toward Highway One, stopping for drinks at a primitive resort in a pristine setting. Sitting on Adirondack like chairs, on a grassy plane above the beach, with tall palm trees above us, and brilliant blue sky beyond, we seemed to be the only humans within ten kilometers in either direction, enjoying the most idyllic setting one could imagine. We had a coffee, served in large, bowl-like cups, reminiscent of the French era, watching the wide bay and the waves lapping against the sand beach.

But Mr. Lee rousted us again from our relaxation. Into the car we went, back to the highway, and "up country" toward Nha Trang. We saw no other cars on Highway One but the traffic was slow nonetheless, for two reasons. One impediment was the slow movement of grossly overloaded and under powered trucks and busses, people and parcels clinging even to the busses' rooftops. The second and further impediments were lane closures. Why? So farmers could use the blacktop of the highway to dry their rice! Here we were, in a country of seventy-five million, and the principal, and only, highway could be closed by a farmer or his wife who wished to dry their rice or manioc root crop! Amazing.

Prosperous Vietnamese built their new houses right next to the main road, I suppose, so that passersby might see evidence of the owner's wealth. Formerly, they would not have done so, lest by their prosperity they be termed "capitalist dogs" and mistreated by the authorities. But that was the "old" Vietnam. Now, since *Doi Moi*, material wealth and prosperity were okay. Large flat roofed houses were built of concrete, stuccoed over and painted with pastel colors such as light green, lavender, or sky blue. Some were faced with decorative colored marble. They looked like gussied up, multistory fast food restaurants. Author Tom Bissell's term is "Lego Deco style."

Along Highway One, the roadside would be empty for five to six kilometers. All at once there would be an irregular grouping of three to four of these boxy houses, quite substantial, right up near the road, followed by several kilometers more scrub land.

Ordinary peasants and farmers, like those in Hai Long, lived in small square concrete block houses with tin roofs (thatched roofs twenty-nine years ago). On the front, these more ordinary dwellings may have had a small porch or similar extension fashioned out of rough cut lumber.

Sure enough, as we drove up Highway One, there seemed to be few if any roads running from the highway over to the South China Sea, six kilometers away, to the east, as the crow flies. Mr. Lee had been right: I could not reach much of my old patrol area, not by car anyway.

After an hour, maybe less, north from Phan Thiet, we came to the northern end of Binh Thuan province, where the U.S. Special Forces camp had been years before and where Highway One again runs alongside the sea. We rounded Point Muy Dinh, this time on the land side, turning west above a long white beach, Con Na Beach, where we had performed evacuations of Vietnamese villagers years ago. Overlooking the beach was a roadhouse looking out on the bay. We pulled in for lunch there.

Mr. Lee ordered. We had a beef and vegetable fondue, or the Vietnamese version of it. Our server bought us a plate of thinly sliced beef (I hoped it was beef, not dog) which we cooked in hot oil. Mr. Lee and I had beers. Thuy had a Coke. I paid less than $10.

Our next stop was the Cham towers above Phan Rang. These ancient monuments sat there, unguarded, no one—tourist or native—around. We climbed the tallest of the towers. Its red brick had crumbled a bit here and there but the tower was in surprisingly good repair. From the tower's highest story, below we could see the houses of Phan Rang, with the former U.S. Air Force base beyond that, and the sand dunes and ocean beyond that.

I saw fifteen or twenty gray fighter jets standing on the flight line of the former U.S. base. Knowing that Vietnam's air power was minimal, I asked Mr. Lee to whom those fighter jets belonged. "Iraq," he answered. After the first Iraqi War in 1991, the United Nations imposed a "no fly zone" on Iraq. To evade the UN sanctions, Saddam Hussein had sought out a renegade country that would allow his pilots and air force to use the country's facilities. Vietnam was the rogue state that stepped forward. Iraqi pilots could train, maintaining their proficiency, far away from the no fly zone that forbade them Iraqi air space.

I was going to telephone the Department of State or Department of Defense in the U.S. but never did. My best guess was that the military intelligence people already knew about Phan Rang and the presence of the Iraqi Air Force.

Mr. Lee had a younger sister who with her family lived in Phan Rang. We paid a short visit to her. Her house was relatively new, plaster over concrete brick walls and square or oblong (but not nearly as sumptuous as the houses I had seen along Highway One), set in a row of fifteen houses. The row houses, each exterior similar to the next, were akin to terrace housing in English and Scots towns but more primitive, of course. We sat in a living room with two overstuffed easy chairs, on a bare concrete floor, with a single throw rung. Nothing else. In back of the living area was a kitchen and, I think, in back of that a single bedroom. The rooms were all lined in a row, like boxcars on a freight train, what in the U.S. is called a "shotgun house."

Most ordinary houses in Vietnam were and are today shotgun houses. They are of brick, covered with a coat of plaster, painted usually in a pastel color (peach, pale blue, light green). These houses have a partial false front (a story and half high), a flat roof, and a tin roofed porch on the front. Sometimes, the inhabitants have painted the exterior trim a contrasting color (orange with peach, dark blue with sky blue) but they do not have the decorative stone or marble richer folks put on their houses. The front wall of the house may consist of a bi-fold door stretching nearly across the front wall. The residents can open the door fully to allow air to circulate. Above the bi-fold door may be a transom, or fan light, to admit natural light when the inhabitants have closed off the front door panels.

The inhabitants of these new houses had electricity and refrigeration. I knew the latter because Nhu, the sister, served me a cold bottle of mineral water. Nhu was welcoming, at ease probably because Mr. Lee had stopped there before with other tourists he had guided.

No grass could grow under out feet, though, as we were back in the car and on the road again. North of Phan Rang, we passed the world class harbor at Cam Ranh, which I had visited many times in 1966-67, but mainly from the ocean rather than the land side. On the land side, the countryside was flat. A vast area of salt ponds, many white or grayish white with salt, with seawater evaporating under heat of the sun, separated the highway and the harbor, which you can see from the road. Mounds of white salt sat on the brims of several empty ponds. No beach or other feature marked where the salt flats ended and the harbor began. The harbor extended ten to twelve kilometers across, with a headland in the distance, with blue sky and cauliflower cumulus clouds above the sand dunes.

Anchored out in Cam Ranh Bay were two large cargo ships. No war ships were in sight. Except for certain areas near the Vietnam-China border, tourists could go anywhere in Vietnam, except Cam Ranh Bay. I did not know what was there, in Cam Ranh. The Russian fleet used to be there, technically at least, but with a vastly reduced presence since the Soviet Union disbanded early in the 1990s. Nonetheless, the area had remained off-limits.

The road began to run farther away from the sea but we turned to the right, came down some hills, past some Cham ruins, and into the resort town of Nha Trang. A world wise traveler once called Nha Trang "Nice in a beggar's clothing," but I think it is much more attractive than that.

Our car went swimming down the streets, honking, stopping,

swerving around pedestrians (all of whom walked in the streets, empty as they were of motor vehicles), cyclos, even an ox cart or two. We stopped, honked the horn, started again, swerved once more.

Then we came out on the wide thoroughfare, Tran Phu Street, which runs along the magnificent beach. Most of the traffic, including pedestrians, had disappeared. The seven kilometer sandy (not shingle) beach was fronted by this broad boulevard onto which fronted hotels and terraced restaurants, most of which had a decidedly French air, with verdant hilly islands off the shore. Posted on several vacant lots were signs for high rise hotels to be built but for which construction had not begun. So far, neither the ground had been broken nor had the tour busses, filled with Japanese tourists and their Sony Handicams, arrived.

Mr. Lee directed the driver to take me to a small white stucco hotel on the beach front road, closer to the town end rather than the port end. It had taken us, with a few stops, nine hours to go 250 or so kilometers, which translates into twenty-eight kilometers, or fourteen-point-eight miles per hour. Mr. Lee and Thuy wished to drive back to Phan Thiet that night. I tipped them, we had smiles, nodding of the heads all around, and soft, Asian style handshakes. Mr. Lee and Thuy headed back toward home, an exhaust cloud spewing from their old Soviet auto.

I put my bag into my hotel room. I headed away from the beach, toward the town center. Here, in early June, few people, tourists or Vietnamese, were about. I found a nice restaurant, with a second floor corner location, on the walking street through the Nha Trang downtown. The restaurant had an English language menu translation. My Vietnamese then or now never was good enough to navigate through even the briefest menu, so I always tried to find a restaurant with an English menu. In a pinch, a backup was a French menu translation.

I was seated and handed the English menu. Eagerly, I opened it. The very first item, the special of the day, jumped out at me: pig brains soup (*Oc Leo*). I wondered how it would go with dog.

****

I hired a cyclo the next day, a Wednesday, from right in front of my hotel. For $2 USD, the cyclo driver took me the length of the seven or eight kilometer Nha Trang beachfront. I passed the Pasteur Institute where the vaccines have been made since the 1930s. I passed the airport. I went to Emperor Bao Dai's summer palace, now a luxury hotel and a small museum. I again passed the sites advertised to be future homes for high rise hotels, to be financed with Filipino and Korean money. It was clear that the twenty-first century was coming. Nha Trang would be markedly different next time I visited.

My cyclo ride took me as far south as I could go, to the port area, where we used to anchor our patrol craft when we came ashore for a night or two. One more war memory came back. It devolved upon an enlisted guy named Moak and I, when our patrol craft had been unattended, to dive under the boats, checking the hulls for bombs VC could have attached there. We would clear fishing nets from propellers and shafts. We did this many times but my memory of doing it in Nha Trang harbor, which I describe in Chapter Six, is the most vivid. I came to hate doing that job; I haven't been scuba diving since.

So although I did not go diving again while in Nha Trang, I did spend two hours on the beach, with kids trying to sell me slices of pineapple or bananas. I took a swim. It was a lazy afternoon; I went back to the hotel for a nap.

Because I had much more on my agenda to see, I decided to fly the next leg of my trip, from Nha Trang to Danang, South Vietnam's second largest city. I easily found the Air Vietnam ticket office in the central city, located in a store front on the main shopping street. There were about a half dozen or so other customers. I watched for a minute. Although all the other customers were Vietnamese, none of the money they used for paying consisted of Vietnamese *dong*. Everyone removed crisp, and presumably new, $50 and $100 US bills from closely guarded white envelopes. In fact, the airline office would not accept Vietnamese money.

Like Eastern European countries in the 1980s, and other under developed countries as well, Vietnam acquired a taste for accumulating hard currencies (English pounds, German Deutsch marks—Euros today) with which they could buy and import needed foreign goods. Vietnam seemed to do so with a vengeance. The currency of choice, with no serious competitors, was the U.S. dollar, which the several million Vietnamese in the United States sent back to family members and other relatives they left behind. The guide books advised travelers to go into Vietnam with a large stock of crisp, new U.S. single dollar and some five dollar bills, for gratuities and grease payments. Few things were appreciated more by Vietnamese than crisp dollar bills.

My hotel was clean, and small, staffed by twenty-something-year-old Vietnamese. I took breakfast each morning on a veranda facing the beach. As elsewhere in Vietnam, breakfast consisted of a fresh baguette and a bowl-like cup of good coffee. My dominant impression of the place, as with many other places in Vietnam, was how young the people were. By young, I do not mean newly hatched, or teenagers, but everyone, waiters, front desk clerks, airline ticket office personnel, airport guards, policemen, everyone save the Saigon cyclo drivers and the workers in the *nuoc mam* factory, seemed to be in their early twenties.

The next morning I took a cyclo to the airport, another converted U.S. airbase, four kilometers south of the hotel, with a runway angling toward the southeast and a flight path over the waterfront drive and the beach. Now as I said, a central mission of the Vietnam government was to gain foreign currency anyway it could. This drive for hard currency included not only promotion of tourism and use of the national airline but gouging the tourists once they got to Vietnam as well. This discrimination took increasingly more insidious forms as I moved up country.

I have paid departure taxes in many countries around the world. You pay it ($20-$25 USD) before you leave the country. Sometimes the airline ticket price includes the departure tax. In other countries, you must set aside sufficient amounts of the native currency so that you can walk up to the booth where it is to be paid, pay the tax, and get a sticker in your passport. You can then leave the country.

Only in Vietnam have I encountered a departure tax to leave a particular city and its airport, charged in dollars rather than *dong*.

Nha Trang added a wrinkle. A tourist in Nha Trang had to pay an entrance tax to get into the airport as well as a departure tax to leave it. There was no use arguing about it. The uniformed guard would let neither me, my cyclo, nor the driver on the airport grounds until I had paid the tax.

Once again the airport aprons and runways were deserted. No airplane would be there until the one we were to board landed. A few passengers milled about a surprisingly large, empty terminal building. The sun shone brightly. It was to be another hot day.

The French built ATR 72 (high wing, twin-engine turboprop) came in from over the ocean, descended quickly, at a steep angle, landed, and taxied to the terminal. The pilot left the outboard engine running as we boarded by the rear stairway and door. The flight attendant shut the door, another fast taxi followed, and we took off, with no delay at all. I was again on the move, up-country, this time to Danang and the imperial city of Hue.

14

Riding the Hard Seat

Driving that train, high on [life],
Casey Jones, you'd better watch your speed,
[Scenery] ahead, [scenery] behind,
And you know that notion just crossed my mind.

—Amended version of "Casey Jones,"
by Jerry Garcia and the Grateful Dead, 1970

THE GRATEFUL DEAD'S "NOTION" HAD JUST crossed *my* mind because I'd spent the bulk of the seven hour, 107 kilometer train trip from Danang to Hue hemmed in by delightful young Vietnamese university students, who wanted to practice their English, with only chances here and there to enjoy the scenery. But I am getting ahead of myself.

I decided to skip Danang (Da Nang to Vietnamese). I was in Vietnam to see the country, not the War, and more than many other places, Danang had come to be a symbol of it.

The first U.S. ground combat troops (U.S. military "advisers" had been there since 1961) in-country landed at Danang. Two battalions of U.S. Marines (3,500 men) waded ashore from Navy landing craft on March 8, 1965. At first the Marines came to provide security for the airbase outside the city. Later Danang and the base at Chu Lai became headquarters for the Marine AO (Area of Operation), which included the DMZ and the far north of South Vietnam. Most of the toughest, most brutal fighting of the war (A Shau Valley, Khe Sanh, Hamburger Hill) took place from Danang northward, in the Marine

AO. China Beach, below Danang on the South China Sea, became an in-country R & R center, a favorite haunt for U.S. troops.

I took a taxicab (automotive, not human powered) from the Danang airport to the train station. I approached the ticket window, confronting there a choice between reserved seating in a passenger coach or a journey on a wooden bench, in a passenger car jammed with Vietnamese (no tourists ride there). I opted for the cheap ticket, "riding the hard seat." I settled down on a train station bench to read my book. I had an hour before the local departed for Hue, 107 kilometers to the north.

When the local train chugged in, I boarded the passenger car, which had rows of wooden seats with backs on them, like church pews. Unlike church pews, the seats were open ended. The car was three-quarters full. I was the only white person in the car. In fact I may have been the only white person who had ever ridden this train. I settled into a forward facing hard seat. Across from me was a rear facing seat into which settled a young (mid-thirties) Vietnamese physician, returning to Hue, and an extremely attractive Vietnamese woman, in her late twenties, I would say. They didn't know each other but were not unfriendly, to each other or to me.

We had four places for three people in our little space. Forward of us, at the head of the railcar, two or three uniformed railroad personnel (conductors?) along with two uniformed security guards (army? police?) had another, larger space. They too were all smiles, not threatening as they would have been on an East German or Czech train. Rather than patrol up and down the cars, they immediately nestled into their set of benches at the front of the car. They dealt out a deck of cards, beginning their game before we left the station, smoking, laughing, and paying some (but not a lot) of attention to what was going on around them. Occasionally one official would rise to go about some assigned task but would quickly return.

Shortly after leaving the station and the suburbs of Danang the train turned inland from the coast and began a slow, slow climb up the mountains. We were headed for Hai Van Pass, (Col de Nuages— Cloudy Pass— to the French), over the east-west spur of the mountains which reaches all the way to the sea north of Danang. The landscape became increasingly barren, as we climbed to an elevation of 1,300 meters.

The pass, and the east-west mountain spur of which it is part, are important for several reasons. One, the pass marks the northern most extremity of the Champa Empire, the Hindu civilization which ruled central Vietnam until the fifteenth century. Two, although several degrees of latitude short of the imaginary line (the Tropic of Cancer at 23.5° N), the pass marks the end of the tropics in Vietnam. Third, the pass marks the North's beginning, not merely for weather but for subtle changes in mannerisms and attitudes, political and otherwise, of the inhabitants. It is not yet North Vietnam politically but from here on up, Vietnamese people are more conservative, more plainly dressed, a tad reserved.

Like the north of Australia (the Kimberly, Darwin, Kakadu), Vietnam has two seasons, the "wet" and the "dry." In the south (Danang, Qui Nhon, Nha Trang, Phan Thiet), the wet, or monsoon, season lasts from June until September or October. The rain is heavy, and the temperature turns cold, at least for a Vietnamese (or a Westerner who has been there for a time). Temperatures sink to 60 degrees Fahrenheit (14-15 degrees Celsius). Most Europeans, and many North Americans, would regard such temperatures as ideal rather than cold.

From Hai Van Pass north (Hue, the DMZ and into North Vietnam), the monsoon season is different, beginning later (late September, early October). The air becomes much colder, at times sinking into the 30s (3-5 degrees Celsius). Some snow falls, usually up in the mountains and passes but not always so confined. The monsoon continues well into December.

Up and up the train goes. Out the side windows you can see the locomotive ahead navigating the curve of a switchback. Later you can see the cars in the rear while your car is in the curve. More hauntingly, you can see the concrete guard towers the Marines built to guard the railroad and mountain pass. Perhaps five meters high, blackened with mildew, and long abandoned now, these towers once held up to five young Marines each, armed with rifles and a machine gun. You can envision just how spooky the place would be on a moonless night, with wisps of fog curling around, the Viet Cong seeming to be everywhere. It makes the hair on your neck bristle.

Over the pass, down a bit and into the forest the train goes. This local train is the lifeblood for the Vietnamese villages through which it passes. At each village, the train stops while passengers unload truckloads of goods purchased in Danang and with which they will stock their shops. There are no trucks to meet the train—everything is carted off by hand. Bundle after bundle is set down on the parallel tracks, then carried off to the platform and beyond. Meanwhile, passengers get out of the passenger cars, squatting by the trackside, smoking, visiting, cooling off. Vendors come through the train selling food, including stew or soup (*pho* is the national broth with noodles, peppers, perhaps meat) from a large pot on a bamboo pole balanced over their shoulder. The pot is counterbalanced by another large pot filled with bowls, cups, and utensils, slung on the opposite end of the pole. Other venders go along the train at track side, reaching up and through the cars' windows. The unloading process takes at least twenty minutes at each stop. You sense that the train stop, at least on a Saturday, is an event.

Eventually, all, or nearly all, of the officials in my car went out of their way to pause or stop by, making it clear how pleased they were to have an American tourist riding the train and in their car, with one exception. At dusk, we stopped for twenty minutes in the middle of nowhere. Twelve to fourteen Vietnamese men in undershirt vests came huffing and puffing out of the forest, a large timber on their shoulders. Sweating profusely, they loaded a score or more large logs or timbers into a box car up ahead. I went to snap a photo but one of the officials, smiling, wagged a finger at me. My guess is that loading timber on a passenger train, in the middle of nowhere, without any modern equipment, or any equipment at all, was not that sensitive from a security standpoint. Instead, the government did not want tourists to bring home indications of just how primitive conditions in Vietnam could be.

All this while the young physician across from me makes fun of and then corrects my halting Vietnamese. He plays matchmaker, telling me how much the attractive woman next to him likes me. She smiles, playing along. The doctor, whose English is quite good, makes not so very thinly veiled references about the sexual relations that could take place between me and the woman, young enough to be my daughter. I am coming down with a cold so the doctor retrieves from a medical bag some medicine for my cold. When you get to know them, many Vietnamese are like that—very friendly, earthy, and sexually explicit.

Halfway through my slow train ride from Danang to Hue, Nguyen Thien Nhan, age twenty, besieges me. Nhan and his brothers (Dung, Tuan, and Hung) grew up in Quang Tri City, close by the DMZ, the scene of much fighting and mostly destroyed in the War. The War, of course, ended before the Nguyen brothers were born: they have no direct memory of it. Now the brothers are students at the University of Hue, returning from a school excursion to Danang.

Nhan claims never to have seen a Westerner. Soon Nhan and his brothers crowd into the facing bench seats and the small space between them.

The Nguyen brothers, at times joined by a friend or two, are curious, friendly, desirous of practicing English, and overall like a pack of enthusiastic puppy dogs. They all speak at once. As many Vietnamese are, they are physical with one another, resting an arm around another's shoulder, sitting close to, almost on top of, one another. Soon one or the other has an arm resting around my shoulders.

The students' English is good, a bit better than the town policemen in Phan Thiet. Because of all the tones (six), glottal stops, and other refinements involved in speaking Vietnamese, the Nguyen brothers have the same difficulty as other Vietnamese do when attempting to speak English. Without recitation and repetition, they do not have a feel how to pitch it right, even though they study incessantly and have become proficient reading and writing it.

So the brothers went quite beyond the English practice directed at me in the street. Everywhere I went, at least off the beaten track (outside Saigon and Hanoi), I got "Hello," "Where you from?," and "You American?," from Vietnamese I passed in the street as well as those who never or seldom had before seen a Westerner, followed me for several blocks.

Here, on the train, with university students doing the practicing, the sophistication level was higher:

"What your job?" Which I corrected to "What is your job?"

"Where you work?" Corrected to "Where do you work?

"Are you married?" They seem to be catching on to the need for verbs in their sentences.

"Do you have children? How many? Boys or girls?" Vietnamese seemed to have an inordinate interest in family details. They would have regarded with suspicion a fifty-year-old male who said he was not married. It also would arouse suspicion if that male said he was married but had no children (I have two daughters and I showed the Nguyen brothers photos I carried in my wallet).

From questions, we went on to practicing declaratory sentences, each of which the brothers, or some of them, would say over and over, trying to find the correct pitch:

"I am studying biology. I will be doctor some day." As with many persons whose first language is not English, early stage English-speaking Vietnamese have a tendency to drop articles, or not to include them in the first place. I kept correcting them on this one but made little headway.

"Good morning. Is it not a beautiful day?" This entry into the conversation sounded as though it was largely from an English-Vietnamese phrasebook. The construction was a bit stilted to boot. But I let it go. "Good. Good English."

And so it went, for three or four hours.

My seatmates, the physician and the young woman, were incredibly patient. These young boys first intruded upon, then took over, our small space. They stayed there for over three hours. The older passengers with me did not object once, smiling and occasionally joining in on our practice session.

Darkness had long since fallen by the time we arrived in Hue. The 107 kilometer trip took seven hours, for an average of fifteen kilometers (nine miles) per hour.

The French colonial Hue train station is painted pink, with white trim, something straight out of Munchkin City in *The Wizard of Oz*. Coming out of the station at the end of the city's main street (Le Loi again), the humidity of the summer evening hits me like a face wash. A crown of cab drivers, hotel touts, and cyclo drivers crowds around, shouting, pleading, and gesturing for business.

I usually cut straight through that crowd. Sure enough, on the backside, a few paces beyond the crowd, I found an older, quieter cyclo driver to take me to my hotel. I sat in the wicker cyclo chair with my suitcase beside me. Soon we left behind the lighted courtyard in front of the station, the cyclo driver pedaling at a medium speed.

There are no street lights. The Perfume River is on my left, as the driver pedals the three kilometers down Le Loi Street, toward the hotel. You sense rather than see other bicycles moving about you in the darkness. Occasionally a motor bike zips by. The breeze in my face feels cool. My eyes adjust. I can see the quarter moon shining on the river. I like Hue instantly.

Portions of the riverside had once been given over to the "social evils" of drugs, drink, prostitution, and gambling. In one of its periodic crackdowns, the Communist government had cleared it all away again, apparently as late as the 1980s. None of that was apparent by the time I got there. I found the riverside and the night journey along it enchanting.

At the opposite end of the riverside drive, the cyclo turned to take me two blocks "inland," back to my hotel. I checked in, stowed my gear, and headed back over to the river where I would eat dinner in the expensive four-star hotel (the New Century, I believe, and the following night in the floating restaurant a short way up river).

Midway there (over to the river), walking up a sandy side street, I am cut off by a very attractive Vietnamese woman, dressed in a plain cotton dress but one which reveals a curvaceous figure beneath it. She cuts me off with her bicycle. "You want to go boom-boom?" she questions, a smile on her pretty face.

Now I knew what she meant and was sorely tempted. My marriage of twenty-three years was beyond being on the rocks; for all intents and purposes, it was over. To boot, it was my birthday. I pondered, thought some more and then, very carefully stated, "No, I don't think so. I haven't eaten yet." Armies travel on their stomachs; I guess tourists do too, at least older ones.

The following morning, at 8:00, the Nguyen Thien brothers came to my hotel. I rented a bicycle (for $.25 U.S.). Together we bicycled the city. We crossed the river on the Trang Tien Bridge to the side (north?) where the precincts of the walled Imperial City, home of the emperors from 1802 until 1945, covers four square kilometers. We don't go in—I'll do that later on my own. Nhan and his brothers show me the university, the quarter of the city in which their apartment lay, and the grounds of the Quo Hoc (National School), the most prestigious secondary school in Vietnam.

All this time we practiced English. Nhan rode handlebar to handlebar with me, calmly speaking and asking questions. Meanwhile, Nhan was running me straight into the face of oncoming traffic. How do you say "Give me some space" in Vietnamese? Later I contrived to position myself on the inboard side, away from the traffic.

That afternoon I took my bicycle (by myself) into the countryside around Hue. My objective was to navigate an eighteen kilometer circle, visiting the elaborate tombs the Nguyen emperors built for themselves. At one point, I took my bicycle across the Perfume River in a *sampan* serving as a ferry boat, in order to visit the tomb of Emperor Nguyen Minh Mang. I got lost on the jungle trails. An older man came by on a motor bike, signaling me to follow him down a series of narrow trails. I thought how twenty-nine years before I would not have lasted five minutes on those trails. The VC or NVA troops would have gotten me if a booby trap had not.

I cut my tour short after seeing only two of the emperors' tombs. The tourist admission for each tomb was $6 USD while for Vietnamese it was free. The price disparity, which got to me from time to time (not always) as I travelled through Vietnam, took a cumulative toll on me personally. I cut short my planned tour, heading back into Hue.

The Vietnamese built the Imperial City along the lines of the Forbidden City in Beijing but with French influences. The City actually is three cities, each one within another. The outer walls are twenty feet high while the innermost sanctum, the Purple Forbidden City, was considered sacred. The enclosure contains the Temple of the Generations, the Temple of Harmony, and the Imperial Temple.

In the Tet Offensive, which began on January 31, 1968, the Viet Cong occupied 100 Vietnamese cities and towns. More than any other of these, Hue became the symbol of the Tet offensive. Hue was a not a military center. No garrison to speak of existed. A small air base existed at Phu Bai outside of town (now the commercial airport).

The VC then had little trouble occupying the city. As the U.S. Marines came to liberate the place, the occupiers withdrew into the Imperial City, raising the red and blue NLF flag with the yellow star over the central tower. Three weeks of some of the fiercest fighting of the War followed, destroying much of the Imperial City. In the United States, nightly televised news casts showed U.S. Marines emptying clips of M-16 ammunition over the walls. Ninety thousand of Hue's 140,000 citizens were left homeless. Viet Cong went house to house, arresting clerics, university professors, anyone with any contact with the government, corporate officials, and suspected "collaborators." They executed 12,000 or more, dumping some bodies in mass graves while leaving others in the street.

In 1995 some breaches in the walls existed while repair workers had bricked up others, which you can pick out because the bricks were new, not moss-covered or weathered. Some of the temples had been rebuilt.

I paid admission to the Purple Forbidden City where all that then remained was the Royal Reading Room. Within those innermost walls, and despite the destruction, I found it serene. I sat on the grass for an hour, bought an inexpensive painting, and walked to the river and across the Phu Xuan Bridge to the commercial side of the city.

At Phu Bai, southeast of the city, the concrete pill boxes and guard towers the U.S. built to guard the airbase still were there, lining the airport perimeter and looking forlorn. The air terminal was a 1930's style barn with plate glass windows out on to the runway, a former hanger perhaps. Unlike Ton Su Nhut in Saigon, or Nha Trang airports, which had been empty, the terminal and even runway aprons at Hue were crowded with thousands of Vietnamese. They were not, however, fellow air travelers.

The Hue professional soccer team, which I think played in a lower division, had won the championship. The team was now flying back from their victory, arriving triumphant in Hue. As the football team's plane taxied into the terminal, fans on the airport apron crowded around. Then all hell broke loose. Fans in cars drove out onto the runway, flags fluttering, passengers sounding large air horns, drivers laying on car horns. Hundreds of them, cars that is, thousands of soccer fans raced up and down, back and forth, on the runway, the taxiway, and the apron. It was the most spontaneous demonstration or celebration I ever saw in Vietnam. No American or European airport would ever permit such a thing.

So the repressive, hard bitten, xenophobic, humorless Vietnamese government had lightened up a bit or, more likely, government officials had let this one get by them. I worried about it though. I had to board an Air Vietnam turboprop sitting at the gate, to which no one seemed to pay the slightest attention. The turboprop would have to navigate its way out from the terminal, dodging cars, people, and other obstacles, and take off on a runway still crowded with gleeful and joyous soccer fans. Despite having fought there in 1966-67, I sized it up as one of the biggest risks I faced during my several times in Vietnam.

THREE TASTES OF NƯỚC MẮM

15

North Versus South

The North is quite different. In the North, the people and the government are one. You need to be more careful what you as a tourist do or say. The Northerners are bigger, heavier, more stoic, and clear on who won the war.

They're real Reds up there.

—Nelson De Mille, *Up Country* (2002)

The Communists of North Vietnam won the War but lost the peace.

—Tom Bissell, *The Father of All Things: A Marine, His Son, and the Legacy of Vietnam* (2007)

MY WORRIES WERE MISPLACED. The runway at Phu Bai airport quickly cleared, as the cars and fans rushed to join the cavalcade which would follow the victorious football team into Hue. The Air Vietnam ATR 72 taxied out, with me on it, taking off toward the ocean.

We were headed for North Vietnam, for Hanoi. Now even though shortly after I returned from my tour of duty I had become opposed to American involvement in Vietnam's war, I felt that journeying to enemy territory, Hanoi and the North, was mildly treasonous. I couldn't suppress feelings that I was about to give aid and comfort to the opposition. Unlike Jane Fonda ("Hanoi Jane"), who had journeyed to North Vietnam during the War, posing for photographs on an antiaircraft gun used to shoot down U.S. warplanes, I was going after the War, and strictly as a tourist, not for propaganda purposes.

Jane Fonda's second husband, Tom Hayden, whom she married a few years later, was a strident opponent of the Vietnam War who said, "We are all Viet Cong now." Well, count me out—I didn't feel that way in the slightest and never have. Viet Cong were ruthless brutal terrorists who murdered hundreds of thousands of innocent people.

Putting my feelings of unease aside, I looked about the Air Vietnam plane. My seat mate was a thin, very old Vietnamese man with a wispy goatee. Vietnamese refer to Ho Chi Minh as *Bac Ho*, or Uncle Ho, which was Ho Chi Minh's favorite nickname late in life, a name he encouraged his fellow citizens to use (Ho Chi Minh, of course, had many favorite names during his life). Born Nguyen Sinh Cung in Nghe An Province, "whose people are known as the most obdurate rebellious of the Vietnamese," says Ho's biographer William Duiker, he renamed himself Nguyen Tat Thanh in 1890. After that Ho used many aliases, sometimes to shield him from official scrutiny and sometimes merely for effect. Tom Bissell, in *The Father of All Things*, reels off twenty aliases Ho used over the years. Ho Chi Minh in fact was an alias meaning "Bringer of Light" (or "Bringer of Enlightenment").

Vietnamese, or some of them, also refer to old gentlemen with wispy beards with the honorific *Bac Ho*. On the airplane, when the flight attendant served the in-flight meal, the *Bac Ho* next to me took the tray but it quickly became evident that he did not know how to use silverware ("the cutlery"). Bac Ho was a poor farmer who had eaten with his hands or with chopsticks all his life. Here on the airplane, Bac ate the entire meal using only the knife.

I could have been mistaken. Bac Ho could have spent his formative years in Paris, where he learned to eat with a knife by watching French people eat cheese. But I doubt it. He seemed as though he had never flown before.

The two-tiered price system existent throughout Vietnam eventually begins to rub its intended victims, tourists, the wrong way but here was one of its benefits. I did not pay an exorbitant airfare for this leg of my trip. I am certain that Bac Ho paid considerably less, which is very much the way I think it ought to be. I did not object at all.

Taxi cabs were scarce so I shared a ride in from the Hanoi airport to the center city with a young German lawyer and a British tourist. I booked in to the small non-descript hotel in which the German had reservations. I hit the streets to begin my three-day stay in Hanoi.

You immediately recognize what Nelson De Mille described as "two distinct Vietnams—sunny, noisy, smiley, somewhat disordered in the South: gray, quiet and sober in the North." Hanoi street life reinforces feelings of unease about being in the North. Two of five adult males wear green NVA uniform shirts; even more wear the pith helmet with the red star, the emblem of the People's Army of Vietnam (PAVN), what we knew as the NVA. An occasional person wears NVA trousers as well. No one in the South wears military garb of any kind.

In Hanoi I got dirty looks and bore-a-hole-through-you stares from other pedestrians, if only as momentary flashes of hostility, for the first time since I had arrived in Vietnam. When I got a bit lost, by mistake turning off into a residential street, some boys threw a rock at me. I didn't know whether it was teenage hooliganism or hostility toward an American, probably perceived as a returning vet. In Hanoi, I received none of the "hellos" which a Westerner would receive walking the streets of a southern city. Northerners, it is said, are reserved, most decidedly not spontaneous, not nearly as relentlessly entrepreneurial as Southerners.

Of course the Northerners won the War, thereby evading re-education camp. You would think that based upon that score alone they would be ebullient, but they're not.

In 1995, who won the War was evident in other ways. Hanoi's old quarter is a knockoff of the shopping district of Paris. Each of Hanoi's thirty-six shopping streets houses vendors of a particular line of goods: pots, pans, and kitchen utensils in one street; shoes and leather goods in the next ; side by side by side electronics vendors in the next;

lumber and building materials around the corner. The quantity and quality of goods available was superior to anything available in the South. I saw booth after booth, fifteen or more of them right in a row, stocked with Scotch whiskeys, Kentucky bourbons, gin and vodka. A block from my tourist hotel was a row of booths selling fruit juices (*nuoc ep*), more than a dozen kinds of juice available at each booth.

I walked to the Hoan Kiem district, which surrounds a lovely mid-size lake. In Hanoi, there are a number of picture postcard small lakes, with parks adjacent to them but Hoan Kiem is the focal point of central Hanoi. Close by Hoan Kiem is the French-built Catholic Cathedral, which faces a plaza near the lake and the park which surrounds it. I went into an art gallery on the side of the cathedral plaza, buying a water color of two Hmong tribesmen in red and blue ethnic dress. I still have it, framed and hanging on my wall.

I turned to grimmer tasks. I wanted to see the Hanoi Hilton, one of the prisons where the North Vietnamese kept downed American flyers, some for as long as seven years. The prison was only a short distance away, purposely located by the Vietnamese to forestall bombing of that district. Occupying a triangular city block, the French built Hao Lo jail dated from 1900 and was painted a deceiving pastel yellow but with tell-tale concertina wire on the tops of the twenty foot walls. Save for one heavy door, there were no openings whatsoever in the enclosure. It was surprisingly small (and, I am told, no longer exists, while a real Hanoi Hilton, this one an actual hotel, does).

A guy a year ahead of me in high school, Ed Mechenbier, graduated from the Air Force Academy and became a fighter pilot. Eddie was one of the first pilots the North Vietnamese shot down and captured. He was one of those who spent the longest in captivity. I walked twice around the Hanoi Hilton, contemplating, praying a little bit, and thinking how, by comparison, I had it easy my year in Vietnam.

My sightseeing done for the day, I headed for the Hotel Metropole, the social center of Hanoi, at least for visiting Westerners. Built in the late nineteenth century and first opened in 1901, but recently remodeled and added to, the Metropole was a center of things for me, including a glass of wine, fine French cuisine, and a bakery with croissants, brioches, and *pan du chocolat*.

The following day, a rainy Sunday, I arose early to beat what I anticipated would be a crowd at the Ho Chi Minh Mausoleum, set in the Embassy District east of the old quarter where I was staying. In 1968-69, television news in the United States reported, seemingly nightly, about the bombing of North Vietnam. You are surprised, then, to find that central Hanoi is, one, largely untouched by aerial bombardment and, two, quaint, in some parts very French and European. Even though the French occupied Saigon and surrounding areas first (as Cochin China, in 1861) and the North last (as Tonkin, in 1891), it was Hanoi, rather than Saigon, which in 1902 became the seat of the French colonial administration.

The Embassy District is filled with broad tree-lined boulevards, lined with grand French colonial residences and ministry buildings colored with that Cheez Whiz orange-yellow stucco. Several of these streets lead toward Ho Chi Minh's Mausoleum, although the tourist is tempted to wander down the side streets. I had to keep on schedule, though, so I resisted the temptation.

As you approach the parade ground area on the side of which the mausoleum is located, the North Vietnamese have built concrete block guardhouses on the wide sidewalks. On each approach toward the mausoleum a guardhouse sits on each block, for three or four blocks, out of character with the otherwise tree-lined European feel of the neighborhood. Security appears to be paramount, as though the North Vietnamese fear an imminent attempt to steal Ho Chi Minh's corpse.

I passed by the first guardhouse I encountered. The three guards inside appeared to be sleeping, or otherwise occupied. I got the sense that they were there for show, not particularly for security.

A block later, as I passed the second guardhouse on that approach, all hell broke loose. One guard blew a shrill whistle. Two others grabbed rifles, scrambling out of the guardhouse, blocking my path. All of this occurred at 7:00 A.M. on a Sunday morning, on deserted rainy streets, mind you. The guards gestured to me that I had to retreat, going back the way I had come.

After several feints, I found the avenue open to the parade ground. The whole episode with its requirement that Ho Chi Minh's mausoleum could be approached in one way, and one way only, seemed emblematic of the rigidity North Vietnamese seem to bring to everything.

Even at 7:30 on a rainy morning the line to the mausoleum was long. You approach on an asphalt pathway through a wide grass parade ground. The mausoleum is a marble columned miniature Greek Parthenon with wings of marble steps radiating out from either side. These wings form the reviewing stands for government sponsored parades and celebrations.

Despite the large amount of open space, eight to ten acres at least, the visitors, all Vietnamese save me, stood in a smallish area, in an orderly single file, like Londoners queuing at a bus stop. Guards in white uniforms with white gloves patrolled the line, maintaining order, although everyone in the line stayed hush-hush, not the least sign of disorder present. Signs forbade bare shoulders, shorts, collarless shirts, cameras, and who knows what else. The gleaming white guards policed these restrictions with stringency.

The line moves quickly. Once in the mausoleum's doors, there are white uniformed guards with rifles and fixed bayonets at every five paces. The air is cool; the lights are quite dim. The line snakes to the left, up a ramp, reverses direction, and goes up another ramp. You go through a doorway and into the crypt for a 270 degree walk-around of the glass case enclosing Ho Chi Minh's body.

To visiting Vietnamese, Ho Chi Minh is a revered figure—a saint to many. Men and women gasp as they view the corpse. People can be seen wiping away tears. In his lifetime, though, Bac Ho was always near gaunt, even as a young man appearing very thin. In death, Ho has gained ten kilograms, or even more. The corpse is corpulent; the remains approach Mao-like proportions. The body is dressed in a plain gray tunic with a high collar, much as Ho Chi Minh was pictured when alive.

Each year the Vietnamese ship Ho Ch Minh to Russia. There, the same technicians who maintain Vladimir Lenin's corpse touch up Ho's remains. Evidently, they do not have available to them a photo, for in death they have made Ho Chi Minh what he never was in life, corpulent.

The entire display smacks of cult creation. Ho Chi Minh was somewhat of a modest man who before death requested that his remains be cremated with his ashes scattered over the region near Hue where he was born. His successors ignored Ho's testamentary directions, creating the cult of Ho Chi Minch.

Outside of the mausoleum, the "Ho Chi Minh trail," the Hanoi City one that is, and the cult creation, begin in earnest. There is a pond. On the shore of the pond, the Vietnamese had re-constructed Ho's rural *pied-a-terre*, which they transported plank-by-plank to the urban site in Hanoi. The house is a simple two room wooden dwelling, up on stilts to let air circulate beneath it, typical of North Vietnam.

After the tour of that station on the trail, the Ho Chi Minh museum is next. The displays in the museum recount episodes in Ho's life interspersed with displays of abstract art objects, most of which have an anti-American slant. My personal favorite is the gallery in which the front of a 1958 Edsel automobile protrudes from the wall—as a symbol of American decadence. Many Westerners visiting the museum may receive an impression other than the commercial, military, and moral bankruptcy of the U.S. Some may feel they are in a Hard Rock Café rather than a museum. Others may find the whole display laughable.

A third impression, however, is of Ho Chi Minh's greatness. From his return to Vietnam in 1939 to his death forty years later, Ho labored first to free Vietnam from oppressive French colonial rule and then to unify the country. Ho's persistence led to the defeat of two superpowers, France and the United States. Although in the last few years of his life, Ho's successors rendered Ho less and less influential, Ho Chi Minh became the symbol, and remains the symbol, of a sizeable nation.

Yet many would say that Ho Chi Minh's obdurateness, duplicity, and hypocrisy lead not only to nearly thirty unremitting years of war but also to Vietnam's ensuing twenty years in the Dark Ages. Recrimination, re-education, brutality, torture, murder, execution, and desecration with the absolute primacy of ideology over economics or anything else followed the War. Six to seven million or more Vietnamese died or fled Vietnam. A small group of aged, rigid, and brutal war mongers, Ho Chi Minh's protégés, ran the country into the ground. You cannot deny Ho Chi Minh's greatness but neither can you affirm it. Certainly many harbor misgivings about certain of the things Ho Chi Minh did or achieved.

****

I spent the afternoon wandering the avenues of Hanoi. Late in the afternoon I stopped in a tourist hotel down the street from my own. I went to the bar for a bottle of beer, meeting two other visitors, a German lawyer and a French-Canadian engineer. Both were frequent visitors to Vietnam, the latter because his company bid on various road construction projects, being the winning bidder on a project to expand Highway One from south of Hanoi to above the old DMZ. Of course there was little or no traffic there: traffic and bottlenecks on Highway One were problems quite far from there, in the South. But, hey, North Vietnam won the War. The Northerners were determined not only to reap the spoils but make very visible their intent to do so.

Neither of my new friends enjoyed their repeat visits to Vietnam. For one thing, both objected strenuously to the way in which Vietnam tourism sites, transportation, hotels, and the like have a two-tiered price structure, obviously to rip-off the foreign visitor. But these fellows went further.

They believed that the Vietnamese government's reason for accumulating foreign exchange, in this as well as in other ways, was not to better the lot of the people, but to replenish and expand military weapons systems. Vietnam's military arsenal, dating from the mid years of the war (1967-69), had long since become obsolete. Spare parts for much of their antiquated weaponry (mostly Russian, some Chinese) were unavailable at any price.

Nor were the Russians and the Chinese prone to give any kind of further foreign aid to Vietnam. Even before the War ended, China and Russia tired of pouring yuan and rubles down what they regarded as a sink hole. Mother Russia and the People's Republic of China wanted the War to end as badly as did the United States. Although each contributed to the North only about 1/7th of the $15 billion the U.S. did annually to the South, nonetheless they contributed a large amount each. Both Russia and China came to regard the Hanoi leadership as truculent, bellicose, intransigent, deceptive, and thoroughly uncooperative, yet always asking for more. The notion that North Vietnamese leaders would even listen to Russian advice was a fiction.

Twenty years after the war ended in 1975, according to my friends, the North Vietnamese leadership remained the same—militant, argumentative, spoiling for fights all over the place. The Vietnamese had occupied Cambodia for eleven years, sending 100,000 troops there. They had two border disputes with China and another with Thailand in the Gulf of Thailand, one of which, in 1989, caused China to invade and occupy Vietnamese territory for seventeen days. Several other disputes concern the Spratly Islands in the South China Sea, to which Vietnam claims title, together with 200 surrounding miles. The rights to explore and exploit the mineral wealth in the Spratly Islands area involved big stakes for countries in the region.

But no country in the region was as bellicose and militaristic as North Vietnam. Although there was no love lost between Vietnam and the United States, Vietnam was eager to obtain the re-establishment of diplomatic relations it achieved via President Clinton in 1994. One reason was to have access to a potential source for updating its arsenal. A second reason was to create a powerful new ally to counter China's influence in the region. In accepting an alliance with Vietnam, my European friends warned, the U.S. should be on guard against Vietnam's deceptive ways and nefarious motives.

This session very much surprised me. The few tourists I had met (Australians, Irish, Dutch) thus far in my travels had all looked upon the end of the War and the re-opening of Vietnam as good things, harbingers of an even better future. Now here were two repeat visitors to Vietnam who painted a distinctly different picture, a Trojan Horse depiction of Vietnam's outward gestures of good will.

That night I paid for my three days' lodging, asking about a taxi for my early morning ride to the airport, thirty-five kilometers away. The Ocean Pacific Hotel manager said "not to worry," he would arrange for a car and driver in the morning. Early the next day, the driver came in a relatively new, clean Toyota, burgundy in color as I remember. After putting my luggage in the trunk and installing me in the rear seat, the driver set off, but not directly for the airport. I objected to his roundabout route. He explained that he had to jog out of the way to get gas. So I sat back, relaxed: I had plenty of time.

We stopped at a place with a gas pump but the driver took very little time. In retrospect, I don't think he got gas at all. Our little detour was just a charade to buy time for the other player in the scam to get out to the airport.

At the Hanoi Airport, the Ocean Pacific Hotel manager was waiting in front of the departures door, his motorcycle parked by the curb.

I greeted him as Vietnamese traditionally would one another: "*Chao anh*," I said, using the familiar honorific ("Hello, brother") for someone you knew. No traditional greeting for him. Waving his arms, he accused me of not paying for my lodging for the past three nights, demanding $90 U.S. on the spot. Well, I had been smart enough (I am not always smart) to obtain a receipt the evening before. I produced it. He waved the receipt away, having the audacity to claim that the receipt was for food: I still owed for lodging.

So there I stand, my backpack and suitcase locked in the trunk of the car. The friendly car driver (friendly to him, not to me) stands there doing nothing, refusing to unlock the trunk. My flight leaves in thirty-five minutes. At best it's a stalemate.

After smiling, attempting to go with the flow, and discovering that such an approach will not work, I bellow at the top of my lungs, "*Cong An, Cong An*," meaning policeman. My few words of Vietnamese work. My shouts for the police quickly end the attempt at a scam. The driver hurriedly unlocks the trunk while the hotel manager hops his motorcycle and roars off. I grab my luggage, shoulder aside the car driver, and disappear into the terminal.

Each and every day of my 1995 journey through Vietnam some misadventure befell me—rip-off by a cyclo driver, pocket picked, interrogation by the immigration police, attempted theft of my luggage (multiple times)—and now this, an attempted holdup outside the airport. But through it all, I survived.

The flight was an Air Vietnam airbus from Hanoi to Bangkok. The flight deck and cabin crews were French (Vietnamese pilots were sent off for re-education and now worked in rice paddies). The pilot himself was a tall, Gallic figure with an oversized nose, prominent teeth, hands on hips, and dramatic pose after pose. All of the flight announcements were in French—crew members did not bother with Vietnamese.

Backtracking, I checked in at the counter. I found that first class was only an additional $75 USD. The notion of first class travel in a

Communist country, on the country's flagship carrier, seemed somehow decadent, which appealed to me. Then I thought of all the misadventures that had befallen me, and the scam that I just had foiled. The older adage, "Living well is the best revenge," came to mind and was the clincher. I paid the $75, boarded the airplane, snuggled into my first class seat, accepted a coffee, and prepared to leave Vietnam for the second time in my life.

16

Legacy of the War and the Dark Ages

Shortly after Saigon's fall... Truong Chinh, one of North Vietnam's most bloodthirsty ideologues, announced that the Party would "level" all differences between the North and the South. The "poisonous weeds" of capitalism had to be pulled up and burned. The long... communist refurbishment had begun.

—Tom Bissell, *The Father of All Things: A Marine, His Son, and the Legacy of Vietnam* (2007)

Yes, we defeated the United States. But now we are plagued by problems. We do not have enough to eat. We are a poor, undeveloped nation. Waging war is simple. Running a country is difficult.

—Vietnamese Prime Minister Phan Van Dong, 1984

ITS IMPOVERISHED STATE DID NOT PREVENT Vietnam from sending 100,000 soldiers to Cambodia, occupying that country for eleven years (1978-89). After it had conquered South Vietnam, North Vietnam waged war with the People's Republic of China—twice. The bellicose Vietnamese government also has had ongoing border disputes with Thailand, China, Laos, and Cambodia.

Vietnam, as it existed in 1995 and to some extent as it exists today, can only be explained or understood against the background of what occurred in the Dark Ages. Fettered by doctrinaire "Marxist handcuffs," an aged Politburo caused Vietnam to be walled off from any significant foreign contact, for nearly twenty years. More moderate Politburo members allowed themselves to be shouted down, overruled by "attack dogs" such as Le Duan or Truong Chinh. Walled off as Vietnam was, the world outside Vietnam could not see the ruthlessness and brutality caused by the many changes the vindictive government attempted to bring about within the country, particularly in the South.

By invading Cambodia, Vietnam bought itself further insulation from the world, as in 1979 U.S. President Jimmy Carter placed a complete embargo on all trade with Vietnam, just as Carter later ordered a U.S. boycott of the 1980 Moscow Olympics, as a sanction for Russia's invasion of Afghanistan. Of course history now shows that, surly and bellicose as they were, the invading Vietnamese ousted Pol Pot, whose maniacal mayhem murdered over two million Cambodians, nearly fifty percent of that small nation's population. In so doing Vietnam did the world a service. Nonetheless, the U.S. embargo stayed in place until 1994 when President Bill Clinton lifted it.

Of course the Vietnamese had mixed motives in Cambodia. After Prince Sihanouk resigned, in 1970, an inept Communist government under General Lon Nol had come to power. Leading his own Khmer Rouge communist movement, Pol Pot ousted Lon Nol in 1975, leading an ideology-driven, maniacal, surreal government. To interdict the senseless mass murder by the Khmer Rouge, Vietnam invaded.

Events in Cambodia also bought about an even more overt movement by the Khmer threatening Vietnam. Vietnamese leaders worried about incursions by the Cambodians into the Delta region (the far south). Over two million (estimates run anywhere from one to seven million) Kymer—smaller, darker skinned than the Vietnamese, ethnically quite different—made their home in the Delta. Kymer also were practitioners of the world-wide dominant strain of Theravada rather than Mahayana Buddhism, which prevailed in Vietnam. To a degree, the Kymer were separate and apart from the Vietnamese, susceptible to cooperation with incursions by Cambodia. The underground name for the Delta, Kampuchea Krom, means "South Cambodia." Some cities of the Delta, such as Tra Vinh, are for most purposes, except for the flag which flies over them, Cambodian.

Of course only with the passage of time have we become aware that by their overthrow of Pol Pot and his crazy regime (think "The Killing Fields") the Vietnamese performed a service for mankind. But the Cambodian invasion by Vietnam also symbolized the head-strong essence of the government that had come to power in Hanoi and in Vietnam, which had been able to solidify its position by virtue of the lengthy and ultimately useless dilly-dallying by Richard Nixon, Henry Kissinger, and the United States.

There were earlier indicators of the nature of this backward look-ing, doctrinaire Vietnamese government, which had begun to assume power even before Ho Chi Minh died in 1969. For example, the North Vietnamese regime closed all media outlets. As author Tom Bissell tallies, the one newspaper, one television station, and one radio station existent in the North, all Communist party controlled, replaced the twenty-three newspapers, three television stations, and ten radio stations that had existed in the South before the War ended.

After the War and the closing of Vietnam's borders, the Politburo and Central Committee forbade all books except those which con-tained "Lenin," "Marx," "Ho" or "Ho Chi Minh," or "Communist" or "Communism" in the title. They closed churches and pagodas. They caused to be desecrated, often by bull dozing, cemeteries containing ARVN war dead. They decreed that all citizens must go out into the streets each morning at 6:00 A.M. to take physical exercise.

Mimicking the progress (downward) of Russian socialism, the North Vietnamese collectivized agriculture, an especially dramatic reform in a country in which land reform had been a burning issue and, during the War, some progress had been made. Under the new ultra-communism, the rural peasant was made to give up the one to two hectares he and his forbearers had zealously sought to obtain.

Shaking his head at the folly of it, one North Vietnamese official captured the excess of it all: "We even collectivized the barbershops."

In 1978, the new government of all Vietnam abolished the institu-tion of private property. In accordance therewith, the government confiscated private businesses. They banned martial arts. They banned women from wearing the traditional *ao dai*. These edicts made Madame Nhu of the early 1960s appear to have been a libertine.

But the most severe government-instituted deprivations referenced personal liberty. The North Vietnamese executed many ARVN officers and South Vietnamese government officials (5,000 according to author Bissell, but other estimates run higher). The new government then ordered South Vietnamese lower down in government or less involved in the war effort to report for *Hoc Tap*, or reeducation camp. The 300,000 originally ordered to a month's indoctrination spent two or three years instead. Others of the one million South Vietnamese who endured re-education spent longer. As Tom Bissell reports, "...throughout the 1980s former ARVN generals were still being set free. In 1988 alone, eleven were released."

So the incredible waste of human capital may stand as the first of many legacies—the loss of great portions of the educated and skilled populace through re-education (effectively imprisonment) followed by relegation of many of the most skilled to menial occupations and callings.

A second legacy, is the loss of skilled and educated populace through ex-filtration from the country and its repressive, backwards regime. The boat people snuck out by sea. Additionally, a steady stream of refugees journeyed down a "trail of tears" through Cambodia and Laos to Thailand, where they spent months in refugee camps. The overall losses may have amounted to a million and a half of Vietnam's citizens, on top of those who left as the War was ending.

Third, 500,000 Chinese are thought to have returned to China or gone elsewhere after, in 1978, the Vietnamese government abolished private property and confiscated all privately owned businesses. The chance ever again of carrying on a business had evaporated. In Vietnam, as well as in most other Pacific Rim nations, large segments of the economy and of investment capital were controlled by the "overseas Chinese" who may have amounted only to two to three percent of the population, but controlled seventy-five percent or more of the capital. There are few, if any, of these skilled Chinese left in Vietnam.

Fourth, government decreed the collectivization of enterprises of all kinds, with the severe decrease in production of what had been the rice bowl of Southeast Asia. Widespread malnutrition and starvation occurred at intervals throughout the Dark Ages. Farmers would could produce three crops of rice in a year became lackadaisical as the government forced the contribution of their land into collectives. Soon, those same farmers produced a single crop per year, cutting production by two thirds.

Fifth, the surly, headstrong, bellicose spirit of the small ruling elite manifested itself in equipping and maintaining a large standing army and military engagements in Cambodia and with China. Arming a large force and sustaining its occupation abroad soaked up billions of Vietnam's gross domestic product.

Sixth, among the legacies of the Vietnam War, there existed a high rate of birth defects among young Vietnamese, attributed to the extensive use of the defoliant Agent Orange by the U.S. during the War. For the period of the Dark Ages especially, these deformed children, who numbered in the millions, had no access to rehabilitation, prostheses, or other medical care.

A principal birth defect has been Spina Bifida, an incomplete formation of the vertebrae, leaving portions of the spinal cord exposed. Effects of the condition include partial paralysis, lack of bowel control, fluid on the brain, and severe learning disabilities. Vietnamese physicians reported stillborn children with no spinal cord at all. Other defects reported as widespread included missing arms, legs, eyes, and organs growing outside of the body.

Operation Ranch Hand (the U.S. spraying of Agent Orange and Agent Blue) ceased in 1971. Estimates of exposure previous to cessation run as high as nearly five million Vietnamese. With birth rates being quite high during the Dark Ages the number of children at risk was correspondingly high. The silver lining, if it can be said that there was one, was that the dioxin exposure, which was the principal environmental hazard, had a half-life in humans of twelve years or less. The rate of defects decreased significantly among children conceived after the mid 1980s.

Wandering the cities and towns of Vietnam in 1995, I saw none, or very few, of these children, who would have been young adults or early middle aged by then. The reason I saw few may be that most of the children were so severely handicapped as not to be ambulatory, hidden away behind walls and in houses, leaving the visitor ill-quipped to judge the legacy's proportions. Or, severely handicapped as they were, many of these deformed individuals had died an early death.

Seventh, a high birth rate and population growth (excess of births over deaths) existed during much of the Dark Ages in Vietnam, a legacy of the War and the repression that followed. As is true in many repressive societies, lack of jobs and forced inactivity led to climbing birth rates, in Vietnam as high as 3.5 percent (the highest rates in the world are in Africa, with countries such as Senegal and the Congo approaching the five percent mark). In the late 1970s, the Vietnamese government issued family planning directives urging married couples to limit themselves to two children, but few obeyed and the government did little monitoring. As a result, by the time the country emerged from the Dark Ages, the population had more than doubled, to eighty-five million in 1999 and ninety-two million today.

Vietnam is now the thirteenth most populous nation on earth, ahead of Japan and Germany, both of which have negative rates of population growth. Catholic countries such as Spain (-.08) and Poland (-1.5) actually have declining populations (deaths exceed births). The United States has a positive but not robust population growth rate, at .97 percent.

Today, according to the United Nations, the birth rate in Vietnam is 1.9 percent, and the population growth stands at 1.4 percent. Vietnam experiences not as many deaths as might be expected because of a disproportionately small number of older people exists, a delayed effect of the War. Worrisomely, though, in 2002 the Vietnamese government rescinded its family planning directives.

Two problems then, legacies of the War, are how will Vietnam accommodate the population bulge of the Dark Ages, which is coming of age now, and the related problem of high future birth rates, which may eventuate, exasperated by the lack of jobs or other meaningful activity.

The eighth legacy: three million unexploded land mines scattered through parts of the Vietnamese countryside. The extent of this lingering aftereffect of the War is unknown, although it will be significantly less than in Cambodia where opposing forces indiscriminately planted a much greater number of land mines. Opposing forces in Cambodia also buried many land mines close in to towns and villages rather than in more remote locations, such as the Central Highlands in Vietnam. In Cambodia, at least where the government does not shoo them away, single and double amputees line the walks and pathways tourists use to explore Angkor Wat and parts of Pnom Phen, holding out begging bowls. I saw none of that in Vietnam.

Ninth, the lack of transparency and the high level of corruption which came out of and grew during the Dark Ages persist. When government holds so much power over individuals' lives, when the ruling elite (the Communist Party, numbered at two million, the Central Committee only 150) is small and distant, and when the front lines of civil servants are maltreated and poorly paid, the ingredients for corruption are present. These latter factors have increased the level of corruption even over what it had been in 1975.

Transparency of Switzerland, an authoritative NGO, each year publishes an index of most countries in the world. Transparency rates Nigeria (134) and Pakistan (143) as among the most corrupt populous countries on earth, while Myanmar, Sudan, and Somalia rank at the very bottom (178 or so). Denmark, New Zealand, Singapore, Finland, and Sweden rank at the top (least corrupt). Surprisingly, the United States ranks not particularly well (22), while its neighbor to the north, Canada, ranks as the sixth least corrupt nation.

Even today, Vietnam is far down that list, ranking 116th (below BRIC nations with which it must compete—Brazil (69), China (78), and India (87). Low paid officials in many countries hold out hands for so-called facilitating, or "grease," payments before they will expedite movement of imports through customs, sign off on safety or other regulatory compliance of a facility or building, or give some other go-ahead or approval. In Vietnam it goes beyond that. Foreigners wishing to progress in businesses there must pay "silent fees" to any number of Vietnamese. A portion of the fees will make their way to Vietnamese government officials.

Over half of the Vietnamese population is under age thirty-five. They have no memory of the War, although the legacies of the War and the Dark Ages greatly affect their lives.

Some of these effects of the War and of the Dark Ages are being ameliorated by more recent developments. For example, many younger persons of Vietnamese heritage, often born elsewhere, including in the United States, are returning to their ancestral country. These Viet Kieu speak other languages as well as Vietnamese, most particularly English. They have university degrees including MBAs. At first unwelcome, the Viet Kieu now have become an integral part of the Vietnamese business community. Their return makes up for some of the brain drain that occurred during the Dark Ages.

In addition, the full effect of the Clinton Administration's 1994 abolition of the Carter-era trade embargo on Vietnam was quickly becoming apparent, even in 1995. Once the embargo had been lifted, multinational corporations (MNCs) and others who located manufacturing facilities in Vietnam could export from those facilities to the United States, a large and essential market for many producers, particularly those in the garment, textile, and footwear industries.

Even before 1994, MNCs wanted to re-locate to Vietnam because of the low wage levels there, the industriousness of the Vietnamese people, and the escalation of wage levels in other countries where they previously had located manufacturing, such as Indonesia and Malaysia. MNCs could not do so because of the trade embargo.

Fast forwarding, those MNCs did re-locate to Vietnam once the U.S. lifted the embargo. In the twenty-first century, garment and textile manufacture has become Vietnam's largest industry, by far.

Many observant Vietnamese view neither the new constitution, nor *Doi Moi*, nor the changing of the guard at the Central Committee and Politburo, nor any other event, as the key turning point for Vietnam. They view President Clinton's abolition of the trade embargo as the beginning of a new dawn and a new day for their country.

Nonetheless, in the 1990s, although seemingly emergent from the Dark Ages, Vietnam was known as "the biggest investment tease in Asia." Foreigners wishing to do business could only do so in a joint venture, with a Vietnamese partner. Capable Vietnamese employees, consultants or advisors were scarce. One-time bribes and more durable "silent fees" had to be paid. Business partners as well as government officials were inefficient and arbitrary. It was clear that those who would succeed had to be prepared to run a marathon rather than a sprint. As Vietnam began the twenty-first century, what was clear was that the country remained less than half emergent from the Dark Ages, with many lingering effects of the War and the bleak years which followed it still present.

So, in 2011, I returned to Vietnam for my third lengthy visit to see if the country had progressed, putting legacies of the War behind it. I intended to determine how, good or bad, ill or nil, the country had fared since 1995. I went back to Vietnam for my third taste of *nuoc mam*.

TASTE THREE

RETURN TO VIETNAM–2011

Boxes of *nuoc mam* for sale in a local store.

17

Places Tourists Don't Go

There are few places in the world where so much has changed in so short a time.

—Mark Ashwill, *Vietnam Today* (2005)

In provincial Vietnam, one saw little of the frantic pace common to Saigon, Danang, and Hue, and as we came into Quy Nhon I noticed the easy manner with which the Qui Nhonese bicycled.

—Tom Bissell, *The Father of All Things: A Marine, His Son, and the Legacy of Vietnam* (2007)

WITH ALL THE CHANGE THAT HAS OCCURRED OTHER PLACES in Vietnam, one would think that in Phan Thiet, where I had been stationed in 1966, there wouldn't be any change, any change at all. The small city was a working town, a fishing town, where still in 1995 all of the streets remained unpaved, no street lights existed, and electricity and refrigeration were in short supply. There was one small hotel, a few guesthouses, a number of makeshift movie houses, chronic unemployment, and an all-pervading smell about the place.

When in 1995 I asked the mini-bus driver to let me off in Phan Thiet, near halfway on his Saigon-to-Nha Trang route, he was flabbergasted. No tourist had ever asked to be let off in Phan Thiet. No tourists, rich or poor, by plane, train, ship, or automobile, ever stopped there.

Those days are long gone. Phan Thiet has now become a destination resort, thanks to the beautiful beaches and sand dunes that had so fascinated me in 1966. It's not bicycles anymore either. You rarely see one these days, not only in Phan Thiet but anywhere you go in Vietnam. It's nearly all motorbikes.

Beaches aside, the city proper also has prospered. The roads and streets are paved now. Street lights show the way after dusk. The temporary movie theaters are gone. The fishing vessels, and there are more than a 1,000, all seem to have more than doubled in size from 1966, to twelve, fourteen and fifteen meters in length. Motorbikes, scooters, and busses (modern ones, not torture busses) fill the streets, as busy citizens go about their business. Phan Thiet has more than quadrupled in population, just since the mid 1990s.

Phan Thiet city remains a working town: no cyclos in sight, no beggars, no evident layabouts. North of the city, for two to three kilometers, new office buildings and factories, many still in the construction phase, not only abut the highway but stretch back from the road. The smell of the place, from whatever source, open sewers or manufacture of *nuoc mam*, is gone. A tourist map lists fifty-five hotels and guesthouses within the city proper. Several (the Diamond, Novotel Resort, Doi Duong) rate three and even four stars. The Novotel Hotel, which includes the Nick Faldo designed Ocean Dunes Golf Course, was the first of the new hotels, opening in 1997, commencing a new era for Phan Thiet.

Why? Exportation of processed food products, principally seafood, is Vietnam's third biggest industry, after production of textiles and garment production and production of offshore oil and gas (all of which is exported as Vietnam has little refining capacity). Phan Thiet is a principal player in the seafood business. Processors there ship shrimp, tiger shrimp, prawns, squid, crab, lobster, fish, fish sauce, and shrimp sauce throughout Asia and the Pacific Rim. The seafood industry is the base upon which the city has been built and now prospers.

I also found that no longer was I the Pied Piper. In 1995, Vietnamese in Phan Thiet, as well as in other out-of-the-way places, wanted to touch my nose ("long nose"), pull hair on my arms, and follow me (sometimes a dozen or more of them), often practicing their English. Today Westerners are old hat, a curiosity no longer, with one exception.

In Phan Thiet, two twelve-year-old boys wanted to pat my middle-aged stomach, which each did several times, in a non-threatening, even courteous fashion. Part of it was curiosity, part good luck. Everywhere I went in South Vietnam, except the North, several times a day Vietnamese would pat my stomach, if necessary crossing the street to do so. Vietnamese women did it. Vietnamese are very direct, very physical. Patting the "Happy Buddha" stomach was part of that.

Tourist business is the other prong of Phan Thiet's development. Even as late as 1995, the only seafront road out of Phan Thiet stretched perhaps ten kilometers from the city, along the north arm of the magnificent bay, to a fishing village where locals still used water buffalo to pull farm carts.

Today the government has pushed through a road on the south arm of the bay, fifteen kilometers or so to Point Ke Ga, where a stone lighthouse stands (built by the French, at sixty-five meters said to be the tallest in Southeast Asia). A dozen or so beach resorts line that road, fronting on the wide beach where once my troops and I had fired at suspected VC running down the sand.

To the north, the government has built two roads to Mui Ne, the point twenty-seven kilometers north and east from Phan Thiet (*mui* means cape or point). The area is known throughout Vietnam and Asia by name, Mui Ne or Point Mui Ne (which actually is redundant).

One road is a shore road. Dozens of four- and five-star beach resorts (Palmira, Victoria, Sea Lion, Blue Ocean, Sea Breeze, Dynasty, Little Mui Ne, Hai Au, Lucy, Canary, Silva, and Malibu—to name a few) line the beach side of the road. Sundry business establishments line the land side (motorbike rentals, dive shops, bars, restaurants, etc.). Although the area is not by any means a 1970s Thailand-like sex haven, a number of massage parlors advertise their wares.

One in particular attracted my attention by advertising the "four handed massage." I must say that the notion intrigued me but I am, after all, a married man, and compared to the "Million Fingers Massage Parlor" in the War days, "four handed" sounded a bit lackluster.

The other road at Mui Ne, halfway up the steep hills which overlook the bay, is a corniche road, a six-lane boulevard, a dual carriageway lined with hand-built stone retaining walls to hold back the shifting sands. Purple flowering bougainvillea line the median strip. Developers have cleared the land on both sides of this spectacular highway. Billboards describe townhouse developments, villas, and golf courses, all of which have yet to be built (except for Sealinks, a golf course and housing development already open). The clear and evident intent is to make the magnificent Phan Thiet Bay another Hawaii. It may take another fifteen or twenty years but the distinct impression is that the development will happen.

At Point Mui Ne, the coast and corniche roads converge. The single highway turns north, into the dunes country. These sand dunes, up to 100 meters high and reaching back as far back as several kilometers from the ocean, are prominent enough clearly to show on Google Earth.

In 1966, of course, not only were there no roads but also no people, save the VC, amongst these towering dunes. The Viet Cong were said to have camps on the far backside of the dunes. Because of the VC presence, U.S. and South Vietnamese charts and maps denominated the area a free fire zone. In fact, one day we (really Captain Munster) had brought in a gunfire support ship, the USS *Morton* (DD 948). The destroyer spent the better part of the day lobbing five-inch shells over the dunes into the folds beyond them (indirect fire, which means you cannot see at what you are shooting).

Today, rather than intimidating VC, those twenty-four pound warheads might distract a Japanese golfer looking for an errant golf ball; take out a tourist on a jeep ride through the dune country; or carve out a deep crater in the path of a visitor sledding down the dunes.

I have travelled all over the world. My 2011 visit to Vietnam confirmed what I had thought in 1966, namely, that the beaches and sand dunes of Vietnam's Binh Thuan Province are the most beautiful in the world, in many ways surpassing the beaches of Brittany, South Africa, Australia, or Hawaii. It is bittersweet that the Vietnamese will develop those beaches for all that they are worth.

A further touch of bitterness is added by the Vietnamese proclivity toward a certain measure of tackiness, at least to the Westerner's eye, to many of the things they develop .

On the other side of the ledger, Phan Thiet and the developments at Mui Ne are proxies for just how Vietnam is booming, developing, attracting visitors, tourists, new businesses, and bringing in dollars and Euros.

For three days, I stayed in a bungalow at an exclusive resort on the Mui Ne road, eight kilometers out from Phan Thiet. Later each afternoon, after the hot sun had relented a bit, I sat on the chaise lounge on the bungalow's patio, a drink in my hand, a book in my lap. In front of me stretched a short expanse of lawn, with tall palm trees spaced along the shore, followed by a sand beach, followed by a medium height surf crashing on shore. Beyond were two to three foot waves. In the middle distance, the waves rocked several fishing boats back and forth but the boat's occupants continued to work, assisted by those round, straw auxiliary craft (coracles) that Vietnamese fishermen use (a few made of fiberglass now). A constant stiff breeze (seven to eight knots) blew in from the bay, cooling me. A greater number of fishing boats worked in the far distance of the huge bay.

I thought to myself, "What a remarkable change since I was here in 1966." I thought too, "What remarkable change since 1995" when the society was more repressed and economically deprived than it had been during the War. If I closed my eyes, I could be in Maui. Remarkable, truly remarkable, but time to move up country.

Well, Da Lat is not a place to which tourists never have gone, at least rich ones, once upon a time. Now, again, after a hiatus, tourists have returned to Da Lat, in greater and greater numbers.

Locals returning to port after a night of fishing

Da Lat is a mile above sea level (1,475 meters, or 5,000 feet, to be exact). Beginning in the 1890s, the French built their summer villas there as did Bao Dia, the last emperor of Vietnam. Until the 1950s, both French and Vietnamese went there to escape the heat and to hunt tigers in the hills and mountains which surround the town. There are no more tigers, but they were in evidence late into the 1960s.

After the French left Vietnam, the little cog railway from the coast up into the mountains and Da Lat, built by the French, fell into disuse and closed. Tourists stopped coming, in numbers at least. Nonetheless, even though the city was not used much and in a state of decline, the South Vietnamese, the Viet Cong, and the North Vietnamese had a tacit agreement to bypass the town at all costs, to which agreement all parties adhered. Da Lat was spared war damage.

After the first stirrings of *Doi Moi*, Da Lat became and still remains the site of many meetings and conferences. My friend, Callie Jordan, now a professor of law at Duke University in the U.S. and at the University of Melbourne in Australia, while an attorney at the World Bank, had a portfolio which included modernization of economic laws in Southeast Asia. Conferences dealing with Vietnam's needs were invariably held in Da Lat. Callie went there a number of times, staying in the majestic Hotel Da Lat Palace, another former royal residence whose spacious grounds overlook Xuan Huong Lake.

Xuan Huong Lake is an artificial lake, six kilometers around, sitting between two folds of hills and the focal point of the town. Early in the morning, the walkway round the lake is crowded with walkers, runners, and badminton players, all of whom are Vietnamese. Beyond the lake is the Da Lat golf course, first laid out in the 1890s as an eight hole course (now eighteen holes) by the French physician and founder of the Pasteur Institute, Dr. Alexandre Yersin, who introduced vaccination to the Vietnamese. Dr. Yersin came up from Nha Trang each summer to escape the heat as well as oversee the Da Lat branch of his Pasteur Institute. Dr. Yersin must have played golf as well.

Da Lat is the Vietnamese equivalent of a Swiss town. One guidebook ascribes to the town a "honeymoon atmosphere." Flowers and ornamental shrubberies decorate every public place, roundabout, public building, and park. The hills surrounding the town are covered with pines and other evergreen trees rather than the palm trees of the coastal plain.

We (my wife Betsy and I) hired a car and driver to drive us from Phan Thiet to Da Lat, as there existed no other convenient way to make the 350 kilometer journey (other than by taking two days to go back from Phan Thiet to Saigon and then up the middle of the country to Da Lat).

Leaving Phan Thiet, Minh, our escort, drove us past a number of farms and plantations growing dragon fruit (red husk, white pulp shot through with black poppy seed like seeds). After ten or so kilometers out of town, the rice paddies began. A further dozen kilometers or so onward the highway started up into the mountains. Less than fifteen to twenty kilometers into the foothills, the highway (Route 28) narrowed to a single track, or a track and a half. From then on, we saw no farms or villages and, save for a few motorbikes, no other cars, trucks, or people, nothing beyond the flatlands.

We went around hairpin turn after hairpin turn. What amazed me was how in a country we view as so densely populated a traveler can sojourn through seventy kilometers of mountain road without seeing a single house or individual. The views and the landscape were spectacular.

When finally we came out "on top," we came to a native village. Vietnam has, of course, over fifty groups of hilltop peoples, who are ethically different and regard themselves as independent of the Vietnamese. Most of these hilltop peoples live much deeper into the mountains and much further north. But you could tell that this village was different. The houses and other buildings all were made of wood, with corrugated tin roofs, different from the brick and plaster construction, flat roofs, and garish pastels of a lowland Vietnamese town. Our Vietnamese driver pointedly made the observation that these people were not Vietnamese and very different from Vietnamese people.

Da Lat was filled with Australian tourists, as were many of the places in Vietnam that we visited. We saw no Americans. In fact, we saw few Americans anywhere outside of Saigon and Hue.

Two reasons may exist for the paucity of American tourists. One is that many American tourists to Vietnam concentrate on the War stuff (Ben Dinh and Ben Duoc tunnels, Cu Chi War Museum, Khe Sanh, the DMZ). Hue is the jumping off place for tours of the DMZ; the Americans go there.

Another explanation is that American tourists are becoming like Japanese ones, following one another to see the same two or three sights. For example, in New Zealand all Japanese tourists go to Queenstown, Mount Cook, and Milford Sound, while in Australia, lemming-like, Japanese visit Sydney, Cairns (the Great Barrier Reef), and Ayers Rock.

We saw fellow Americans only in Saigon and at Hue, seat of the Vietnamese emperors after 1802, and as I said, the gateway to the DMZ, but nowhere else. In Phan Thiet, the tourists whom we saw were all French. After Australians, French ranked second among visitors, although the ratios would be disproportionate, something like fifteen Australians for every three or four French, followed by one American or European other than French (we did see a German group, and an Italian group, but only in Saigon). My wife speculates that after the Bali bombing in Indonesia (by Islamic terrorists, murdering 210 people, including 150 Australians on holiday), Australians have substituted Vietnam for Bali as their exotic get-away.

I talked to an Australian bloke from Adelaide whom I ran into several times in Da Lat. He was with a large group of Australians (about a dozen middle-age men) who had come to Da Lat for motorcycle excursions. Da Lat is the jumping off point for two to three day rides up into the mountains and amongst the hill people.

A Vietnamese acts as guide and driver. They call themselves "Easy Riders." Motorbikes and scooters, of course, flood Vietnam but they have relatively small engines (100, 110, maybe 125 cubic centimeter (cc) engine displacement) and are easy to operate. Larger (175 cc and above) two-wheeled conveyances are classified as motorcycles. Operation of one requires a special license and payment of additional fees. They cost more, too ($1,000-$2,000 USD for a motorbike but $3,000-$5,000 for a motorcycle).

Honda, BMW, Harley Davidson, and other motorcycle manufacturers sell 250cc, 350 cc. and 500 cc machines. Their largest have engines of 750cc, 1000cc or 1500 cc, approaching a medium size car's engine size. You will see none of the latter in Asia (too expensive to buy, too expensive to operate). So Easy Riders operate 250cc and perhaps 350cc machines, big by Vietnamese standards but small to medium size elsewhere.

The whole Easy Rider thing can be dangerous. The Australians we saw all had purchased helmets, as Vietnam has a mandatory helmet law, but the helmets available and which they purchased were cheap, flimsy plastic things similar to the ones most Vietnamese wore. The image one has is of a human head, like a basketball, bouncing down the pavement. Nonetheless, a lot of thrill seekers do the Easy Rider bit with Da Lat the place to hook up with a ride.

We went to the market in Da Lat, the central point of any Vietnamese town. Cho Da Lat is known for the foodstuffs grown locally (pyramids of oranges, stacks of strawberries, baskets of papayas, mangos, lettuce, spinach, or tomatoes, even Da Lat wine, the grapes for which are gown outside of town under thousands of hectares of plastic tents). Da Lat wine is seen throughout Vietnam but still is not quite up to Western tastes. The Da Lat market spills over into the surrounding streets, with squatting merchants guarding their wares.

At the market, as well as elsewhere, motorbike and scooter drivers are imperious. They push their bike through any opening, however small. They drive up onto the sidewalk. They toot their horns, over and over, but, regardless (horn or no horn), motorbike drivers expect the pedestrian to get out of the way. A few of them drivers will nudge a pedestrian with the bike's front tire if she does not step aside. A constant stream of motorbikes comes through the streets surrounding the market and even parts of the market itself. They and their drivers are a colossal pain in the butt. (More on my annoyance with Vietnam's motorbikes and their drivers in following chapters.)

Inside the market merchants sell nearly everything: hardware, kitchen utensils, cups and plates, footwear (lots of footwear), and all manner of clothing (jackets, trousers, underwear for men and women, dresses, bolts of cloth, shirts, suits, ties...). The merchandise reaches from floor to ceiling and spills out of the booths, leaving an aisle barely wide enough for one person.

Many (all?) of the outer wear items for sale in the market are knockoffs. Ralph Lauren labels and their polo player logos are very popular. And the prices, oh the prices. Even though you have to bargain for everything, which gets tiring after a while, asking prices come quickly down. If you bargain well at all, you are going to get what seems to be a deal, say, $8 or $9 U.S. for a logo sweater.

Ah, but all that glitters is not gold. Out walking around the lake in the mornings, I saw several Vietnamese women wearing Ralph Lauren knockoff sweaters, with the polo logo on the chest. Although it probably looked great in the market's artificial lighting, and the price was cheap, in daylight a passerby could see right through the sweater. The women's white brassieres actually stood out.

Logo tee shirts for men (333 Saigon Beer, Good Morning Vietnam, Tiger Beer, Hanoi, what have you) can be had for 70,000 *dong* ($3.50 USD) in the market. After one laundering, though, a South African man remarked to me, "They're only good for washing your car, that's it." At a minimum, then, you have to be careful at the market, inspecting goods closely. Even at that, at best you get what you pay for.

Vietnamese in these parts dress as would Americans for a Midwestern autumn. While the temperature down on the coast may be as high as 36 or 37 degrees Celsius (102-104 Fahrenheit), up in Da Lat it may be twelve to fourteen degrees cooler (say, 23 degrees Celcius, or 75-77 degrees Fahrenheit). To us, that is ideal. To Vietnamese, even those who live up here, that is cold. So in Da Lat, Vietnamese wear sweaters, jackets, and woolen stocking caps (it was mid-May). We saw Buddhist nuns shopping for gray woolen stock caps which would match their light gray habits while keeping them warm.

Although in the Dark Ages, the doctrinaire Marxist government repressed all things French, now the powers that be permit the French influences to rebound, or not rebound, as the case may be. No one, save oldsters, speaks French any longer but in Da Lat French influences have made a comeback. A restored 1930's Citroen sits in front of the Palace Hotel, itself very continental, very French. Next door is the Art Deco Café de la Post, French to the core.

Across town stands Boa Dai's last palace, built from 1933 to 1938 in what can only be termed French Modern (post Art Deco?), with a flat roof but rounded corners, two stories high, large but not immodest. The palace still contains the original furnishings, which Vietnamese visitors test out after hopping over the rope barriers. The Vietnamese docents in the rooms permit this although the wear and tear on the furnishings shows. Fabric coverings on many of the chairs are shiny and threadbare, about to be worn through. The Vietnamese and their children go all over the place, trying everything out, posing, taking pictures for the folks back home.

Emperor Boa Dai lived here with his five children until Queen Nan Phuong left him in 1949, taking the children to Paris and raising them there. Boa Dai, an imposing man (tall for a Vietnamese—in one photo Bo Dai towers over French Legionnaires he is inspecting), was a gambler and a womanizer who went to Hong Kong after he abdicated the first time. He periodically returned to Vietnam, attempting and failing to become head of state in the new 1954 government. Ngo Dinh Diem outwitted Bo Dai, becoming both head of government (prime minister) as well as head of state (president, king or queen, emperor). Boa Dai then fled to France, first to the Riviera and then to Alsace. He changed his name to Jean Robert, converted to Catholicism, and married a French citizen. He died, in Paris, in 1997, at age eighty-five.

****

Quy Nhon was my favorite Vietnamese town, although we stayed only a night. A city of 280,000 halfway up the coast, Quy Nhon is a place truly where few tourists go, then or now. During the War, Quy Nhon was home to the U.S. Navy's Coastal Surveillance Center for II Corps. I went there once in 1966 but had little memory of it. Quy Nhon also was the site where the second contingent of U.S. Marines (the Second Marine Battalion) conducted a full scale amphibious landing a month after the first contingent of Marines had landed at

Danang. In April 1965, 1,000 or more Marines, bristling with weapons and driving armored vehicles, came ashore, startling the locals beyond belief. Today the Marines are gone and Quy Nhon is more than any other a true Vietnamese city.

Highway One runs ten to twelve kilometers west of Quy Nhon. So, beginning about twenty-five kilometers south of the city, the Vietnamese built a spur road off Highway One leading along the coast into Quy Nhon. The spur road has the usual underpowered and overloaded Vietnamese trucks, but not a lot of them. The road runs up and down on the cliffs over the ocean. Islands dot the distance while immediately below and to the right are hidden coves with sandy beaches. In the distance you often see a dozen ocean-going freighters at anchor, waiting for berths to clear in Quy Nhon. The spur road into Quy Nhon may be the most beautiful highway in Vietnam.

Quy Nhon is known for its beaches—forty-two kilometers of them, according to the hype: Queen's Beach where Queen Nam Phuong used to take her children; Bai Bau Beach south of town; and Quy Hoa Beach, just to name three.

But the city is chock-a-block against the coastal mountains, sort of a Vietnamese Rio de Janero. The hills and mountains, says Tom Bissell, present "an arcadia of rough, beautiful triangles of fuzzy jade and sharp spurs of exposed white rock, a few sparkling white waterfalls pouring down the hills' faces."

The in-town ocean front is a continuous seven kilometer beach that curves toward the northeast. The beach is more spectacular than the seven kilometer beach in Nha Trang, commonly billed as the best in Vietnam (a land of uncommonly beautiful beaches). Another difference is that few, if any, persons visit the spectacular Quy Nhon beach while Nha Trang beach is crowded with thousands of tourists, Vietnamese families, swimmers, waders, and walkers.

Fronting onto the Quy Nhon beach is a manicured park strip with flowers and shrubbery. There are several medium rise hotels (the

Seagull is one). A broad boulevard runs the entire length of the beach, with the city behind that.

Another salient feature of the town is its wooden boat building. In Quy Nhon, craftsmen build the large wooden vessels used for offshore fishing and cargo hauling. Using techniques passed on from generation to generation, these ship builders have more than a dozen vessels, up to twenty-five meters in length, in various stages of construction.

Craving western food, we ate at Barbara's Kiwi Rest, facing onto the beach road northeast of the downtown area. Barbara's is emblematic of the one, enduring non-Vietnamese influence here, that of New Zealanders (Kiwis). Kiwi NGOs have been sending aid workers and helpers here at least since the 1950s. Throughout the War the Kiwis continued their mission in Quy Nhon. They are still there. We did meet one American, a USAID public health worker from Hanoi (Xeres), in Quy Nhon to speak at a Vietnamese public health workshop held at one of the beach hotels the next day.

Quy Nhon was evocative to me. If I wished to go to a very foreign town, but one with a few Western creature comforts available, Quy Nhon would be it. Difficult to get to, and beautiful in its setting, Quy Nhon seems quintessentially Vietnamese.

18

Places Tourists Do Go

Called "Nice in beggar's clothing," Nha Trang still retain[s] some of its
French heritage but these days the beggar [is] living on velvet.

—Tom Bissell, *The Father of All Things* (2007)

*A visit to this old world gem [Hoi An, a UNESCO World Heritage Site]
is sure a cultural highlight of any tour of Vietnam … [f]rom the 16th to
the 18th century Vietnam's most important port and trading post,
particularly of ceramics with nearby China.*

—Sherisse Pham, *Frommer's Vietnam* (3rd ed., 2010)

*Palaces and pagodas, tombs and temples, culture and cuisine, history and
heartache, there's no shortage of poetic pairings to describe Hue, a UNSECO
Heritage Site since 1993, the capital of Nguyen emperors … where tourists
come to see something of the old, pre-communist Vietnam … .*

—Yu-Mei Balasingamchow, *Vietnam* (10th ed., 2010)

TODAY MOST OF THE NHA TRANG BEGGARS (good natured ones, kids mostly) are gone; the beggar does rest on velvet (high rise hotels, numerous restaurants), and the Nha Trang beach is world class but, other than the Catholic cathedral, no French influences remain.

Hoi An is small and compact, scenic, and good for walking (at least earlier in the morning, or in the evening, after the heat subsides), but a tourist trap extraordinaire. In Hoi An, my wife finally was pushed over the top, coming to the conclusion that "Vietnamese are always trying to sell you something, aren't they?" Hoi An is the epitome of the Vietnamese psyche, good and bad, emblematic of how capitalism suits the Vietnamese psyche to a T.

Hue, my favorite place in Vietnam when I visited in 1995, has an enchanting setting along the Perfume River, with tree shaded Le Loi, the main street, running along the river's edge for several kilometers. The walls of the Imperial Purple Forbidden City and the block-like citadel at the front, with a huge red Vietnamese flag flying, are always visible across the river. But there are more tourists now and, while it may seems callous to say, there are several things about Hue the guide books do not point out:

- While it may not be strictly true that "seen one pagoda, seen 'em all," a few here and there will usually suffice. There is a sameness to them. A tourist would waste her time trying to visit all the pagodas with which guide books fill their pages, including those in and about Hue.

- Attempts at Western cuisine in Hue not only fall flat but result in horrible food. Hue Vietnamese cuisine is known throughout the country as being hot and spicy, even for Vietnamese, and not well suited for most Western palates. You can tell your server to go light on the chilies, or eliminate them altogether, but it is problematic whether or not your request ever will reach the kitchen.

- The Nguyen dynasty of emperors only begins with 1802, with the construction of the Forbidden City only in 1805. As monuments go, the Imperial Purple Forbidden City is not that old.

- The guidebooks lay most of the blame for destruction of the citadels, temples, and pavilions within the Forbidden City to the three-and-a-half weeks in which U.S. Marines used tanks and howitzers to blast out the Viet Cong. The VC had seized control of Hue, retreating into the walled inner compounds suring the 1968 Tet offensive. What the guide books do not tell you is that in 1947 the Viet Minh occupied the Forbidden City. The French blasted holes in the walls and destroyed many of the structures in rooting out the Viet Minh. Many of the treasures were destroyed at that time, not in 1968 by the Americans.

• Then, too, the guidebooks also do not tell you that, after emperor Bao Dai abdicated in 1945, the Imperial Palace and the Forbidden City fell into abandonment and disrepair, a state of steady deterioration that had left the remaining structures, and all but the brick compound walls, crumbling by 1968, when the U.S. Marines arrived.

****

Often when I go to a sporting event (baseball, basketball, football game), the next day when I read the sports writer's newspaper account I soon am wondering if the writer saw a different game than I did. Travel guidebooks are that way, too. Did the writers really visit the places you went, or did they go somewhere else, or did they make it up, some of it or all of it, cut from whole cloth? Many things I see or experience in my travels bear little or no resemblance to what is in the guidebooks.

I read Tom Bissell's book, *The Father of All Things,* an excellent memoir and travelogue about modern-day Vietnam. I agreed with much but not all of what he said about places he and his father (a Vietnam vet) visited (Quy Nhon and Nha Trang, for instance).

But the guidebooks *cum* guidebooks—they are so full of hyperbole and hype, misdescriptions, semi accurate descriptions, misleading characterizations, and on and on, that you wonder if the people who wrote them spent most of their time in New York or in Melbourne. There, you imagine, these "travel writers" paged through and paraphrased what previous generations of travel writers had written. The thought does cross your mind as you see how imperfectly the real things before your eyes match up with what the books say.

Still, many travelers rely heavily (too heavily?) on them. At breakfast in Hoi An, we sat a table away from two women from New York city who were ultimate power tourists. They had a stack of guidebooks to Vietnam piled on their breakfast table, including those with the color plates in them (*National Geographic*, I believe) which weigh several pounds each. These two energizer bunnies had yellow highlighters, felt tip markers, bookmarks, paper clips, and pads of Post-It Notes. The women were assiduously marking up each book's entries. I am certain that, focused as they were on all the different guidebooks and the hype they carried, these women failed to see much of Hoi An itself or to soak up any of the atmosphere. The women tourists may also have needed a handcart (or wheelbarrow) to carry around all the guidebooks they had.

I don't mean to be a nattering nabob of negativism. I thoroughly enjoyed my visits to Nha Trang, Hoi An, and Hue, "the places tourists do go," but for reasons somewhat different that what the books say.

Business interests in Nha Trang have turned Hon Tre, the largest of the eighteen or so islands offshore, into a Disneyland-like amusement park. They sunk towers down to the sea floor in the bay, crossing over between the port area to the south and the island. From these towers, the park's promoters strung a cable for cable cars which now carry patrons the one-and-a-half kilometers over the water out to the island. Little cable car gondolas now go back and forth.

On Hon Tre, which also has a luxury hotel and an aquarium adjacent to the amusement park, a mountain rises up behind the park. On the mountain overlooking the park , large, white letters, visible for several kilometers, spell out the name of the place: VINPEARL, ala the fabled HOLLYWOOD sign overlooking Los Angeles.

The introduction of a capitalistic economic model into a country whose political-governance model remains socialist has produced amazing results for Vietnam and its people. VINPEARL is not one of them.

Another tacky (or kitschy) landmark spoils one of the world's most beautiful beaches. It sits on the sand side of Nha Trang's beach road, Tran Phu Street. Smack dab in the center of the urban stretch of beach the Vietnamese have built a multi-story memorial of some kind, in various shades of pink, shaped like a rocket ship, or perhaps a flower bud (a tulip?).

Much like public spaces in many U.S. cities (the Washington Mall, Central Park, Chicago's Grant Park, etc.), the long Nha Trang waterfront has been crapped up with memorials, monuments, play areas, tacky and not-so tacky sculptures, and so on. Natural beauty, here a glorious seven kilometer long, sandy beach, never seems to be enough, at least when the politicians, for whom every lobbying group represents votes, get control over it. Same deal in Vietnam, I guess.

Long a vacation destination for Vietnamese, Nha Trang has also become a destination resort for international vacationers. The north end of the beach area has five or six, fifteen to twenty story hotels (Sheraton, Crown Plaza, Nha Trang Lodge, Novotel, etc.). These were vacant lots when I visited in 1995. The first new hotel, the Evason, a low rise on the beach side, and where we stayed, opened in 1997.

Much of all the high rise construction has been financed by Korean interests. Khanh Hoa Province, of which Nha Trang is the capital, was the seat of Korean military operations during the War.

North of the nest of high rise hotels, the wide shallow estuary of the Cai Lai River empties into the sea. Two causeways span the water, the one nearest the ocean is a continuation of Tran Phu, the beach street. The other causeway is several blocks back from the seafront, leading out from Nha Trang's downtown. Just beyond the second causeway lies a steep hill or mound, possibly once the tip of an undersea mountain. One the top of that hill, the Chams built their towers.

Climbing up several flights of stairs, the tourist comes upon three Cham towers, of varying heights and well-preserved. Preserved in fact so well that two of the towers are functioning Hindu temples. The temple to the Hindu Goddess Yan Po Nagar was built in 817 A.D., but the Champa did complete the complex until the thirteenth century.

Behind the Nha Trang Cham temples is a small museum. The whole complex is surrounded by a brick and stone patio approaching half a hectare in size. There are benches upon which to sit. The view is of the wide estuary, with nests of bright blue fishing boats anchored in the stream and several large boulder formations forming small islands, or islets. The larger green, forested islands are in the distance. Shade trees keep the near relentless Vietnamese sun at bay. We spent an hour there but could have spent longer. It's peaceful, spiritual perhaps, and cooler up there.

The Nha Trang beach's bookend is the Bao Dia palace complex at the opposite end (southern end) of the beach. There, a wooded peninsula juts out in to the bay. On that peninsula Bao Dia caused to be constructed five buildings, which formed another summer emperor's palace (Bao Dia had many palaces). Of the buildings which remain, the furthest out on the peninsula had a watch tower the emperor would use. Today the building has sample furnishings, clothing, and photos of the past emperor. It is a small museum, open to the public. Another of the buildings has been converted into a hotel but to a degree has been eclipsed by the beach front hotels. It has fallen to three stars.

The view from the end of the little Bao Dia peninsula is magnificent. You can see the entire curve of sand beach, with the city proper toward the northern end and the high rise hotels in the distance.

Below the summer palace is the port area, where I used to come in 1966 and 1967. In 1966, and still in 1995, the road came to a dead end at the port. The road goes through now. Several kilometers below the port area is yet another golf course development called Diamond

Bay. A coast road has been built, at places seemingly cut into the oceanfront cliffs, making the drive along the road spectacular.

Thirty-two kilometers down that coast road is the new Nha Trang Airport, which was the U.S. airport for the sprawling Cam Ranh Bay military complex, where 40,000 U.S. military were stationed during the War. That is where in 1967 I, along many others who had completed the standard one year tour of duty, flew back to the U.S. from Vietnam. As the chartered DC-8's wheels left the tarmac, a loud and long cheer went up. We were going home. The plane's captain ordered the flight attendants to open the bar even before the plane had climbed out through 5,000 feet.

Today Nha Trang has closed the in-town air strip with its short angled runway, which had served as the city airport. The city now has, on the Cam Ranh Peninsula to the south, a 14,000 foot runway, built by the U.S., and a state-of-the-art airport, capable of accommodating the heaviest and largest of jet aircraft. Although a bit ahead of much of the rest of the country (quite a bit, actually), Nha Trang nonetheless remains on the move. The not-too-distant future will bear witness to international flights into Cam Ranh and Nha Trang where beaches and dunes (Cam Ranh has beautiful white sand beaches, backed by the dunes) will attract vacationers. Already, a billboard between the airport and Nha Trang city promises a seaside Westin Hotel to be built there soon. More East Asian Hawaii on the way.

While in Nha Trang, we went to the Catholic cathedral, perched on a small hill facing one of the city's main roundabouts. Built of concrete and stone, the cathedral is, as many of the Catholic churches in Vietnam, well tended, picturesque, and a prominent landmark in the city. Contrary to what the guidebooks say, however, the cathedral and its interior were the only French influences we saw in Nha Trang, but even these had a Vietnamese twist. Jesus on the crucifix above the altar had a red neon halo above his head. On the side altar, the statue of the Blessed Virgin had as background a blue arch, also bright neon, which reflected over the white of the statue's gown. Tacky? Yes, but I thought it was really cool.

****

The road to Quy Nhon and then to Hoi An is, as seemingly is the road anywhere in Vietnam, Highway One. The highway passes through miles of rice paddies of varying shades of green. The color helps the farmer determine the optimal time for harvest. This, mid-May, was harvest time. As we drove northward, farmers in the paddies (men and women), dressed in white conical hats, brought in a crop. They gathered rice straw for their animals. The smoke from burning stubble here and there drifted across the highway.

Highway One is a two-lane, rough highway, with deformed pavement over long stretches, forcing motorists to slow to five and ten miles per hour, cars bottoming out and scraping on the up and down road surface. If an international organization wanted to do something meaningful in Vietnam, the highest and best use of resources might be to improve Highway One (it is improved and a four-lane, divided highway south out of Hanoi but, hey, we know that the North won the war—even though the South is where the traffic is).

Buses passing buses, thousands of motorbikes, overloaded trucks, slow moving trucks, even more slowly moving trucks, farmers' wagons (overloaded with rice straw)—all creep along, honking horns, passing on the curves, looming out into the oncoming traffic, ducking back into their proper lane with only a few meters to spare. At one point, as we journeyed northward, we had a two-hour delay, for the most part sitting in parking lot ten kilometers long. Finally, we crept up on the obstruction. A truck, no longer in evidence, had dumped its cargo of scrap metal on the highway. The mound of metal just sat there, blocking one of the two lanes. Plenty of Vietnamese policemen were on the scene but they did nothing. Finally, as we approached, the policemen took action. They all crammed into the king-cab police truck in which they had arrived, and drove nonchalantly away, probably to find some lunch.

On the way to Hoi An, we passed what had been the major U.S. airbase at Chu Lai, south of Hoi An and Danang. The Vietnamese have converted most of these major U.S. bases (Chu Lai, Bien Hoa) into industrial parks. Fronting the highway at Chu Lai was a large Chinese owned and operated factory that manufactures buses. Other large factories and warehouses sat behind it, as multinational and other corporations re-source production to Vietnam, taking advantage of the low wage levels there.

Finally, late in the day, after an eight hour drive from Quy Nhon, we arrived at Hoi An, an ultimate tourist trap but a thoroughly enjoyable one. Old Hoi An, the tourist part, is five or six blocks long, two to three blocks deep, along the lazy Thu Ben River, forty minutes south of Danang. It is one of those places where young travelers, backpackers and the like, stop for a few days, getting laundry done, writing postcards home, and visiting with one another. In that manner, Hoi An resembles Luang Prabang in Laos, or Victoria Falls in Zimbabwe (now, since Mugabe's antics, Livingstone, in Zambia, on the other side of the river), or Interlocken in Switzerland (because it is a principal railroad junction), or Queenstown in New Zealand—places that have a similar air about them. Hoi An has that air about it, full of many young European and Australian travelers.

There is a market, full of trinkets and souvenirs as well as foodstuffs, although you have to put up with motorbike riders. It is a fun market that stays open into the evening.

Several Hoi An old town streets front directly onto the river. Several are walking only streets (no motorbikes). There are restaurants of all kinds as well as art galleries and shops on that street and on the next street back, which also parallels the river. A 16th Century Japanese style covered bridge spans a tributary of the river, leading to two additional blocks of the old town.

A big attraction seems to be Hoi An's tailors. Dozens of them have shops with fronts open to the street. The shops contain dummy after dummy dressed with samples of the particular tailor's wares, mostly women's outfits (not many men's). I thought that most of it looked dated, 1950s-ish. But later, in Hanoi, we met and had several conversations with an American husband and wife, both physicians from Santa Fe, New Mexico, and, indeed, former medical school professors from the University of Pittsburgh. They travel quite a lot in East Asia. He has his clothes tailored in Bangkok. She has hers tailored in Hoi An, Vietnam.

The guidebooks ballyhoo Hoi An's antiquities, the Japanese style bridge, and numerous houses of Chinese traders, built in the 16th century and well preserved. You can buy a ticket, with five tabs on it, entitling you to visit five of these houses. Don't bother. It's a complete waste of time.

We bought tickets. We went to two of these houses. Inside neither was architecturally distinguished or even particularly interesting. A young woman Vietnamese guide expected the entire group of tourists (up to a dozen in number) to be seated and listen carefully to a boring spiel ("In the great flood of 1999 the river water reached up to this point"). Then she tried to sell things—jewelry and trinkets.

I left when the guide began her talk. My wife thought I was being rude, an insensitive tourist. I was vindicated, however, when an Australian couple got up off their stools, following me out. We all waited in the shop across the street, I for my wife and the Australians for friends who were travelling with them.

These Chinese traders' houses seem a good example of travel writers' fraud. It seems clear to me that these people who write the Vietnam books never went into those houses. Otherwise, they never would recommend a visit to them. You have to ask yourself, "Who writes this stuff?"

Instead, do a drive-by or look-see on these houses. Don't buy the tickets; don't go inside the houses. Instead, enjoy the ambiance, the restaurants, and the shops in Hoi An. Several street leading away from (perpendicular to) the river are tree lined. Sit in the shade at an open front café. Have a beer (Vietnamese beer is quite good) or a tea, watching Hoi An go by in front of you.

****

Again, we had to hire a car and driver to take us from Hoi An to Hue, about 125 kilometers away. On the way, between Danang and Hoi An, we passed three golf courses, all in a row, one complete (the Da Nang Golf Club), and two under construction. The first course was "Montgomerie Links," named after the Scottish professional golfer, Colin Montgomerie (aka "Mrs. Doubtfire"), and the third was "Greg Norman Estates," after the eponymous Australian professional (aka "the Shark"). While some Americans may play golf there, the Vietnamese intent is to attract Japanese tourists.

Crazy about golf, many Japanese pay upwards of $500 USD greens fee for a round of golf in their homeland. Here, in Vietnam, the Japanese golfer can stay in a luxury hotel, play golf every day, and enjoy a sight or two, for $220 or $250 per day. The principal aim of golf courses outside Saigon, near Danang (there are three or four), or Phan Thiet (there are two, with two more planned or under construction), and Hanoi (I saw advertisements for three golf courses near Hanoi) is also to attract the Japanese. Danang already has a gateway, an international airport capable of accommodating flights directly from Japan.

From Hoi An, our driver skirted south to Danang and then along the east side of the metropolis. We joined the ubiquitous Highway One, crossing the broad estuary of the Touraine River, with Danang's skyline visible ten kilometers away, over our right shoulder. Highway One then enters a tunnel, newly constructed, under the mountain spur, but the old road, which we took, climbs, up and up, in order to cross a spur of the Troung Son mountains that reaches all the way to the sea. Finally the road crests the spur at Hai Van Pass, 496 meters (1,620 feet) above sea level.

This pass, Hai Van (Sea Cloud), is important for several reasons. It is scenic. The turnout-overlook at the top gives way onto breathtaking views of Danang and the ocean. The pass marks the line of demarcation between the North and South, not politically (the DMZ did that) but culturally and weather wise. Beginning here, and on northward, Vietnamese people tend to be more reserved. The seasons are different. South of the spur monsoon comes in June, lasting until September or October. North of the spur the monsoon comes in October, lasting into December. "Chinese winds" make winters to the north more severe while the mountains protect Danang from these gales. In Hue and to the north, the cuisine is also different (hotter and spicier).

The pass is eerie. There stands the French-built brick guardhouse, pockmarked with bullet holes. Up the hillside are concrete pillboxes-guard towers built by the Americans and the South Vietnamese, now blackened with mildew. On dark nights, with the wind howling and the fog swirling, Viet Cong crept through the surrounding forest while young American and ARVN soldiers stood guard, attempting to keep the pass and the highway open.

****

What can be said about Hue that has not already been said (see Chapter 14)? It is a lovely city, built up with several new four-star hotels and resorts (Huong Giang Hotel, the Saigon Morin Hotel, in addition to the venerable Century Riverside) along the Perfume River and La Loi Street. Unlike Hanoi or Saigon, however, Hue does not seem to have spread out much or otherwise grown in the sixteen years since my last visit.

We stayed in La Residence, to the east side of the city, toward the pink Hue train station and Hue University. The original hotel building was the home to French administrators and civil servants when they visited Hue. The developers of the hotel added two other buildings, each angled away from the main building, which opened in 2005. La Residence is decorated, floor to ceiling, including the geometric tile on the floor, the doors and light fixtures, and everything else, top to bottom, in Art Deco. Our room had a balcony from which we could view the river, with long-tail fishing boats and put-put wooden cargo lighters carrying sand and gravel down river. La Residence was my favorite hotel not only of the trip but in recent memory.

We did many of the same sightseeing ventures that I had done sixteen years earlier. We took a riverboat up-river to the Thien Mu Pagoda, where we saw the tower, pagoda, and monks, first at worship and then at lunch. We went to the pier between La Residence and Ho Chi Minh Museum next door. Ho Chi Minch moved to Hue as a young boy, when his father became a mandarin at the emperor's court and for a time young Ho attended the famous, Truong Quoc Hon high school, where many prominent Vietnamese were schooled. The school, and the separate girls' school as well, were across Le Loi Street and down a bit from the museum.

As soon as we had boarded the little, rickety tourist boat and had left the pier, ready to chug up the Perfume River to the pagoda, the lady of the house (the father was driving while the children—the family was said to live on the boat—stayed in the stern) began laying out her merchandise. My wife observed again: "Every Vietnamese is trying to sell you something." The Vietnamese hostess laid out stacks of shirts and blouses and Vietnamese mass produced prints. I ignored it all. The constant selling and badgering gets to me at times.

My wife fell for the captive selling effort, buying four Vietnamese prints, for which we have no use, for $17 USD. To boot, she didn't bargain, or bargain very hard. To me, those prints, identical to ones you can find in Vietnamese souvenir shops, were, and are, worth no more than $1 each.

We did the tombs of the Nguyen emperors, jaunting twelve to fifteen kilometers into the countryside south of Hue to see several. We drove to the tomb of emperor Minh Mang (1789-1840, ruled 1820-40). I had bicycled down a jungle trail in 1995 to reach this same royal tomb. Save for one other couple, we were the only tourists there. Deep in the forest, the tomb and its walled grounds take up twenty-eight hectares. The guide told us that Minh Mang had forty-three wives, 142 children, and all told, 500 wives and concubines. He died at age fifty-one, probably of exhaustion.

Hue is a touristy city, so you see a number of cyclos. The city government in Saigon is trying to phase them out, I suppose because they clog up traffic lanes in what has become a very crowded city. In Saigon, you see very few cyclos, say, only outside Ben Thanh Market or the Reunification Palace, while once they were plentiful throughout the city. For whatever reason, cyclos are scarce as well, albeit not nearly so, in Hanoi. And in a working town like Phan Thiet there never were many cyclos in the first place.

In Hue you see them. I counted eighteen outside the Houng Giang Resort alone, but who would want to ride in them? The cyclos' drivers have become a decidedly gray group, who wear raggedy clothing and flip-flops, dozing off in their passenger seats and appearing not to bathe too often. Their vehicles are dinged up, with frayed and unclean cushions for passenger seats.

I used to take cyclos all the time in Vietnam, and pedicabs elsewhere in Asia. Many of the cyclo drivers then (not all) were clean-cut, younger and healthier looking, not so off-putting as they appear today in Saigon, Hanoi, or Hue.

In Hoi An, many cyclos patrol the streets, including the walking streets. The drivers there are not so young anymore either but they appear neat and clean. Many wear uniforms: short sleeve blue shirts with "Hoi An Drivers" printed on the back.

****

The War was a long time ago but I did see evidence of it. On the second morning in Hue, I walked across the Perfume River on the Phu Xiang Bridge, over to the river's north side, where few tourists go. I was on my way to the Dong Ba Market, a produce and foodstuff place (I like the hurly burly, sights, and sounds of an early morning market). In between the Phu Xiang and the Trang Tien bridges, the latter a historic older steel truss bridge built by the French in 1897, I passed a park on my right, between the street and the river.

On top of the footings for the fence, separating the park from the sidewalk, various merchants were laying out their wares: cups and saucers, plates, old tarnished cutlery (silver), old coins.

Most of the merchandise seemed intended for Vietnamese customers. So I walked quickly by, at least until I came alongside the fourth merchant. Interspersed with the crockery and cutlery was a pile of "dog tags," the identification plates all U.S. military used to wear on a chain around their necks. I stopped. The first couple of dog tags I picked up I could not read because they were so coated with tarnish and dirt. The fourth set I picked up were clear. They read, "Gary Havelock, USMC." I cannot tell you the emotions that seeing those dog tags bought forth, or the questions they prompted. Is Gary Havelock alive or dead? Was he killed in action (after all, we are only sixty kilometers from the DMZ and here in Hue, it was U.S. Marines who stormed the Citadel)? Is he MIA?

Dog tags for sale on the street struck me as very irreverent, disrespectful in the extreme of the men who wore them. It did not dawn on me until a day or two later, however, that I should have retrieved my wallet from the hotel, gone back, and bargained to buy the whole lot. But then, the moment the thought came to me about what I should have done, I was in Hanoi. It made me very sad that I had not thought of that earlier.

THREE TASTES OF NƯỚC MẮM

19

Motorbikes and Memories

Saigon has been described as a city of nine million and thirty million motorbikes. That's an understatement. It's an infinity of motorbikes.

—Columnist Daniel Henninger, "The Motorbike Economy,"
Wall Street Journal, February 3, 2011

War is simple, peace is complex.

—Nelson De Mille, *Up Country* (2002)

ACCORDING TO ANOTHER ESTIMATE, IN Ho Chi Minh City alone there are seven-and-a-half million people with over five million motorbikes and scooters. Projecting that ratio on the country as a whole (ninety million people, more or less), Vietnam would have sixty million motorbikes and scooters. I am certain the number is less than that but "who's counting"? Anyway you estimate, it's a heck of a lot of motorbikes.

Overall, my concluding assessment of the modern Vietnam, finally at peace, is a robustly positive one. True, in the previous chapter, I griped a bit, but that was about the wiles and deceptions of travel guidebook writers rather than about the Vietnamese.

In this chapter, I want first to inform the reader in that I will gripe a bit about modern Vietnam and the Vietnamese, or at least one aspect of it and of them. That aspect is the motorbike, what it is doing and has done to the Vietnamese, and what negative effects the motorbike and the scooter have on the tourist.

Typical commuter traffic scene.

In 1966, traffic on the highways and streets in Vietnam consisted of military jeeps and armored vehicles, a few privately owned automobiles (many French), and thousands of bicycles. Later, in 1995, when the country had just emerged from twenty years in the Dark Ages, and economically was far worse off than it had been in 1966, the automobiles were gone. The old Renault buses from the 1930s limped along without radiators (long ago rusted away), the bicycles still were there in the thousands, and for every twenty to twenty-five bicycles, there were two or three motorbikes.

Today, the ratio has flip-flopped, and then some. Boy, has it. In a crowd of 150 motorbikes, which can congregate at a red light in a matter of twenty seconds, one searches in vain for a bicycle or two. The bicycles may well be there but they are difficult to find amidst all the cacophony of engine noises and horns emanating from the motorbikes, hundreds and thousands of motorbikes, motorbikes everywhere.

Vietnamese use their bikes and scooters for everything. We saw a bike carrying a full length mirror on the rear seat, as well as one with the passenger holding a four-meter stepladder. We saw a motorbike carrying a door, another carrying seven full-sized cartons, another with a large TV set, one carrying nine oblong boxes, and one carrying a full size door and frame, all fastened to the rear cargo carrier or passenger seat with a bungy cord.

On a day-long excursion from Saigon to the Mekong River, a fellow tourist was a young Vietnamese engineer, Nguyen Thranh Trang, who befriended us. One positive aspect of the new Vietnam is that income levels have risen to the point at which some Vietnamese are able to tour their own country.

Anyway, Trang regaled us with several motorbike stories. He predicted, "You'll see one with a refrigerator on the back." Sure enough, fifteen minutes later we did. "The Vietnamese two-wheeled truck," he called it. (Twice more we saw motorbikes with three-quarter size refrigerators laid horizontally and strapped across the rear seat.)

Of course later, Trang revealed that he and his wife had taken eighteen days to go from Ho Chi Minh City to Hanoi, zig zagging much of the length of the country, riding double on his scooter. Trang told us that while technically it is illegal to carry more than four people on a motorbike, which you often see (mom, dad, and two children), we saw five on a bike several times and, once, four full-sized adults on one bike. Guess it is the "two-wheeled bus" too.

Often you see saddle-bag-like cages slung over the rear wheel of a motorbike. The cages carry six pigs, or twenty chickens, or eight dogs, which many Vietnamese regard as a delicacy (On information and belief, Hanoi has a street with sixty or more restaurants, all in a row, serving dog meat as a specialty. I did not go there.)

So, why my personal vendetta against motorbikes? One, the bikes, numbering in the thousands, make it difficult to cross a street of any consequence, even when a traffic light exists and it is in your (the pedestrian's) favor. Two, bikes parked every which way on the sidewalks make it equally difficult for a pedestrian to navigate the designated walkways. Three, motorbike drivers are arrogant and pushy, taking bikes up on the sidewalk or through a crowded market, nudging with their front tire pedestrians who do not immediately get out of the way. Fourth, the motorbike, motor scooter, and motorcycle have eliminated altogether an elegance and style which must have reached an apogee in the dying days of the bicycle.

The bikes are Japanese, Korean, Taiwanese, and Italian mainly. The principal manufactures are Yamaha, Suzuki, Kawasaki, Vespa, and Honda. Thang told us that while his bike is Korean, more Vietnamese prefer Honda than any other brand. Popular models include the Airblade, the Wave, and the Wave II (all Honda). You also see Ciris, Sirius, Saphire, Taurus, Lead, Diamond, Sapphire, and others. Whether the latter are model names or manufacturers' names I do not know. Some of both, I guess.

When a pedestrian crosses the street in the U.S. or Europe, she strides purposely across the street. If she missed seeing oncoming traffic, she'll hop, skip, or run to the curb. Big mistake in Vietnam. There literally are tens of thousands of motorbikes passing any corner in a short period of time, whether it be in Saigon or Hanoi, or in some lesser city, such as Nha Trang or Hue. To cross the street, the pedestrian first picks her spot, one in which the traffic has let up a bit. She then ventures across, slowly, so as to give the oncoming bikes a chance to navigate around her, avoiding a collision. Some Vietnamese pedestrians hold out their arm and hand toward the oncoming traffic, but I could not see what that accomplishes. It is an altogether harrowing experience to cross the street in Vietnam—like playing a game of "Whack the Mole" where you *are* the mole.

I almost got hit by a motorbike every day. To make it worse, much worse, many Vietnamese drivers in the oncoming rush of motorbikes today are talking on cell phones, or texting. They may be in the middle of a pack of twenty bikes, serenely texting away. One young driver and his passenger were both waving to a friend on the corner. The motorbike missed me by inches as I tried by fits and starts to make my way across a busy street in Hoi An.

Even when the traffic light is in your favor, a few bike riders ignore the traffic light. Worse are those planning to turn right on a red light. They always may look left but never right and, at best, they do a "rolling stop" at the intersection, never thinking about a pedestrian who may come from their right. I nearly got nailed a few times that way as well. "To cross the street needs nerves of steel, or Buddha's inner calm. Or, failing that, a stiff drink," says Vietnam hand Mark Ashwill.

Vietnamese sidewalks are equally difficult to navigate. Along the walk are small *pho* (Vietnamese noodle soup) restaurants with plastic chairs or stools taking up much of the sidewalk, two or three restaurants to a block. Vietnamese on their way to work in the morning stop by these makeshift sidewalk restaurants, eating their noodles with disposable chopsticks. Lunch draws another crowd.

On the sidewalks, besides portable restaurants, there are lottery ticket sellers, sandwich makers with little glass cabinets full of small baguettes, chess and majong players, and spectators peering over chess players' shoulders. The players are seated on plastic stools or overturned boxes, further blocking the sidewalks. Along Le Thanh Ton in downtown Saigon, there are shoe cobblers, with their tools and shoes awaiting repair spread before then on the sidewalk. For several blocks, as one approaches Ben Thanh Market, cobblers sit every couple of meters, with customers squatting in front of them, blocking the way.

Now factor in motorbikes, parked every which way, completely blocking what openings remain on the sidewalk. Some of the scooter drivers still sit on the bikes, reading the newspaper, smoking a ciga-rette, or eating a bowl of *pho*. In Hanoi, the bikes may be parked a lit-tle less haphazardly but they present an even more daunting obstacle. The parked bikes, 100 or more in a neat row, are all parked with their front tires six inches, or less, from the adjoining building's wall. If room exists on the sidewalk, another row may be immediately behind the first, or even parked in street.

In Vietnam, the pedestrian is damned if she does, and damned if she doesn't: walking either in the street or on the sidewalk each presents challenges and dangers. "No one in Vietnam is 'marching' to the future. There's nowhere to [march] ... [t]he sidewalks are covered with mo-torbikes," reports Daniel Henninger, quoting a Saigon waitress.

Just enough bike drivers are pushy to the point that the pedestrian must be careful. Threading through a narrow opening at the Da Lat market, I got sideswiped by just such a pushy bike driver, nearly forc-ing me into a lady vegetable vendor and her wares. I got brushed back several times in crowded circumstances, in markets and in narrow passageways. Seems as though the motorbike riders in Vietnam al-ways have the right-of-way, or act as if they do.

The last deleterious effect of the motorcycles' and motor scooters' ubiquity may be subtle but nonetheless is real. In the age of the bicy-cle, 1995 or so, Vietnamese bicycle riders, particularly the female ones, had a great degree of elegance and style. Not only did they pedal stately along, with perfect posture, they also were absolutely beauti-ful. In order to protect their complexions from the hot sun's ravages, young Vietnamese women wore large brimmed hats with roses or other flowers, artificial or real, pinned to the side. Some bike riders wore lengthy opera gloves as well, pulled up to the elbow, for further sun protection. These ethereal young women wore light fabric silk-like dresses (few back then wore *ao dais*, of which you see a number today, but in restaurants, travel agencies, hotels, and in the hospitality industry generally rather than on a bike or scooter).

Fast forward to the present day. A young Vietnamese woman rides a motorbike rather than a bicycle. This entails a completely different costume than a spring dress and a broad brimmed hat.

The bike rider may wear a surgical mask. About twenty percent of Japanese wear masks, particularly during cold and flu season. The Vietnamese, however, wear a white or green mask with other purposes in mind: protection from the sun's rays, the exhaust fumes of other bikes, and the dust and debris stirred up by other vehicles' tires.

The Vietnamese bike rider's next step up from the surgical mask is a decorated mask. It may be striped, or plaid (Scottish tartan masks are popular—I saw a Dress Stewart and a Lindsay in Saigon), or it may have a smiley face, teddy bear, kewpi doll, or squirrel logo sewn onto the mask—or small flowers, or some other decoration printed onto the fabric. I saw a beige mask with black and red snowflake decorations on it, a flannel type mask with tiny red roses printed on it, and a white mask with small blue designs on fabric that could be used for a baby blanket.

The ultimate motorbike rider protective devices, of which you see many in Vietnam, is the full head wrap, or the three-quarters head wrap. The full wrap is much like a baklava, or a firefighter's protective head gear. It fits over the head. Loops which fit around the ears hold the three-quarters wrap in place. There will be a slit for the eyes; there may or may not be a flap for the mouth, which fastens by means of Velcro swatches.

Now Vietnam has a helmet law, rigorously enforced, but motorbike riders may comply with the law by buying an inexpensive plastic shell. These shells have no visor or just a hint of a visor, so, before putting it on, the bike rider fits a baseball hat (say, Houston Astros) over the full wrap before she puts the helmet (the shell) over the baseball hat. Then she, the motorbike driver, puts on sunglasses.

To further protect herself, the bike rider wears a cheap jacket, usually with one or more zippers too many for American tastes, and

A motorcyclist wearing the "full wrap."

denim jeans (Levi's, or some such). In short, she dresses like young persons now do all over the world, which is to say not too well.

So now, in 2011, because of the motorcycle's ubiquity, we have gone from sprightly, beautiful Vietnamese damsels riding bicycles, a near ethereal sight, to mummies, devoid of any style whatsoever, roaring along on motorbikes. Routinely, as a pedestrian, one can face a crowd of up to fifty mummies and their motorbikes coming straight at her. Not only is the graph on elegance and style on a downward curve, in Vietnam it has taken a rapid and pronounced nosedive.

****

The other criticism I have, again, relates to travel writers and, only indirectly, to the Vietnamese government. This diatribe relates not to motorbikes, scooters, inept characterizations, and inaccurate descriptions or characterizations of things. This gripe relates to travel writer's expression of opinions, most specifically about the Vietnam (American) War.

For example, Englishman Nick Ray, the author of much of *Lonely Planet's Vietnam* (Melbourne, Australia, 2010) lists the War Remembrance Museum and the War Remnants Museum as two of his top sites in Ho Chi Minh City. Both museums are tired looking and moth eaten, somewhat run down, filled to the brim with North Vietnamese anti-American venom and plain old-fashioned propaganda. Turning a corner, you come upon an out-dated poster celebrating the ongoing class struggle. The museum celebrates the triumph of "a unified proletariat over the running dog bourgeoisie U.S. capitalists and their elitist oppressive schemes." Retro, camp really, if the displays and rhetoric stopped there.

But it does not stop there, some old musty museum in Saigon or an out-dated political statement the North Vietnamese politicians long ago forced down the Southerners' throats. The guidebooks' and their writers' treatments of the war keep the propaganda effort alive. Moreover, the guidebooks, and the war museums, are badly warped, one-sided and just plain wrong.

The guides similarly point tourists, especially American and Australian tourists, to the scene of the 1968 My Lai massacre (the Son My district of the central coast, above Quy Nhon and below Hoi An). There a deranged U.S. Army infantry platoon led by a morally and mentally deficient Lieutenant William Calley murdered 504 Vietnamese villagers in cold blood (the U.S. count is 347, but it doesn't matter—the conduct was horrendous and the conduct and cover-up that followed inexcusable).

The Lonely Planet Guide to Vietnam terms the My Lai massacre "one of the most horrific crimes of the American War." Of the Saigon propaganda mills, author Ray writes, "[s]eldom do Westerners have the opportunity to hear victims of the U.S. military action tell their stories." He continues with more: "Even those who supported the war would have a difficult time not being horrified by the photos of children affected by U.S. bombing." In his glossary, Ray defines napalm as "jellied petrol (gasoline)...used by American forces with devastating repercussions during the American War."

Well, what Ray and the Vietnamese propaganda mills do not tell you is that the VC and the NVA had napalm, lots of it in fact, which they used whenever they could. The VC and NVA used napalm over a much longer period of time, too, in many more locales than the Allies did, with similar devastating consequences.

Oh, all of this is so one-sided. The Viet Cong were vicious terrorists, terrorists extraordinaire. In 1968, the same year as My Lai, where errant U.S. troops murdered 500 civilians, the Viet Cong executed 100,000 Vietnamese civilians in the first days of the Tet offensive alone. The Viet Cong executed an estimated 12,000 civilians in the small city of Hue.

Every year of the War ,Viet Cong executed 10,000, 20,000 or 30,000 civilians. The Viet Cong assassinated village leaders, tortured and then executed village headmen, murdered anyone thought to have had any connection with the Saigon government, pulled childrens' and women's arms from their sockets, burnt people to death, assassinated physicians and other professionals, and every day committed hundreds of atrocities in order to coerce villagers into taking sides. For every U.S. atrocity, and there were some and they are unforgiveable, the Viet Cong committed not fifty, not 100, not 500, but 1,000 or more atrocities, all aimed at civilians .

Second, the Viet Cong committed these acts as a matter of policy. It was no matter of aberrant behavior, as was My Lai. Coercion and terrorism were the *raison d'etat* for the underground VC organization. No authorities ever punished a Viet Cong or an NVA soldier for wreaking havoc on the civilian population. "Extort, coerce, blackmail," backed by intimidation, torture, and murder were official VC policies. On the United States' side, while there were unfortunate, nay, horrendous, incidents, too many in fact, never were these sorts of things any part of the U.S. policy.

Lieutenant Calley's slap on the wrist by an Army Court Martial at Fort Benning obscures the reality. In fact, U.S. policy in Vietnam was the opposite of a slap on the wrist given Calley. It was, or became, quite severe. Parties suspected of retribution, revenge, or other crimes, especially against Vietnamese civilians, namely, U.S. military, faced grave consequences. Soldiers, Marines and Navy personnel had to follow rigid rules of engagement. Material deviations from those rules, including any significant harm done to a Vietnamese civilian, would result in a court of inquiry, a court martial, or both.

Read Philip Caputo's *A Rumor of War*. As a Marine lieutenant, leading his weary platoon back from a several day mission, author Caputo was in charge when one of his men accidentally killed an elderly Vietnamese. Subsequently Caputo was relieved of duty, faced a several-day court of inquiry at which he testified, and narrowly escaped a general court martial.

Travel writers like Nick Ray have absolutely no idea of what occurred from 1963 until 1975.

Few Vietnamese have direct memories of the War. Those that do are in their sixties and seventies now. But, as with many societies, the Vietnamese have a strong tradition of oral recounting and story-telling. Vietnamese in their thirties, forties, and fifties, while having no direct memories of the War, have been told about it by parents, grandparents, aunts, and uncles. As I travel about, I tell these younger Vietnamese, as best I can, that I fought in the War.

Due to language barriers, I do a pantomime. I motion as though holding a rifle, saying "boom, boom," and then saying "VC." I cannot tell you how many times the Vietnamese person shook my hand, gave me a thumbs up, or at least smiled, indeed beamed, at me.

Vietnamese lacked any respect for the VC. Most South Vietnamese detested them. They reviled the VC because of the havoc and destruction the VC incessantly reaped on the populace and their villages, for thirteen long years.

On the other hand, most Vietnamese, while they may not have agreed with the U.S. position, tactics or methods, respected, even liked Americans. That bond is still strong, even stronger, today than it was forty years ago.

What about the "Lest we forget" aspects? "Lest we forget" is the Australian and New Zealander means of holding in their consciences the deeds and bravery of the Australian and New Zealand (ANZAC) troops who gave so much in wars, especially in World War I, but also World War II and Vietnam. Each ANZAC and Remembrance Day, and at other times throughout the year, Australians and New Zealanders remember their veterans and their war dead. I think that as Americans we do need to hold in our memories the history of the War, if not those who fought in it, so that it does not happen again (even though it seems to, over and over). But these reminders should be here, in the U.S., as they are, for instance in the Vietnam War Memorial in Washington, DC.

We need reminders of terrible atrocities that were committed as well, hopefully to stamp out any chance that they could re-occur. But let's be fair and impartial. For every memorial such as that at Son My, there should be 500 or 1,000 memorials scattered through Vietnam to commemorate the Vietnamese victims of Viet Cong depredations and terrorism. There should be prominent and lasting emphasis that the end, in this case a change in the form of government, does not justify the means, here the extreme ones of torture and murder.

But that is not going to happen. That is why when I pass close by My Lai and Son My, I bow my head and say a short prayer but I do not go there. I do not need a one-sided reminder of what bad guys we were when, by and large, we were not the villains at all.

Many of the travel writers, such as the *Lonely Planet's* Nick Ray, seem to want Americans, Australians, Koreans, Filipinos, New

Zealanders, and other tourists to go through these museums on their knees, beating their breasts, mouthing *"mea culpa, mea culpa, mea maxima culpa."*

My advice? Skip them. The War was a long time ago. The Huey helicopter on the museum lawn is covered with dust; over the years it has picked up more than a few dings in its hide. It is time to move on. There is so much more to see and do in Vietnam than to be assaulted by some out-dated, one-sided propaganda machine whose sole purpose seems to make Westerners feel bad about themselves.

A street vendor selling delicious french bread—a common site on the streets of Hanoi.

20

Capital Cities

The grand old dame of the orient, Hanoi, is perhaps the most graceful, atmospheric and exotic capital in Asia. Its appeal is instant, with sweeping boulevards, tree-fringed lakes, ancient pagodas and a relatively compact historic center….

—Iain Stewart, *Vietnam* (2010)

Ho Chi Minh City (Saigon) has long been a hotbed of activity but it only recently became the overcrowded powerhouse it is today. The French made it the capital of Indochine. During the Vietnam War… international journalists were captivated by its exotic nature. Today Ho Chi Minh City continues to remain on the cusp of all things new and in vogue.

—Marianne Cook, *Let's Go: Southeast Asia* (2005)

VIETNAM, OF COURSE, HAS ONLY ONE POLITICAL capital, Hanoi, in the north. But most Vietnamese will tell you that their country has two commercial and cultural capitals, Hanoi and Ho Chi Minh City, which all but government officials refer to as "Saigon." Estimates vary but many say that Saigon has ten million inhabitants in the greater Saigon area. Hanoi is smaller, 3.7 million residents, but its population must be augmented by that of its port city, Haiphong, 103 kilometers to the east. Haiphong has 1.9 million inhabitants.

The day I began my journey to Hanoi was May 19, Ho Chi Minh's 121st birthday. Before my journey, I set out for a 6:00 A.M. walk around Hue. Next to our hotel was the Ho Chi Minh Museum. Ho Chi Minh attended the prestigious Truong Quoc Hoc national high school, across Le Loi Street from the museum. Everywhere you go in Vietnam there are paintings, prints, busts, and museums of Uncle Ho but the museum in Hue is particularly important because of Ho Chi Minh's associations with the town.

Already, at that early hour, messengers had delivered twenty or more lavish floral displays to the museum, which sat on the front steps, waiting for the museum to open. When I returned from my walk, a little after 7:00 AM, the museum doors had opened; officials had taken the displays indoors. In the courtyard in front, school children, eight and nine years old, were gathering. Later they were to march and sing in honor of Uncle Ho's birthday.

The children dressed in garb identical to school children throughout Vietnam: white shirt or blouse, red scarf around the neck, and blue pants or skirt. The only exception I saw was that in some high schools, and in a nursing school I saw outside De Lat, the young women wear white *ao dais*. But it was Ho Chi Minh's birthday—what more fitting day could there be for a trip to North Vietnam?

The wooden 1930's Hanoi air terminal is gone, replaced by a soaring tinted glass structure with a three- or four-story arrivals hall. Outside the terminal is the chaos I usually associate with Asian airports, but at least there are cabs. Sixteen years ago taxis were few in number. Moreover, the private car I hired back then to take me to the airport (after my visit) played an integral part in an attempt to scam me.

The airport is a long way from the central city (thirty-five kilometers), on the north side of the wide Red River, opposite of the city. What was farmland just sixteen years ago now is filled with patches of urban sprawl, which become more or less continual urban sprawl as you get nearer to and then enter the city.

Hanoi itself is surprisingly more French than Saigon. There are a half dozen French restaurants, several hotels tracing their lineage back to the French colonial days (the grand dame of Hanoi and a five-star hotel, the Metropole, is very French, in the same location, near the

Children celebrating Ho Chi Minh's birthday.

colonial French opera house, where the hotel has been since 1901). In fact, there are two 1930's Citroens parked in front of the Metropole's main entrance. In the northwest quadrant of the city, surrounding the Ho Chi Minh Mausoleum and Museum, is a large, well preserved French quarter, with large houses, many of them now embassies of foreign nations.

Some other surprises include the following:

• Young Vietnamese are a head taller and at least ten kilograms heavier than their grandparents and half that when compared to their parents. A young Vietnamese lawyer with whom I had dinner in Hanoi, Ba Truong Grang Ngo, told me that the youngest generation of males averages 1.75 meters (5' 8 1/4") in height. This compares with Vietnamese with whom I served in 1966, who were small (5' 1" or 5' 2") and, if you'll excuse the expression, scrawny. I suppose the increased size is due to much improved nutrition. One hopes that none of the improved stature is due to farmers' use of steroids and human growth hormones in order to fatten poultry and livestock. Like Americans, modern day Vietnamese are meat eaters, especially when compared to other Asian populations (fish eaters) such as the Japanese. You notice this "bulked up" aspect of Vietnamese more in cities such as Hanoi than in the country.

• The beggars and street urchins are gone. They were always much more plentiful in Saigon than in Hanoi. In Hanoi, in 2011, shoeshine boys accosted us, one or two each day. I suppose they were de facto beggars. They stayed with and badgered us for several blocks. I say de facto because I was wearing gray running shoes that could not possibly have been shined. The shoe shine boys were nuisances who wanted money.

• Other than war propaganda (for example, a downed B-52 which has been left in the lake where it fell, or the threadbare Army Museum), little evidence of the War survives in Hanoi, even less so than in Saigon where the government has left reminders in place to keep the memory of the horrors of war alive amongst the population of the South. In addition to guidebook authors, travelogue writers such as Paul Theroux (*Ghost Train to the Eastern Star* (2008) want to make readers believe that Vietnam is honeycombed with undetonated land mines and filled with amputee victims of explosions. That is Cambodia; Theroux tries to be melodramatic, attempting to incite breast beating by bleeding heart Americans and other foreigners. In truth, Vietnam has a small problem with land mines, confined to remote areas of the Central Highlands, the principal place where mines were left; and the Vietnamese have cleared many of those areas. In my visits to and travels all over Vietnam, I would estimate that I have seen two, maybe three, amputees, none of whom held themselves out as a victim of an exploding land mine. In Cambodia, each day you pass dozens, sometimes scores, of single and double amputees, all land mine victims. But that's Cambodia, not Vietnam.

• A rising tide floats all boats. In Vietnam, the tide has steadily risen, with over seventy-five percent of the population under the poverty line (according to the World Bank) in 1985 being reduced to twenty-one percent by 2002 and down to fifteen percent today.

• Bigger, stronger youth and the near disappearance of street urchins are two results of a reduction in poverty. Another is the absence of scams. In 1995, among other things, pickpockets took my wallet, thieves twice rifled my backpack, the tourist police attempted to extort a bribe, and a hotel operator tried to coerce me into paying twice, among other things. With one exception (a taxi driver in Hanoi), nothing like that occurred on this trip, which I interpret as a result of increased levels of prosperity.

As you drive into Hanoi, and further as you wander about the city, it becomes apparent that here in the North the number of privately owned automobiles exceeds the number in Saigon by a factor of twelve-to-one, perhaps even greater. They are not all smaller Japanese or Korean cars, either. The autos are Lexus, Mercedes, BMW, Land Rover, and other brands of full-size SUVs. My former student, Dang Chi Lieu, now practicing law in Hanoi, says there are even Rolls

Royces and Bentleys, although I did not see any of those. I thought that the number and make of the automobiles might indicate over-the-top economic successes, successful real estate developers, ala the Donald Trumps of the world, who tend to drive fancy cars every-where. Not at all, according to Lieu, as Saigon has benefited much more from direct foreign investment than has Hanoi. Haiphong, the port city adjacent to Hanoi, remains very poor. Alternatively, I thought the surfeit of large, fancy autos might be another sign that the North had won the War, or evidence of the fruits of corruption, most of which would filter down to Hanoi, the seat of government. Corruption, after all, remains Vietnam's Achilles heel. According to Lieu, I guessed wrong again.

"It's a cultural thing," Lieu told me. "In Saigon, even billionaires ride motorbikes." He asked me how many times a passerby had patted my stomach while I was in Hanoi. Thinking about it, I had to say, "none," while in Hoi An, Nha Trang, and Phan Thiet it had happened several times a day. "That is because in the north people are much more reserved," Lieu said. Author Mark Ashwill notes, and Lieu agrees: "Northerners are considered to be more intelligent, conser-vative, austere, serious, and frugal … South Vietnamese say that north-erners' aloofness can border on arrogance."

The one backlash against that natural reserve seems to be in the selection of modes of transportation. Northerners who can afford it buy big fancy, even brassy, automobiles. Of course, it may not be wholly cultural. Wealthy persons in the South might fear that if they permit their wealth to show too much, becoming ostentatious, the government would unleash upon them another wave of repression. The days when Vietnamese people pretended to be poor so it would not appear that they had become greedy capitalists may not be totally gone.

According to Ashwill, "Southerners are perceived as fun-loving, easy going, open people who rarely think of saving money for a rainy day. They are also seen ... as more direct ... [a] style more compatible with that of most westerners." The reluctance to buy fancy cars, and of Saigon billionaires to drive motorbikes, are notable exceptions to Mark Ashwill's characterizations.

Those billionaires, as well as many other Vietnamese, put their money in gold. They have little faith, no faith really, in the *dong*, which has, I believe, been devalued seven times since the mid 1990s. In 1995, you bought 1,500 *dong* for one U.S. dollar. Today you buy 20,500 *dong* for the dollar. A short taxis ride costs 150,000 or 200,000 *dong*. The restaurant tab easily can top one million *dong*, two million if you have a bottle of wine. To tamp down the potential profit, in 2010 the Ministry of Finance proposed a flat twenty percent export tax on gold. The State Bank of Vietnam and the Ministry of Industry and Trade regarded the idea favorably.

It seems surreal but you get used to it. It's like play money. Then, too, many hotels, restaurants, sellers of big ticket items, or purveyors of antiques quote prices in U.S. dollars, or both in *dong* and dollars. While I was in Vietnam, the government announced that going forward all prices had to be expressed, and presumably collected, in *dong* only. The government must have concluded that through exports the country obtains a sufficient amount of foreign exchange (hard currency such as dollars or Euros). The banking system need no longer rely on consumer transactions to obtain dollars.

Officials in Saigon backed the government's *dong*-only edict by fining twenty merchants for listing prices in dollars. Ironically, the *Vietnam News* reported the total of those fines in U.S. dollars, not *dong* ($1,100, as I recall). Presently, merchants use the *dong*, almost exclusively, for smaller items but above the $40 or $50 range the dollar takes over exclusively. Anyway, I wish the government the best of luck in making the *dong* the exclusive coin of the realm. With perseverance, they may accomplish the goal in 100 years. Vietnamese people have no faith in the *dong*.

In Hanoi, we made the obligatory journey to see Ho Chi Minh's remains. The crowd was a large one, made up almost exclusively of Vietnamese. You must enter the labyrinth leading to the Ho Chi Minh Mausoleum by a precisely defined pathway, which winds around for several blocks additional to what the gauntlet used to be in 1995. Guards screen everyone, as at an airport: no cameras, no shorts, no bare shoulders, etc. A new wrinkle is that authorities had added an additional layer of security before you reach the guards garbed in spotless white uniforms, who guard the corpse. A cadre of middle aged Vietnamese women, dressed in *ao dais*, now forms the outer screen. They are extremely bossy. They are equipped with bullhorns, which they use with a loud voice even though they may be a meter or less away from you.

Nonetheless, the tourist gets through the various obstacles and the several blocks of designated pathways quickly. Last time I saw Uncle Ho, he appeared much heavier than he ever had been in life. In fact, when I saw my friend Lieu that evening and told him where we had been, his first question was, "Do you think that he has gained weight?" I told him maybe, but my first impression this time was that Uncle Ho now appears to be made of plastic. Or at least his corpse had been covered with a layer of clear plastic or some other protective coating. He's 121 or 122 years old now.

That day, election day for the National Assembly's 500 delegates, was hot and humid. My leather watch band, inundated with sweat, was bleeding all over my shirt and pants, staining them. So we hailed a taxi.

It was in the taxi that the only scam of the trip came down, the well-known (in Hanoi) scam of the "rigged taxi meter." The guidebooks warn about this. On the near exact reverse of an outbound trip, to the mausoleum, costing 30,000 *dong* ($1.50 USD), we were not halfway back when the meter hit 69,000 *dong*. When we looked away and looked back, the taxi's meter had jumped another 12,000 or 14,000 *dong*. I asked the cabbie to stop, paid him 60,000 *dong* (the exact change

I had), and got out of the cab. No fuss, no ruckus, although perhaps I should have reported it (I got the cab's number: 101).

So we decided to go to the National Art Museum, to see the collection but also to get out of the heat. A few blocks short of our goal we came upon the Goethe Institute, which had a restaurant full of Vietnamese families. We were the only Europeans in there but all the Vietnamese were eating schnitzels, bratwurst, or goulash, washing it down with German beer. The world is indeed shrinking.

The art museum was empty, save for one other American family with children. The sculptures and paintings were far more appealing than I had thought they would be but it was here that the cult of Ho Chi Minh, which the government perpetuates, goes too far. Even here, on the third or fourth floor of a museum, every gallery, or at least every other gallery, even in the nooks and crannies of the museum, contained a bust of Ho, a painting of Ho, a painting of Ho with young children bringing him flowers, Ho with workers in a rice paddy, Ho resting with troops, and on and on. Every town in Vietnam is filled with billboards depicting Ho, banners lettered with sayings of Ho, busts and other statues of Ho. Even Ho himself would not have wanted all that attention.

Everywhere you go in Vietnam are government sponsored pocket billboards and banners stretched over streets and highways. All these propaganda tools are red with yellow lettering, the colors of the Vietnamese flag. They are a constant reminder to you that you are, after all, in one of the world's four remaining avowedly communist countries (Vietnam, Peoples' Republic of China, Cuba, and North Korea).

But the exhortations on the billboards and banners are not the fire-eating ones of your parents' day, such as:

Those who take part in civil defense, an iron wall for the country, guard our strong nation [picturing a woman with a baby on her back and an AK 47 in her hands].

The youth of the capital join the army to keep us free [depicting several males in NVA uniforms, also holding automatic weapons].

The peoples' war effort will triumph over so-called Yankee air superiority [a farmer's cart, pulled by a water buffalo, contains the tail of a downed fighter plane, with U.S. insignia prominent].

Spilling our blood demands the spilling of Nixon's blood.

Our Hue never takes a step backward; our Hue holds firmly the gun [picturing a young woman advancing, an AK 47 pointed forward].

Repel the invaders.

Those were the old days. Today the exhortations are more fitting of a Girl/Boy Scout camp than they would be of a rally of war-mongering communists:

The best time to plant a tree was 20 years ago. The second best time is now [picturing Ho Chi Minh with several children].

Unity, unity, great unity. Success, success, great success [quoting Ho Chi Minh].

• *Celebrating eighty years of having the party in our life* [1930-2010].

• *Land is like gold. Five tons of rice per hectare will insure our nation's success.*

• *Vote Sunday for delegates to the National Assembly.*

****

Saigon is very different from Hanoi. Hanoi is old, dating back to 1011. Saigon is new, having been a fishing village until 130-40 years ago. Saigon is an exemplar of "red capitalism" ("a market economy with a socialist orientation"), producing over thirty percent of Vietnam's exports. Hanoi is the more austere seat of the national government.

Intel just opened a 500,000 square foot production facility outside Saigon. From the air, as you approach Saigon, you peer down on the metal roofs of fifteen, twenty and twenty-five hectare campuses, housing factories which produce garments and textiles (#1 export), shoes and leather goods (#4 export—Vietnam produced 110 million pairs of shoes for Nike alone in 2011, equivalent to China's output), furniture (#5 export—wicker furniture is a specialty), rubber and latex products (#8 export), and more.

Nha Be, the river port where the minesweepers and patrol craft were kept to clear the Saigon River for merchant ships coming up river to berths in Saigon (call sign "Moon River"—now how did I remember that?) in the War, used to be considered in the middle of nowhere. Now Nha Be is an epicenter, with miles of factories manufacturing items for export, principally garments and shoes.

Saigon is brash, busy, and frantic, inebriated with its own nonstop pace of life. Today there is a skyline when sixteen years ago the tallest building was nine stories. A dozen or more new buildings reach up twenty-five, thirty or even forty stories. Although there are far fewer automobiles than in Hanoi, to and from the airport we passed modern brightly lit BMW and Volkswagen dealerships.

The airport, by the way, is far different than it was in 1995. Air Vietnam, Singapore Airlines, and Thai Air airplanes, even a United Airlines 747, fill the tarmac. In 1995 the only airplane in evidence was the one I had flown in on.

Some things stay the same. I counted eighty concrete fighter plane revetments along the airport taxiway, left over from the War, now blackened with mildew. The Vietnamese have put several to good use (three or four as a fire station, several for storage, with wooden walls at either end) but most are hauntingly vacant and unused. The old wooden terminal building, now re-modeled, is the domestic terminal.

As in Hanoi, the international air terminal is a new, tinted glass structure with a soaring arrivals hall, efficient immigration (although indifferent, bordering on abrasive, just like anywhere else), and no-hassle customs.

Saigon seems to me have more and more assumed the feel of a business city. A few blocks from Notre Dame Cathedral is a new Park Hyatt, where business people have evening drinks, seated in high back wing chairs, talking in hushed tones. Even the old watering holes are different. The rooftop bar at the Caravelle, where war correspondents had their nightcaps and watched the firefights at the airport, is still there, atop the nine-story original hotel, now a wing of the main structure, twenty-five stories tall.

From the Caravelle bar, you cannot see the airport anymore (too many high rises in the way). The gracious older tuxedoed waiters are gone. The Caravelle wait staff consists of shapely young Vietnamese women, wearing single strap, form-fitting red Lycra tops. To say service is indifferent is a gross overstatement. These young women, with attitude only the father of teenagers can fully appreciate, stand near the bar, texting on their cell phones and giggling amongst each other. Serving patrons is the last thing on their minds. Ah yes, the Caravelle has changed; I would never go there again.

In six days and two visits, the place we came to be drawn back to was the rooftop bar at the Rex Hotel, another watering hole famous in the War years. U.S. headquarters, intelligence, and other military types gathered there nightly. Although only five stories up, the Rex roof is spacious, the food good, the service excellent. A band plays nightly, often a golden-oldies band (Vietnamese or Filipino) playing '60's and '70's rock music.

But, the War stuff aside, Saigon lacks tourist sights. The Hotel d'Ville, the opera house and the post office are splendid French colonial buildings but they're all drive-byes (or walk-byes). The tourist cannot go into them. Motorbike traffic is horrendous. Only a few of

Posters announcing the "36th anniversary of the complete liberation of the South," in both Vietnamese and English.

the French street names remain (Rue Pasteur, for example). The North Vietnamese required all street names changed to commemorate the struggle: Dien Bien Phu Street or Tu Do (Freedom) Street, for instance. None of the French ambiance remains.

Rue Catinat, the main shopping street, is now Dong Khoi Street. We went into an art gallery. A portrait of a hilltop tribeswoman that cost $300 USD (asking price—you always bargain) in Nha Trang and $65 in Hoi An (although probably not as good in quality) has a $1,200 asking price in Saigon.

Navigating the shore along the Saigon waterfront is impossible. Concessionaire booths, ferry docks, and sundry other obstacles line the entire shoreline. Construction is everywhere, as are motorbikes (parked or driven).

Except for the museums, and the trips to the tunnels, evidence of the War is scant. You also learn that fallout from the War struck very unevenly. Our friend Trang, a thirty-something engineer, told us, "My dad was an engineer in a cement factory. My mother was a nurse. Even though my dad worked almost all the time for the South Vietnamese government and army, we escaped re-education or rehabilitation." Thang, his brother, and his sister had a normal upbringing, at least what passed for one during Vietnam's Dark Ages.

Another friend we made was Nguyen Thi Thu An ("Thi" is sort of an honorific, indicating that the holder of that name is female). An is the proprietor of a small French restaurant, the Augustin, in downtown Saigon. We ate there two nights. An has the opposite story to tell.

"My aunt started this restaurant in the '60s to take advantage of all the Americans who were beginning to come to Saigon. My uncle, though [the aunt's husband], was a major in the ARVN. So when the North Vietnamese occupied the city, they forced the restaurant to close down." The North Vietnamese also confiscated the tables, chairs, kitchen equipment, and everything else in the restaurant. "They sent my uncle to re-education camp where he stayed for a long time."

In 1995, An was fortunate enough to procure the same location, on Nguyen Thiep Street, opening the tiny restaurant again. "But the trials of those years were hard on my family. Many of my relatives escaped and now live in Massachusetts, Texas, and California." An was particularly proud of her niece, who had entered NYU Law School in fall, 2010.

So, Saigon residents want to forget the War and the years following. The latter, especially, were not good times. The effects of North Vietnamese repression fell very serendipitously, as Thrang's and An's stories attest, but they were hard on everybody.

Saigon people, though, are not morose. On the contrary, they are open and friendly. Our friend, Thrang, tried to persuade us to order "weasel coffee." Country farmers feed coffee beans to captive weasels. The beans pass through the weasels' digestive tracts undigested. The farmers then remix the weaseled beans with regular coffee beans. Weasel coffee is a Vietnamese delicacy. Or at least Thrang joked about it quite a bit.

So comes the inevitable: Saigon or Hanoi? Well, I am about to commit heresy, contradicting every travel and guide book about Vietnam. I would limit my stay in Saigon to one or two nights, or skip it altogether. I would put my bet on Hanoi, even though when I visited there in 1995 I felt like a traitor. Those feelings are gone now and, here are some additional reasons for my decision:

• Hanoi has a focal point, Hoan Kiem Lake, in the middle of the city. Saigon has none. The walk around Hoan Kiem ("Lake of the Restored Sword") takes an easy half hour stroll.

If you go early in the morning, there are thousands of Vietnamese doing exercises at the lake. Hundreds do Tai Chi, large groups do stylized exercises with swords, or with fans, and several morning groups do ballroom dancing and jitterbugging. Three hundred women do aerobics in the park-strip leading from the lake to the main post office. Then there are hundreds of walkers and a few runners (expats mainly).

• And then there are the badminton players. Every wide sidewalk in Hanoi has badminton courts lined off on it. The triangular pocket park across from our hotel had fourteen badminton courts laid out with white lines painted on the sidewalks. A hotel staffer told me that a designated player from a foursome (it's all doubles) will get there as early as 4:00 A.M. to stake out a claim to a court. Vietnamese are early risers: exercise time is 5:00 A.M. to 7:00 A.M. If you went around Hoan Kiem at eight o'clock in the morning, the exercise groups would be gone, by then showered and at work, or otherwise going on about their day's business.

• The shopping is better, much better, in Hanoi. There are wooden statutes, paintings and other artwork, antiques (probably fake), silk scarves and pajamas, and countless other items to bring home and put away in your attic or hall closet. In Saigon, you can find some of those things but they are harder to discover.

• Moreover, in Saigon you always have the suspicion that merchants might be cheating you. There is far less of that uneasy feeling in Hanoi.

• Hanoi has a place to wander, namely the Old Town and the thirty-six guild streets, a kaleidoscope of colors, sounds and smells. Saigon has nothing comparable. True, even in Hanoi's old town you do not escape the motorbikes but at least there the narrow streets and crowds of people force the motorbikes and scooters to go more slowly.

• Hanoi has a real and evident French influence. Saigon has the white and yellow French Hotel d'Ville, opera house, and post office but the French overlay on Vietnamese society seems to end there. The French influence in Hanoi goes deeper, is more nuanced and, if anything, seems to be making more of a comeback.

There are, however, also some reservations about choosing Hanoi over Saigon:

• Too much Ho Chi Minh. Uncle Ho's image and sayings are everywhere throughout the country, but Ho artifacts and prop-

Young women in Vietnam in 2011
(*clockwise*): Clad in traditional *ao
dais*; wearing the "new" *ao dai*—
with denim jeans; and posing with
flowers in a more formal style.

aganda seem to reach an apogee in Hanoi. Ho was a great man but enough is enough.

• Crushing humidity. Hanoi is quite a bit north of Saigon but its residents complain of the humidity, especially in summer months. Combined with high temperatures, the humidity takes it out of you. On the other hand, Saigon has higher temperatures, at times a searing heat, but less humidity. Choose your poison, I guess.

• It's more expensive to get there. All the flights I checked went through Hong Kong. Hanoi is a one hour flight from Hong Kong, while Saigon is a longer haul (two hours fifteen minutes). Yet airfares from the U.S. to Hanoi were approximately $1,500 higher than airfares to Saigon. Why? Most who travel to Hanoi are business people, who have appointments with government officials, lawyers, or prospective business partners. Their travel is less discretionary. The airlines, bless their hearts, charge what the traffic will bear.

• Saigon, on the other hand, is perceived of as a tourist destination. Tourist travel tends to be discretionary. If the airfares are too high, tourists will go elsewhere, or not at all.

****

So there you have it, heresy and apostasy. *Three Tastes* may be the only Vietnam book you will ever read that expresses a preference for Hanoi, once the enemy's capital city, and once the seat of Richard Nixon's and Henry Kissinger's nemesis.

21

Vietnam's Future

The Vietnam of today is full of promise and potential, pulsating with energy and steeped in dreams. At the same time, Vietnam has entered the twenty-first century faced with a range of pressing political, social and economic problems – some as the result of bad plans, mismanagement and ideological rigidity, others the legacy of colonialism, war, and subsequent attempts to punish [the South] for political reasons.

—Mark Ashwill, *Vietnam Today* (2005)

Our worst enemies are not the ignorant and the simple, however cruel; our worst enemies are the intelligent and corrupt.

—Graham Greene, *The Human Factor* (1978)

This, perhaps, is what it means to love a country: that its shape is also yours, the shape of the way you think and feel and dream... [But] As the gulf widens between the feast of the haves and the famine of the have-nots, the stability of the country must be more and more at risk.

"I haven't seen you dance for years," I said. "Come back soon," she says, "Then I'll dance."

—Salman Rushdie, "A Dream of Glorious Return," *The New Yorker* (2011)

IN THE SALMAN RUSHDIE QUOTATION ABOVE, I think that "she will dance" refers to Vietnam itself. But corruption and the expanding gulf between rich and poor are two of among several problems modern Vietnam faces.

The multinational corporations are not coming, they are already there, learning that, according to Mark Ashwill, "patience and perseverance [gets] you a long way." A word of caution for those businesses not already there, Ashwill adds: "Don't come here with the feeling that you are going to 'save' anyone. The gold rush of the 1990s notwithstanding, Vietnam is not a place where get-rich-quick schemes are likely to succeed."

Neither missionaries nor get-rich-quick gold diggers need apply. Today, Ashwill reminds us, "…one must be a marathon runner, not a sprinter, to be successful in Vietnam." Business is said to be relational, as in Japan, rather than transactional, as in Germany or the United States, involving gestures, slight bows, cultivation, thoughtful little gifts (and later often big ones, which is part of Vietnam's problem). Vietnamese are reluctant to say "no" (*khong*). "Yes" (*vang*) means merely "I hear you," not I agree or I consent. Use of understatement generally is also frequent. It takes time to win acceptance and then confidence from the Vietnamese.

Doing business in Vietnam today is not nearly the problem it was even fifteen years ago, as the effects of legacies left by the War wind down. Agent Orange victims (said to number over four million) have reached middle age and beyond. Fortunately, the genetic mutation and destruction Agent Orange could cause have a short half life, not extending into the generation following those born during the War. Unexploded land mines, while never a significant problem as in Cambodia, are being systematically cleared by the Vietnamese government. Retribution against the South is mostly past history, rearing its ugly head now and then but only in small ways. Chinese business people, and their investment capital with them, are gone, not likely to return in numbers, but that is water under the dam.

First of Vietnam's problems, and carrying over from the War and the Dark Ages years, are the high birth rates and population growth. The birth rate in Vietnam ebbs and flows, but mostly flows, reaching a high of 3.5 percent (the United States is around .9 percent, thought to be ideal). In 1976, the government issued a two-children per family directive but did little to monitor the birth rate or enforce the directive. Nonetheless the birth rate fell but then the government rescinded its guidance in 2002. Neither it nor other organizations have done little since that time. Back then (1975-76), and now, the government refused to follow Beijing's "One-Child" policy. The birth rate has dipped as low as two percent but climbed again toward three percent. Vietnam now is said to have, by the most generous estimates, ninety-two million inhabitants.

By one measure, population growth may not be a problem. Vietnam does feed its populace, with enough left over to have become the number two rice exporter in the world. Together, the forty-eight nations classified as "The Least Developed Countries" (LDCs), have birth rates of 3.0-3.5 percent, with their collective population of 900 million predicted to more than double by 2050, to two billion. Governments in many of those countries take the seemingly easy way out, saying that as in China and India, "more mouths to feed means more hands to produce." Perhaps Vietnam could say the same.

Vietnam no longer is an LDC. But much like an LDC, the country faces a host of second generation problems related to population growth: beyond hunger, Vietnam faces a scarcity of housing, dilapidated housing, poor sanitation, inadequate water supplies, and schools that are sparsely attended at times because of low teacher salaries and inadequate facilities. The Vietnamese government must take action of some sort with regard to Vietnam's excessive (not runaway) population growth and the problems thereby engendered.

A second problem is the widening disparity in wealth among Vietnamese. Although the country has bifurcated the governance system (still communist) and the economic one (capitalism), resulting in "red capitalism," extreme accumulations of wealth seem out of tune with the country's history and socialist background. On the other hand, my Vietnamese friends tell me that only one "corporate jet" exists in the entire country, that being owned by the "furniture king" who needs expeditious transport to visit his far-flung factories (well, they didn't use the word "expeditious"). Another friend said, "Yeah, that is true but it misrepresents the situation." He said, "A number of Vietnamese are so wealthy that they own helicopters which they use to commute to work" and also for recreation.

Periodically, governments around the world have used progressive taxation to cut the very wealthy back to size, narrowing the gap between rich and poor. In the mid 1960s and 1970s in the United States the highest marginal rates were seventy percent on passive income (interest, dividends, royalties) and fifty percent on "earned income" (thirty-five percent now). Scandinavian and other Christian Democrat nations of Europe have had sixty to seventy percent or higher marginal rates on all income, but they all have reduced rates of taxation now.

Taxes in Vietnam are simple. Everyone pays a ten percent value added tax (VAT) on goods and services they purchase. Further, a progressive income tax exists, with brackets from five to twenty-five percent, modest by U.S. standards.

Being a libertarian of sorts, albeit one with a not particularly high income, I would never recommend a progressive tax or higher tax brackets for anyone. In fact, I favor a modified flat tax scheme. Nonetheless, the government and other policy makers in Vietnam must remain acutely aware of the gulf between rich and poor and especially political unrest that would result.

The third danger Vietnam faces is a return to bellicosity. Vietnam invaded and occupied Cambodia (1978-89), had two border wars with China, and has border disputes with China, Laos, and Cambodia, and offshore with the Philippines, China, and Taiwan (over the Spratly Islands). These "don't tread on me" episodes seem flashbacks to the policies and attitudes that prolonged the Vietnam (American) War.

While I was in Hanoi, in summer 2011, the *Viet Nam News* reported that "Viet Nam has affirmed its sovereignty over the Hoang Sa (Paracel) and Truong Sa (Spratly) archipelagos and protested China's recent actions concerning the two island groups." China Mobile (a private corporation) had evidently extended mobile service coverage to include the islands.

The dispute quickly escalated, seemingly on Hanoi's motion. The Vietnamese accused the Chinese of harassing a seismic research vessel working in the area, trailing a long cable behind it (which would limit its mobility). Very soon thereafter, the Vietnamese announced that the Vietnamese Navy would be conducting live-fire exercises in the disputed areas. Vietnam seemed to be attempting to send a signal not only to China but also to the Philippines, Malaysia, and Taiwan, each of whom has territorial claims in the South China Sea that conflict with Vietnam's assertions. Whatever the facts, from both its "Don't Tread on Me" and "Quickdraw McGaw" persona, a pattern of truculence emerges from Vietnam's history of foreign relations.

Fourth, the ever present danger exists that the government could regress, tripping over its political ideology and venturing too far back into the economic sphere. After the iron curtain fell, many former socialist states followed the "big bang theory" to move towards capitalism. In Russia, for example, the government privatized all state-owned enterprises at once. They did so by giving vouchers, representing ownership shares, to the workers. Then matters went awry. Certain unsavory elements, including the Russian mafia, bought up those vouchers for a few rubles each. Quickly, thugs and the like owned everything, thoroughly infecting the economic sector with corruption and inefficiency, a state in which Russia finds its economic sector still to be in today.

Learning from Russia's experience, China went much more slowly after it had made the decision to leave central economic planning behind. The Chinese government first "corporatized" state-owned enterprises (SOEs), spinning the enterprises out from departments of government into free-standing corporations, the shares of which still were owned by the government. The managers of such enterprises, though, had become employees of the corporation, not of the state, and their performance or failure, as the case may be, was more visible than were it enmeshed in some government department. Subsequently, the PRC then caused these corporations (China Airlines, China Mobile, PetroChina) to go public (selling shares), but by tranches, five percent here and ten percent there, rather than all at once.

The PRC government "privatized" state-owned "corporatized" enterprises but only partly so and in stages. Today, it is estimated that 1,800 SOEs still exist in China but with public ownership of slices of many of them.

Vietnam followed China's example. The state corporatized most enterprises but did not privatize them, at least not all at once. At one time, the state owned 12,000 enterprises. Today the Vietnamese government owns 4,000 enterprises which employ approximately one-third of Vietnam's workers. But more recently the Vietnamese government is known for its failures rather than its success.

The headline-grabbing failure is the near collapse of one of Vietnam's flagship state-owned enterprises, Vinashin, the Vietnam Shipbuilding Industry Group. My Vietnamese friends, Lieu and Ngo, could only shake their heads, and shudder a bit, when the subject of Vinashin came up in conversation.

Some central planner somewhere (probably Hanoi) saw a window of opportunity in shipbuilding, a heavy industry in which Korea has counterprogrammed (steel production, shipbuilding, automobile manufacture, etc., rather than high tech). Seeing Korea's remarkable success, and to some extent China's, Vietnamese planners thought that the modern shipbuilding industry left room for Vietnam to become a player. The government created and rapidly expanded its shipbuilding effort.

Early on Vinashin, Vietnam's state-owned shipbuilding company, prospered with a growth rate of thirty percent per year. It quickly grew to 20,000 workers and twenty-eight shipyards along Vietnam's coast, but Vinashin had hiccups along the way. One angle Vinashin thought it could play was to refurbish older ships, but freighters Vinashin purchased in Poland, for example, had too many cracks in their hulls to be seaworthy enough to make the voyage to Vietnam. Nonetheless, despite these and similar pratfalls, propped up by the government, Vinashin expanded aggressively.

In the global crash of 2008, Vinashin, already not well managed, lost $8 billion worth of shipbuilding contracts, choking off the company's cash flow. Effectively, Vinashin was bankrupt with its debts ballooning to $4.7 billion U.S. and beyond. The government arrested the chairperson, Pham Thanh Binh, the controller, and two other managers, for falsifying financial statements.

In Vietnam, the state owns and thus has ultimate control over key industries such as oil, mining, and shipbuilding. Rumors are that Vietnam Oil & Gas Group, known as PetroVietnam, teeters on the brink of trouble. The solutions to the predicaments in which state-owned enterprises find themselves are the stock and product markets, which will discipline errant managers much more quickly than government overseers ever can. More privatization rather than less is the key, although there may be pain in the transition to private companies. The Vietnamese government must avoid the normal political reaction, certainly rejecting the idea of more government control and embrace the alternative of additional privatization.

Fourth of the future problems facing the modern Vietnam is the problem of what has come to be known as "plantation production." Twelve years ago, or even fifteen, if you bought a golf shirt, a nice one, or a mid-price blouse, chances are that the labels would have read "Made in Indonesia." Twelve years previous to that the labels might have read "Made in Malaysia." Before that, the label said "Made in Korea." Perhaps sometime in the distant past, workers in Japan assembled sportswear. Today many of those labels read "Made in Vietnam." My wife says that nearly all her mid-priced outer garments, and nearly all her under garments, have that "Made in Vietnam" label. The same with male sportswear.

As standards of living have risen in a particular country, wages and demands for higher wages have risen as well. When the expectations for an improved life style, and higher wages which support it, reach a certain level, the multinational corporations move the production to a lower cost base country, particularly in those industries employing unskilled or semi-skilled workers, such as garments and textiles or manufacture of footwear. Rightly or wrongly, the U.S. company Nike, which produces athletic shoes and sportswear (now extensively in Vietnam), has been a poster child for moving production from country to country. This is the "plantation production" problem.

Actually, it is not the multinationals, which have adverse public relations to worry about, but their faceless subcontractors who move the production. At the insistence of NGOs and other international organizations, multinationals require their subcontractors to sign a "Supplier Code of Conduct," forbidding child labor, limiting working hours, specifying minimum working conditions, and the like. But the devil is in the details, or rather in the auditing of compliance with and enforcement of such agreements. Monitoring and enforcement range from hit-or-miss, to spotty, to non-existent.

In 2000, when I was in Indonesia as a consultant for the U.S. Department of State, I saw that, with no notice whatever, a Reebok subcontractor, whose factory produced athletic footwear, announced that it was going out of business. Suddenly, 7,000 out-of-work Indonesians staged a sit down strike on Jakarta's principal freeway. I could see the unemployed workers from the windows of the Crown Plaza Hotel where I was staying. The sit-down tied Jakarta in knots. It was unannounced but in all probability that production, and the jobs that go with it, were going to Vietnam.

In symposia at which I have spoken, I am frequently asked, "Isn't that Vietnamese woman who sews running shoes better off?" The answer is "yes" and "no." She does have higher wages but those high wages may only be perhaps conducive to a higher not necessarily a better standard of living. Let me explain the "perhaps" with another Indonesian story. On one of my trips to Jakarta, having finished my business there, I stowed my luggage at the airport. Taking a backpack, I flew to Medan and then traveled the length of the island of Sumatra, north to south, 600 or more kilometers.

In the far north, at Medan, while out on a walk, I was dragooned into practicing English with a number of young Indonesian women. I learned that three of these women were scheduled the next week to cross the Malacca Straits to Malaysia, where they would work as guest workers. They had three-year contracts to work for Nippon Electric (NEP). They would join the three million other guest workers in Malaysia at that time.

Sounds like a grand adventure. These young women would be moving to a foreign country, from an economy in which their wages would have amounted to no more than $1,000-$1,200 to one in which NEP would pay them $4,000 per year. But they would be leaving their families and friends. They would be living in a dormitory, where they would become incredibly homesick. And they would be moving from a subsistence economy, with chickens and pigs in the backyard and homemade clothing, to a market economy in which everything had to be purchased and would be more, much more, expensive. After their contract ended, they would find themselves betwixt and between, not yet capable of functioning in the big city but now ill-equipped or less desirous of returning to their native village.

The same phenomenon occurs on a domestic basis, when men and women, say, from a rural area of Vietnam, move to the sprawling Saigon region where the jobs making garments and footwear are. The wages are higher but the workers move into a less forgiving, sometimes harsh, market economy and existence.

The other downside to plantation production is that while the wages may be decent, and working conditions okay, if the past is any guide to the future, those multinationals will again move the production when wages become too high or worker demands too insistent. Then, as the production is moved to another country, there is a big sag, and possibly an unfilled black hole, in the domestic economy. Workers, like those in Jakarta, are left high and dry.

Semi-skilled workers in Vietnam such as those in the garment and textile and footwear industries, earn about $150 U.S. per month. Way back in 2000, the garment workers in Indonesia already were making $400 per month, or slightly less. Little wonder that the production moved from Indonesia.

One of the principal problems China presently faces is inflation in wage rates, said in 2012 to have reached $400 USD per month and higher in some industries, raising the prospect that production now in China may move elsewhere.

Factories on China's East Coast, where most of the factories are located, report demands for or having to pay workers an additional $.30 or $.50 per hour in each of last few years. *Bloomberg Business Week* (2011) reports that workers' wages in the vast Chinese toy industry have risen just in the last two years to $308 U.S. per month, on average.

Will it happen to Vietnam? Although no signs indicate that wages and costs are rising precipitously in Vietnam, and in fact production is now moving there from China and other countries, chances are that they will rise sometime in the future. Where might the multinationals move the production? Some say Central China, which has not at all benefited from the boom on the Chinese Coast. Others say Africa, where the track record is scant but does exist. For example, Soweto, land locked all-around by South Africa, has an established garment and textile industry.

No one knows where the plantation production mentality may in the future move manufacturing and production now taking place in Vietnam. The prospect is that the production may well move as wages rise, Vietnam becoming the victim of its own success and the plantation production phenomenon. Policymakers, officials, and others in Vietnam need to discuss the probability that it will occur, laying out contingency plans accordingly.

And the winning problem? By unanimous consensus among the Vietnamese with whom I spoke, in Saigon, in Hanoi, and in cities in-between, the most serious problem facing Vietnam is corruption, and the corrosion which accompanies it.

Corruption pervades the scene in many of the LDCs and the newly industrializing ones, in the Middle East (*Baksesh* in Egypt and other nations), in South and Central America (the "little bite"), and in Asia). Laws (for instance, the U.S. Foreign Corrupt Practice Act of 1978), the new comprehensive anti-bribery statute in the UK, and Codes of Conduct (the Organization of Economic Cooperation and Development's [OECD's] Convention Against Bribery [formally The OECD Convention on Combating Bribery of Foreign Officials in International Business Transactions—1997], to which Vietnam is not yet a signatory) help confine payments to smaller bribes, grease or facilitating payments. UK's new statute even makes criminal payment of the latter. Those enactments help keep bribery and extortion in check.

In a few especially corrupt countries, the monetary amount of bribes is greater than in others. An amount of ten percent of the amount of any bid or contract may have to be paid, collectively, to the dictator, the minister of defense, or the minister of trade and commerce. In Vietnam, the amount that one doing business with the government must pay, is a whopping twenty-five percent of the total bid amount, contract price, or construction cost, according to my sources.

Speaking with a young architect in, of all places, Seattle, he told me that he was acting as a subcontractor for a large architectural firm, drawing plans for a high rise office building to be constructed in Hanoi. Time after time, the large U.S. firm for whom he worked submitted complete plans and an application for a permit. Time after time the Vietnamese official rejected the application. Finally, the Vietnamese official suggested that the U.S. firm might want to associate a particular Hanoi architectural firm, which he named. Ever obedient, the American firm hired the Vietnamese firm, and paid a large fee to it, for which it did no work. Thereafter the American firm re-submitted its application for a permit, with the Vietnamese firm's name prominently displayed on the application. The permits were speedily granted.

The American firm never saw the Hanoi firm of architects again. Who owned that firm? The head of the planning department did, the Vietnamese official who told them that they had to have a Vietnamese partner and who it should be.

What makes Vietnam particularly fertile ground for extortion and bribery? Well, the usual suspects are undoubtedly present: a background of extreme poverty; low salaries for government officials ($76 per month, as compared to $151-205 per month for employees of foreign owned firms, according to recent statistics); and a centralization of power in which too few "gatekeepers" control the eye of the needle though which foreign firms or business persons must pass ("rent seekers" to economists).

But Vietnam's particular circumstances added to the impetus the usual suspects create. Under the Foreign Investment Law of 1987, foreign concerns finally could do business in Vietnam but they only could do so via a joint venture, with a Vietnamese person or entity as their partner. The 2000 law, as well as previous liberalizations, softened that requirement quite a bit. Only areas deemed sensitive, imbued with national security concerns, such as aerospace or telecommunications, retain the joint venture requirement.

As a practical matter, however, the necessity in Vietnam of having a domestic joint venture partner remains strong. To this partner, who does little actual work, the foreign investor must pay what Mark Ashwill terms "silent fees." The silent fee recipient, much like the Hanoi architectural firm above, then engineers a way in which to channel economic benefits to government officials.

Vietnamese land law creates an additional incentive to have a Vietnamese partner. Vietnamese law is a mixture of French and Soviet civil law. The Soviet part dictates that in a socialist state a private individual cannot own real property. The state owns everything.

To a large extent, state ownership of everything is a fiction. In Vietnam, the farmer, the apartment resident, the shopkeeper, and the factory "owner" have rights in the land they occupy superior to everyone's but the state. And the state, as the true owner, still will not take the farmer or shopkeeper's land away without paying just compensation. The practical effect is the same as in the United States—with one exception: to take away your land by "eminent domain," the American government must not only pay you just compensation but also only take land away only to serve "a public purpose" (build a road, construct a school, widen a highway). Of course what is a public purpose has widened considerably over the years (mark out an industrial park for private users, etc.). Under Vietnamese soviet-style law, the government owns the land and can take it away from you for whatever reason it may have, or for no reason at all. No proper purpose required.

Because the government owns all real property, foreign owners cannot own real estate in Vietnam, which may be a good thing. Were it otherwise, Korean and Japanese interests would have bought up the whole country by now.

Additionally, foreign interests can lease real property only for up to fifty years. These legal factoids add to the incentives in Vietnam to do business through a joint venture, even though a joint venture may not strictly speaking be legally required. The joint venture arrangements provide a conduit for payments of bribes.

What is wrong with cronyism and corruption? After all, Vietnam has achieved astounding economic progress. This is what author Andrew Wedemen in his book, *Development and Corruption* (2002), calls the "East Asian" paradox. In many of those Asian counties that achieved astounding success in the late 1980s and 1990s (the "Asian Tigers"), the level of corruption has been high—as in many U.S. cities, such as

Chicago. Despite high levels of cronyism, corruption, and its incidents (nepotism, bid rigging, bribery, etc.), Chicago has become known far and wide as the "city that works."

Eventually, high levels of corruption may slow or halt direct foreign investment (DFI) in host states, be they Indonesia, the Philippines or Vietnam. That may become even more true as stringent anti-bribery laws in multinationals' home states, which include severe criminal penalties, take hold. Corruption prevents prompt and efficient responses by governments in times of crisis such as the East Asian economic crisis of 1998. When "reforms" do address the crisis, they come belatedly, take the form of selective bailouts, selective enforcement of existing regulations, selective enactment of new measures, and generally lopsided reforms.

A laundry list of reasons why high levels of corruption lead nation states astray, despite the "East Asian Paradox" phenomenon, might include:

- Corruption masks the true costs of government services, as contracts and awards do not go the most efficient or lowest cost producer but to those with influence or who have paid bribes. Innocent third party citizens pay the added costs, eventually becoming frustrated and then losing patience.

- Democracy, even in the limited form which exists in Vietnam, is subverted by bribery and corruption, as those result in the secretive funding of politicians and bureaucrats who are not necessarily best suited for their jobs.

- Corruption makes it difficult for countries to develop lines of authority clear and visible to those who wish to do business there.

- Bribery and the like favors larger, more well-connected organizations that can pay the bribes and know or can find out whom to pay.

Bribery, cronyism, and corruption all entail costs. The effect of those added costs will come home to roost in the not-too-distant future if Vietnam does not reduce the level of corruption now rampant in its society.

****

So much for being a policy wonk. I would like to finish this book by reverting to the tourist mode. Overall, I recommend that you go there, preferably soon, before the Vietnamese turn large portions of the country into a large resort. Here goes, downside first:

• Very little or no French influence any more. A travel writer pens: "[t]he French presence still remains … lingering not only in the minds of the older generation but physically in the legacy of the colonial architecture and the long, tree-lined avenues, street and highways [the French] left behind." I don't know who writes this stuff but it's wrong. Traces of French culture remain in Da Lat and Hanoi. Saigon has considerably less, only one typically French restaurant and three grand colonial buildings from the French days. Remnants and reminders of the French days are much more plentiful in Phnom Penh, in Cambodia, or in Luang Prabang, in Laos.

• A scarcity of antiquities. Myanmar has Began, with 10,000 Buddhist temples in a few square miles, a spectacular sight. Cambodia has the incomparable Angkor Wat. Vietnam has no showstoppers like that. Travel writers might urge upon you sights such the Forbidden Purple Imperial City in Hue but they do not come close. In Vietnam, the man-made sights are often limited to pagodas here and there, along with Cham towers. In many towns, an attractive Catholic church, built in the French colonial times, and well maintained today, is the principal sight but that hardly qualifies as a showstopper.

Some who do not know any better might attribute that condition (lack of showstoppers) to destruction which took place in the Vietnam War, but that is not the case. I think it may be that historically the Vietnamese have been a more practical and industrious group of people than the Cambodians, Laotians, or Burmese, less concerned with frills and adornments.

• Too many motorbikes and scooters running about uncontrolled if not wildly. This phenomenon certainly takes the bloom off the rose for tourists but, hey, I wrote most of a chapter already complaining about it (see Chapter Nineteen).

Advantages, surprises and things I liked:

• Vietnam has finally assumed its rightful place in the community of nations. During our last visit, the Governor General of Australia made an official state visit to Vietnam. She was very quickly followed by a delegation from the Indian Parliament. Recently, Vietnam ascended to membership in the World Trade Organization (WTO). The nation is also a full-fledged member of ASEAN (Association of Southeast Asian Nations), in which it actively participates.

• The most beautiful scenery and natural settings in Asia. My favorites long have been the beaches and sand dunes east and north from Phan Thiet. But the entire Vietnamese coast, at least the one I know, from Vung Tau in the south to Hue and above in the north, has miles of secluded, pristine beaches, along with hidden coves ringed by expanses of sand and palm trees. Nothing in Europe, Africa, or South America compares. As you journey northwards, visible to the west in the near distance, are the Trung Song mountains and later the Annamite Cordilla.

• Friendliness, industriousness, and apparent contentment of the Vietnamese people. In 1995 Hanoi, each day I saw six, seven or eight men wearing the olive drab pith helmet of the NVA. Unlike 1995, when I received baleful stares here and there, and flashes of hostility from Vietnamese in Hanoi, particularly those in military garb, I experienced nothing of the kind on my latest trip. A few of the helmeted Vietnamese did have the Red Insignia of the Vietnamese Army on the helmet. But the oldest helmet wearer was fifty-something, too young to have fought in the War. I concluded that the men I saw wearing helmets had just bought the hat from a vendor. Those were the only artifacts I saw coming even close to or reminding me of attitudes a half generation ago. All I encountered this trip were smiles and help-fulness, along with a salesman or two along the way (well, more than a few, actually).

In days gone-by, say, after the French left, Vietnam could be seen as halfway up a steep hill. Following the Geneva Convention in 1954, the partition of the country, and a war lasting thirteen or fourteen years, however, Vietnam descended to the floor of the valley that lay at the foot of the hill. It stayed there for a long while. The repression and rigid doctrinaire communism dictated by Vietnam's septuagenarian leaders took the country to new depths of the valley, so deep and so dark that the country was one of the poorest and most secluded on earth.

With a new set of leaders, a new constitution, the separation of many political and economic spheres, and foreign investment, which has helped create jobs and new wealth beyond measure, Vietnam has left the valley behind, beginning to climb the mountain at the other side of the valley. Vietnam has made significant progress up that mountainside, now standing above the crest of the hill on the opposite side of the valley, the hill on which it stood in 1954. The climb, though, upon which the country is now embarked is a mountain rather than a hill. Looking ahead and above, the nation is a ways from reaching the pinnacle but the progress so far has been remarkable.

One measure I use to take the pulse of a country is the number of flags. Because Vietnam is a communist country, and propagandizing extensively in the communist way, most towns and cities in Vietnam have a red flag on every other light pole, red banners stretched across the highway, and billboards with slogans and often pictures of Ho Chi Minh. Yet citizens, far greater than just the two million Vietnamese who belong to the Communist Party, put out flags as well. The fishing boats I saw, and many of the private homes, fly the national flag, a red square with a large yellow star. The number and placement of the Vietnamese flag by the country's rank-and-file citizens bodes well for the country, far above what I would have predicted based upon my combat experiences in 1966-67.

Intuition gained from my travels up and down the country tells me that in the future they will "put out [even] more flags," to quote Evelyn Waugh. That's a good sign.

About the Author

DOUGLAS M. BRANSON IS THE W. EDWARD SELL CHAIR in Law at the University of Pittsburgh. Following military service, including a year in Vietnam, he attended Northwestern University, practicing law in Chicago, before receiving an advanced degree at the University of Virginia. He is the author of fourteen books, including *The Last Male Bastion* (2010) and *No Seat at the Table* (2007). He and his wife, Betsy, divide their time between Pittsburgh, Pennsylvania and Seattle, Washington.

To learn more, visit the author's website:
tastesofnuocmam.com